LITERARY AUTHORS, PARLIAMENTARY REPORTERS

Samuel Johnson, Samuel Taylor Coleridge, William Hazlitt and Charles Dickens all worked as parliamentary reporters, but their experiences in the press gallery have not received much scrutiny. Nikki Hessell's study is the first work to consider all four of these canonical writers as gallery reporters, and it provides a detailed picture of this intriguing episode in their careers. Hessell challenges preconceived notions about the role that emergent literary genius played in their success as reporters, arguing instead that they were consummate gallery professionals who adapted themselves to the journalistic standards of their day. That professional background fed in to their creative work in unexpected ways. By drawing on a wealth of evidence in letters, diaries and the press, this study provides fresh insights into the ways in which four great writers learnt the craft of journalism and brought those lessons to bear on their career as literary authors.

NIKKI HESSELL is a Senior Lecturer in English Literature in the School of English, Film, Theatre and Media Studies at Victoria University of Wellington in New Zealand.

LITERARY AUTHORS, PARLIAMENTARY REPORTERS

Johnson, Coleridge, Hazlitt, Dickens

NIKKI HESSELL

CAMBRIDGE
UNIVERSITY PRESS

CAMBRIDGE UNIVERSITY PRESS
Cambridge, New York, Melbourne, Madrid, Cape Town,
Singapore, São Paulo, Delhi, Tokyo, Mexico City

Cambridge University Press
The Edinburgh Building, Cambridge CB2 8RU, UK

Published in the United States of America by Cambridge University Press, New York

www.cambridge.org
Information on this title: www.cambridge.org/9781107013575

First published 2012

Printed in the United Kingdom at the University Press, Cambridge

A catalog record for this publication is available from the British Library

Library of Congress Cataloging in Publication data
Hessell, Nikki.
Literary authors, parliamentary reporters : Johnson, Coleridge,
Hazlitt, Dickens / Nikki Hessell.
p.   cm.
Includes bibliographical references and index.
ISBN 978-1-107-01357-5
1. Journalism and literature–Great Britain–History–18th century.
2. Journalism and literature–Great Britain–History–19th century.
3. Great Britain. Parliament–Reporters and reporting.   4. Johnson, Samuel,
1709–1784–Career in journalism.   5. Coleridge, Samuel Taylor, 1772–1834–
Career in journalism.   6. Hazlitt, William, 1778–1830–Career in journalism.
7. Dickens, Charles, 1812–1870–Career in journalism.   I. Title.
PN5124.L6H47 2012
820.9–dc23
2011026080

ISBN 978-1-107-01357-5 Hardback

Contents

v

Acknowledgments

This book would not have been possible without the support of the Royal Society of New Zealand's Marsden Fund Fast-Start Grant that I received in 2006 or the Visiting Fellowship at the University of London's Institute of English Studies that I held in 2007. I am grateful to the staff who assisted me at various libraries around the world, especially those at the Henry W. and Albert A. Berg Collection at the New York Public Library and Nicholas Mays at the News International Archive. Christopher Reid, John M. L. Drew, Ian Harris and Thomas Kaminski were extremely generous with their time and offered a great deal of advice about possible sources and approaches to this project. For their advice and ongoing professional and personal support I would like to thank H. J. Jackson, Heidi Thomson, Sara Malton, Ingrid Horrocks, Elizabeth Gray and Sarah Ross. Finally, my thanks to my family for their patience and love.

Preface

What are reporters? They are the humblest craftsmen in the profession of journalism. They are not the creative writers whose names are known to thousands of readers and whose work is printed over their signatures. They are those who write down patiently the exact words of public men and transmit them faithfully to the channels of publicity. They are anonymous, but indispensible.

William Law, *Our Hansard: Or, The True
Mirror of Parliament* (1950)

Parliamentary reporting and literature might seem to have very little in common. As William Law articulates in the epigraph, the distinction between a reporter and an author has traditionally been a catalog of opposites: the humble journalist and the exalted writer, the anonymous craftsman and the literary celebrity, the faithful recorder and the creative genius. Yet there is a small group of parliamentary reporters who were also "known to thousands of readers," both in their own time and beyond. Some of the most famous, influential and canonical figures in English literature worked in the press gallery during their careers. Samuel Johnson wrote or edited reports for the *Gentleman's Magazine* for six years, although he apparently only attended the debates once. Samuel Taylor Coleridge reported for the *Morning Post* in 1800; William Hazlitt did the same for the *Morning Chronicle* in 1812 and 1813. Charles Dickens got his start as a shorthand reporter for the *Mirror of Parliament* in 1831; he would go on to work in the gallery for another five years.

Despite the differences between the writers included in this study, the critical reception of their parliamentary reporting manifests some remarkably consistent themes. Scholarly and biographical work on these authors typically presents parliamentary reporting as a rather unpleasant interlude or stepping stone in their careers, one that is left behind with relief as they rise above its petty demands. This is perhaps unsurprising;

there is a sense in which critics – and perhaps readers – want writers to be devoted to literature and to operate beyond the realm of day jobs and wages. We feel for Coleridge, for example, when he writes to a friend that he thinks he might be forced to work in journalism in order to gain those things "yclept BREAD & CHEESE," and perhaps rejoice when he manages to avoid this fate, even if his reprieve is only temporary.[1] At the same time, the parliamentary reports of these four authors are presented in the existing scholarship as exemplars of the genre that manifest the peculiar strengths of the emergent literary genius, the narrative of such accounts being that if literary figures find themselves forced into Grub Street, they will nevertheless certainly shine.

As a genre, parliamentary reporting poses particular challenges for anyone who would like to submit it to a literary analysis, not only because it captures other people's words rather than the author's language but, most significantly, because it is guided by the rules governing Parliament and the newspaper business rather than the author's instincts about quality writing. These difficulties manifest themselves in the scholarship on the reports of literary authors as a tension between accuracy and creativity, a tension which seeks to praise these writers for a unique creative take on the debates, or an accurate rendition of what occurred, or some combination of those two virtues. This is, in fact, an entirely reasonable approach to analyzing parliamentary reports but it emerges from a source different from that which was used at the time when they were composed. As this study will demonstrate, editors, journalists and the reading public of each era wanted to see the debates published in as accurate a form as possible, although it is important to be clear about historical notions of accuracy, as I will discuss later. At the same time, however, the practical and logistical constraints of reporting Parliament hampered the ability to produce accurate reports, while the commercial pressures of the newspaper and magazine business meant that different titles attempted to differentiate their coverage and thus inject some creativity into the content. In other words, the tension between accuracy and creativity was built in to the journalism industry in which each of these authors worked. It did not emerge from, nor is it necessarily indicative of, a transcendent literary talent. Journalists like Johnson, Coleridge, Hazlitt and Dickens certainly did possess the skill to deliver reports that brought together elements of the accurate and the creative. But without an adequate understanding of

---

[1] Coleridge, *Letters*, I: 227.

the business of journalism in the eras in which they worked, it is easy to overlook just how *normal* was such a skill. Consequently, it is easy to overlook the degree to which these literary writers operated as highly successful journalists, not frustrated novelists, poets and literary essayists, during their time in the gallery.

Previous scholars have come to a different conclusion, assuming instead that the gallery successes of these authors stem from being outside or beyond the norms of their profession. Thus Johnson, unlike his peers, "dedicates his hack work to the ages," while Hazlitt is portrayed, in a similarly exceptional fashion, as "no slavish stenographer" but rather someone listening to the debates "with the ear of a connoisseur in rhetoric."[2] There are two reasons why earlier scholars have reached a conclusion different from the one that I reach in this book. The first is simply that many of the works in this area are decades old, and critical scholarship on journalism and periodical publishing has moved on since they were published. In 1989, a special issue of *Victorian Periodicals Review* outlined the need to come to terms with such issues as joint or corporate authorship, the heterogeneous reading habits of periodical readers, the relationship of the periodical text to time and the connection between the physical form of the periodical and its contents.[3] However, while these well-established tenets of periodical research have been used to analyze other journalistic works by the authors in this study, such as *Household Words* or *The Rambler,* they have not yet been applied comprehensively to the field of parliamentary reporting even in the most recent literary and biographical works, which still tend to rely on a much older idea of the role of journalism when it comes to considering the press gallery. Perhaps this is because parliamentary reporting does not, by and large, consist of original work, whereas other forms of journalism, such as periodical essays or even editorials, can be more easily incorporated into an interpretation of an author's individual voice or style. Gallery journalism thus remains a stagnant area of research within periodical studies, even as that field provides new and exciting insights in literary criticism more generally.

The second reason that earlier scholars working on the parliamentary reports of these writers have reached conclusions that differ from mine is that they have been involved in a different task. Most analyses of this

---

[2] Lipking, *Samuel Johnson,* 74, and Birrell, *William Hazlitt,* 96, respectively.
[3] See for example Beetham, "Open and Closed," 96–100; and Latané, "Birth of the Author," 109–17.

phase of the literary subject's life are situated within wider studies – critical and biographical – that aim to show the development of the writer and his or her characteristic strengths and distinctive charms. Since in all four cases parliamentary reporting occupied these authors only briefly and temporarily, and since the point of wider critical and biographical studies is to develop a fuller picture of the their lives and works, such studies consider the reports *only* in terms of what light they can shed on the mature author. My aim in this book is not to criticize these scholarly decisions. The existing studies are typically undertaken by literary critics writing for an audience interested in literary authorship; understandably, such criticism is focused on literary analysis and achievement, and there would be little appetite for a book-length study of any gallery journalist if he or she were not also known for something else. However, while the relative neglect or misapprehension about the authors' gallery careers might be understandable, it does not have to be the final word. There is no compelling reason why scholars and readers should not want to understand this aspect of the authors' writing lives as fully and precisely as they understand other aspects; its potentially minor significance in an illustrious literary career is not an excuse for misrepresenting it. There is thus a need for a study that analyzes the relevant parliamentary reports within their true genre and contemporary environment, seeing them not simply as curious precursors to more important later writings but as pieces of journalism composed within a particular context, if only because any work by a major literary figure should be thoroughly understood if we are to make sense of the entire career.

The divide between literature and journalism might seem like a straw man, a rather dated concept that is no longer accepted in literary criticism circles since periodical studies has emerged and introduced more robust theoretical and scholarly approaches. As I hope to show, however, it is surprising how often even recent critics and biographers slip back into the notion of the redeeming superiority of literary sensibilities when approaching both the reports themselves and the experience of reporting. This study aims to address this problem by shifting the criteria for analyzing the parliamentary reports of these authors in order to show that their achievement is journalistic rather than literary, by which I mean that their reports might succeed as journalism while failing as literature. They might not be aesthetically pleasing, characteristic of the author's usual style, witty, fluent or even particularly interesting, and yet they could still have been extremely fine pieces of parliamentary journalism by the standards of the day. Using evidence from the newspapers and magazines of the time and from notes, diaries, memoirs and biographies of journalists and politicians, I will demonstrate the ways in which Johnson, Coleridge, Hazlitt and Dickens operated within the normal journalistic practices of their day, blending the accurate and the creative as required to produce successful parliamentary reports. My approach thus attempts to meet Michael Wolff's challenge, issued when revisiting his seminal paper "Charting the Golden Stream: Thoughts on a Directory of Victorian Periodicals": "Why is it so hard to study the press on its own terms and not as though it was an anomaly, and for many a regretful, disturbing, even pathological anomaly within the tidy world of traditional letters?"[4] Rather than comparing these authors' reports with their other, better-known writings, I will compare them with the work of contemporary reporters. This study may do little to enhance their literary reputations, but it will reinstate their important achievements as journalists.

It will also attempt to overcome an ongoing schism between periodical studies and literary studies that makes effective consideration of the journalism of literary figures extremely challenging. Periodical studies is a booming sub-field in the humanities, and Sally Mitchell recently documented the high number of new, large-scale works in the field. But the major figures of the periodical world are not necessarily the major names in literature; Mitchell's survey includes studies of Grant Allen, Rosamund Marriott Watson, Ella Hepworth Dixon, John Chapman, Charles Knight, Douglas Jerrold and Florence Fenwick Miller, important or interesting figures in the history of periodical publication, but hardly household names.[5] Katherine Ledbetter's *Tennyson and Victorian Periodicals: Commodities in Context*, which Mitchell also highlights, has as its subject a major literary author, but is concerned with poetry rather than journalism. It is much rarer to find studies devoted to the journalism of major literary figures – literary studies and periodical studies inform one another, but do not always overlap enough to generate analysis that is concerned with the familiar faces of the literary world but grounded in the theories and practices of journalism research.

In some senses, this book is simply an exercise in the recovery of evidence; I present some source material that has not been scrutinized before, and some that has not been given its due, in the hope that the weight and

---

[4] Wolff, "Damning the Golden Stream," 128.
[5] Mitchell, "Victorian Journalism in Plenty," 311–21.

nature of this information, presented as a whole, make us more know-ledgeable about this aspect of my subjects' work as reporters. But this method is also designed to ask a wider question about the existing scholarship on these authors, and indeed on any author who has worked in a minor genre in his or her career. Why is it that this evidence has not been recovered or adequately assessed already, when one considers how thoroughly these writers have been researched, how often their parliamentary reporting forms a set piece – albeit a small one – in literary and biographical studies, and how comprehensively the notions of literary originality and the hierarchy of genres have been challenged at least since the 1970s in both theoretical and empirical studies? This question is one I will return to in the following chapter and in the conclusion.

Because parliamentary reporting is by its nature rather dense, I have tried to set workable parameters for this book. I have chosen to focus only on those writers who can be considered truly canonical and have thus been the subject of sustained literary analysis. Some obscure literary authors did work in the gallery from the eighteenth to the twentieth centuries, but I have chosen to omit these figures because I am interested in the way that the journalism composed by canonical literary figures is interpreted in the extensive secondary research that surrounds them. I have also restricted my selected sources for the four subjects of this book to a small group of London periodicals, chosen for their prominence or for their direct rivalry with the publications for which my subjects worked. Provincial publications are not discussed because they were not directly in competition with the London papers and most did not have their own reporters at Parliament.

My work draws on that of a number of literary scholars who have made similar attempts to analyze parliamentary journalism *as* journalism. It is a testament to the limited attention that has been given to this approach that I can name only, at most, two or three principal scholars or studies for each of the authors under examination. Benjamin Beard Hoover's 1953 book *Samuel Johnson's Parliamentary Reports: Debates in the Senate of Lilliput* remains the authoritative study of Johnson's career as a parliamentary reporter, although the edition of *Debates in the Senate of Lilliput* in Yale University Press's Works of Samuel Johnson includes valuable new insights. As well as providing an elegant summary of the background to Johnson's reports for the *Gentleman's Magazine* and readings that compare Johnson's versions with those in the *London Magazine*, Hoover produced a measured and clear-sighted evaluation of this body of work. More recently, Thomas Kaminski devoted a chapter of his *The Early Career of Samuel Johnson* to the question of the reports.[6] (The timing of my book means that I have unfortunately not had the opportunity to consult the forthcoming Yale edition of the *Debates*, but I am extremely grateful to Professor Kaminski, one of the volumes' editors, for allowing me to read his general introduction before the new edition went to press.) The early work on Coleridge's parliamentary reporting, and indeed on Coleridge's journalism generally, was produced by David V. Erdman. Through his introduction to *Essays on His Times in the Morning Post and the Courier* for the Princeton *Collected Coleridge* and in the article "Coleridge in Lilliput: The Quality of Parliamentary Reporting in 1800," Erdman undertook an important analysis of Coleridge's notes from the gallery. Hazlitt's reports have only been considered in any detail (and then largely in an editorial, rather than a critical, context) by Duncan Wu in his edition of *New Writings by William Hazlitt*.[7] Kathryn Chittick discusses Dickens's reporting in her *Dickens and the 1830s*, as does Matthew Bevis in *The Art of Eloquence: Byron, Dickens, Tennyson, Joyce*.[8] John M. L. Drew's *Dickens the Journalist*, the only major modern study of the novelist's journalism and one of the few recent works that brings together the fields of canonical literary studies and periodical scholarship, includes an excellent chapter on the reporting.[9] Much of this research is now many years old, and a fresh approach to the subject, informed by some of the new directions in periodical and print culture studies, is certainly warranted.

My study aims to contribute to this important body of work by adding detail about the practices and norms of parliamentary journalism and providing more readings of the reports themselves than some of these studies, particularly those which are focused on journalism generally, were able to do. It will also be more comparative in nature than the works mentioned above, placing the reports of each author alongside reports by their contemporaries in the gallery as well as considering the links between each of my subjects and their approach to reporting. In order to achieve these goals, I have drawn on a second group of texts: the numerous histories of journalism and memoirs by gallery journalists published from the mid nineteenth century up to Andrew Sparrow's 2003 book

[6] Kaminski, *Early Career of Samuel Johnson*, 123–43.
[7] Wu, ed., *New Writings*, I: 31–45 and I: 94–120.
[8] Chittick, *Dickens and the 1830s*, 1–17, and Bevis, *Art of Eloquence*, 86–144.
[9] Drew, *Dickens the Journalist*, 5–20.

Obscure Scribblers, the first history of British parliamentary journalism to appear in ninety years.

What this book does *not* attempt to do is provide close readings of the later literary works of these authors in light of their experience as parliamentary reporters, although it will make a contribution to our understanding of their careers as a whole. This literary analysis has been undertaken in some detail by the scholars already mentioned (particularly in the cases of Johnson and Dickens). But it is also a form of analysis that runs counter to my central argument in this book: namely, that focusing on the literary aspects of reporting and the reporter's life tends to crowd out comprehensive and sustained analysis of the journalism as journalism and the journalist as journalist. In his biography of Charles Dickens, Grahame Smith makes a crucial point about the difficulties of coming to terms with the "complex" of a literary life, arguing that "there is a tendency to privilege a single strand of this complex in relation to the discourse that currently preoccupies the reader and critic."[10] My study is as guilty of this tendency as any other, in that it ignores other facets of the subjects' lives and writings in favor of microscopic attention to one genre from their bodies of work. It does, however, have two redeeming features that other studies perhaps do not. The first is that its particular area of attention is one that has not received much scrutiny, making the decision to isolate it from other, heavily documented aspects of the authors' works perhaps more justifiable than another analysis of well-worn ground. The second is that it deliberately does not offer a superficial reading of the authors' literary texts in order to justify its claims about their parliamentary reporting, in the manner that much of the existing scholarship uses brief and sometimes unsubstantiated accounts of the reporting to support readings of literary works or interpretations of literary lives. This book does not, therefore, aim to provide a new way to read *David Copperfield*, for example, although I would be delighted if someone used it to undertake such a study. My contribution will instead be to make the case for removing literary genius from the journalistic equation to see what new insights emerge in our quest to understand the full range of each writer's work.

Of particular importance to this study is Dror Wahrman's 1992 article "Virtual Representation: Parliamentary Reporting and the Language of Class in the 1790s." Wahrman argues that the different press reports

[10] G. Smith, *Charles Dickens*, 1.

of speeches from the period he considered ought to be read as "distinct reconstructions" of parliamentary proceedings, influenced by political allegiances, rhetorical strategies and reporting practices.[11] For readers in the 1790s, Wahrman suggests, "there was no single image of parliament available to and shared by everyone. Instead the public was confronted with a plurality of representations."[12] While his evidence is drawn from a single decade, and his focus is on the papers' political allegiances, his summary of the nature of parliamentary reporting as a genre is valuable in analyzing other historical periods and other motivating factors.[13] Wahrman's sensible analysis of the way parliamentary reports were constructed reminds us of the importance of treating each publication's coverage as a hybrid product, forged by professional practices, competition in the marketplace, political allegiances and interferences, journalists' abilities and readers' expectations.

The notion of the report as a "distinct reconstruction" is one that guides this study. The reports that will be examined in later chapters are considered alongside alternative versions of the same coverage in competing publications, authorized speeches published by the orators themselves, the other speeches that made up the debate in which an individual address was delivered, and the rest of the parliamentary coverage that each publication ran. They have also been considered in the context of contemporary attitudes to parliamentary reporting as expressed by politicians, journalists and ordinary readers. The assumption behind this approach is that it is only in combination and comparison with other examples and relevant contexts that the particular "distinct reconstructions" created by the writers who form the subject of this study can be adequately identified and analyzed.

My approach to reading a report is thus to see it as, inevitably, one journalist's response to the range of forces that acted upon reporters at that time. Taking Wahrman's term as indicative of normal journalistic practice throughout history, I interpret the reports as products of a peculiar assembly line, one that renders the same raw materials into related

---

[11] Wahrman, "Virtual Representation," 85.

[12] Wahrman, "Virtual Representation," 85.

[13] A similarly helpful summary of the usefulness of eighteenth-century parliamentary reporting is provided by Brycchan Carey, who reminds us that, despite the flaws in the way Parliament was reported, the existing records are still important to scholars for the "echo" of the original spoken rhetoric that they preserve. Carey also notes that the very diversity of the accounts of Parliament produced by journalists in the eighteenth century allows researchers the unique opportunity to see a single rhetorical event from different angles; see Carey, *British Abolitionism*, 145 and 159.

but unique products. These products derive their value simultaneously from their resemblance to the blueprint of the real speeches delivered in Parliament and their difference from one another. The identity and talent of the individual reporter are some of those raw materials, but the status of the report produced shares an important characteristic with every other report. What they have in common, paradoxically, is their claim to uniqueness. By acknowledging the inherent logic of viewing a report as a "distinct reconstruction," I hope to shed light on the forces that create it and thus counter some discredited but still influential assumptions about transcendent literary talent and its effect on parliamentary journalism.

Throughout the book, I refer to "accurate" reporting, and it is perhaps worth explaining how I am using this term. In this study, accuracy is always assumed to be historically mediated; even with modern technology, it is worth remembering that the age of audio- and videotape is also the age of sound bites, Photoshop and video-editing suites. It is difficult to be sure exactly what was said in Parliament today, and it was much harder in the periods under examination in this book. When I talk about accurate reporting, then, I am not appealing to the idea that the exact words of speakers were captured (or, if there is some evidence to suggest that they were, it will be provided). I am, however, appealing to the contemporary understanding of accuracy, within whatever constraints operated at the time. I am also proposing that the evidence suggests that editors, journalists and readers placed a high value on such circumscribed accuracy, making it an important measure of effective reporting.

This book consists of six chapters. The first, "Reporting and the individual talent," examines the critical heritage of each author's career as a parliamentary reporter. It proposes that despite the differences between the authors in terms of their eras and the genres of their later literary work, and despite the advances in periodical studies that propose that there should be no special divide between the literary and the journalistic, there are consistent themes in the way scholars approach their careers in the gallery. In every case, there is a tendency to regard these authors as exemplary parliamentary reporters, so good that they are recognized as masters of the genre and thus too good to remain in the gallery, journalists so excellent that they must stop being journalists. There is likewise a tradition, in every case, of examining the various reports for stylistic clues that point to the emerging talents of the canonical author. I characterize each of these critical heritages using a phrase that describes the manner in which this persona, transcendent of contemporary journalism and yet consistent with the later literary figure, has been presented: the creative Johnson, who, in his own words, invented speeches for parliamentarians in "a garret in Exeter-street"; the poetic Coleridge, too imaginative to discipline himself to the work of reporting speeches; the critical Hazlitt, sneering at the mediocrity he witnessed; and the accurate Dickens, capturing the voices of MPs in the way he would later capture the voices of his most memorable characters.[14] This chapter thus establishes the critical orthodoxy that can be questioned when the norms of parliamentary journalism in each era are considered.

The next four chapters treat the authors in chronological order. Chapter 2 considers Johnson's gallery journalism alongside arguments about fact and fiction in parliamentary reporting in the late 1730s and early 1740s in order to question the emphasis on the creativity of his reports. It begins by sketching the conditions governing parliamentary reporting in that era, when Johnson contributed the "Debates in the Senate of Lilliput" to the *Gentleman's Magazine*. I explain the way in which my research differs from Benjamin Beard Hoover's invaluable but dated study in its use of the manuscript notes composed by Lord Hardwicke, who was present in the House of Lords during some of the debates that Johnson reported but whose notes do not feature in Hoover's account, nor in any other scholarship on the subject as far as I am aware, and in providing a more complex understanding of the balance between fact and fiction in the magazines' reports than Hoover allows. The chapter outlines the ways in which Johnson's recollections of his days as a parliamentary reporter colored subsequent readings, which tended to stress his creative powers and his ability to dupe readers into thinking they were reading verbatim accounts of the speeches, and shows that contemporary readers, editors and journalists were in fact very sophisticated in their understanding of the relationship between fact and fiction in the reports. The second half of the chapter considers examples from Johnson's career as a reporter, in comparison with the work of his rival, Thomas Gordon of the *London Magazine*, to demonstrate both the high value that he and his editor, Edward Cave, placed on factuality, and the way in which his creative contributions were influenced by the magazine's style. The chapter concludes that Johnson's creativity was tempered and shaped by the norms of parliamentary journalism.

---

[14] Murphy, *An Essay*, 44–45.

Chapter 3 reconfigures the notion of the poetic Coleridge, familiar to us through his biography and major poems, to suggest instead the ways in which his shrewd journalistic vision manifested itself in the pages of the *Morning Post*'s parliamentary coverage in 1800. The chapter begins by outlining the changes in the status and practices of parliamentary reporters between Johnson's era and Coleridge's. Using memoirs by his contemporaries in the gallery, this chapter demonstrates that Coleridge occupied an unusual role in the world of parliamentary journalism in 1800: part reporter, part subeditor and part commentator. This finding is then used to build on David Erdman's work on Coleridge's parliamentary reports, which concluded that he was an outstanding exponent, to argue that some of the characteristics of his reports can be explained by his unconventional role.

Chapter 4 argues that Hazlitt was more fully integrated into normal gallery practices than critics have allowed in their focus on his critiques of Parliament and his typically skeptical manner. The chapter explains the important events of 1803, when parliamentary reporting received a degree of official recognition from the Speaker of the House, and the developments in gallery journalism between Coleridge's tenure in 1800, and 1812, the year Hazlitt joined the parliamentary corps for the *Morning Chronicle*. It considers Hazlitt's preparation for the task of reporting in light of his 1807 work *The Eloquence of the British Senate*, as well as the intense scrutiny that parliamentary speechmaking and reporting were under in the period. The chapter then turns to the substance of Hazlitt's parliamentary reports. I examine the so-called "Christabel notebook," which belonged to Hazlitt's wife Sarah and which he used during his time in the gallery, to demonstrate that he reported six debates in May and June 1813. Although the existence of these notes has been documented in earlier scholarship, this is the first time that they have been correctly dated and that the subsequent six reports in the *Morning Chronicle* have been attributed to Hazlitt. Using these six reports, I analyze his reportorial technique, demonstrating that it was a combination of attention to some of the exact words and phrases used by the speakers in the House, abbreviation where necessary of speeches that were unlikely to stir public interest and, in some cases, reliance on memory when his notes were inadequate. This evidence about the norms of parliamentary reporting in the period, and the characteristics of Hazlitt's style, is then applied to Duncan Wu's attribution of two reports in *New Writings of William Hazlitt* (2007) in order to demonstrate that these attributions need further refinement. The chapter concludes with an analysis of a famous speech Hazlitt reported – Plunket's address on Catholic Emancipation in February 1813 – to show how his technique played out when confronted with a speech he particularly admired. In addition to making new attributions to Hazlitt, and refining those already made, this chapter proves that there were several occasions on which Hazlitt's report became part of the official record.

Chapter 5 takes issue with the longstanding assumption that Dickens's parliamentary reports cannot be traced because his highly accurate shorthand texts have blended in with the rest of the newspapers' reporting. The chapter outlines the evidence that shorthand was in fact a rare skill in the gallery when Dickens joined in the early 1830s, and that accuracy was a contested notion in the world of parliamentary reporting. As well as analyzing the coverage of the one speech that can be confidently attributed to Dickens – Stanley's February 1833 speech on Ireland – this chapter tentatively proposes two further reports from his time at the *Morning Chronicle* that might be attributed to him, using a combination of evidence about the system of turns that governed gallery reporters, his movements on particular dates and the presence of shorthand sections in the *Chronicle*'s coverage. The evidence for these attributions is inconclusive, and they are offered not as definitive findings but as the basis for further research and questioning. The chapter concludes that Dickens's accuracy might actually have made him a slightly anomalous – and thus slightly more visible – figure in the 1830s press gallery than has previously been assumed.

The concluding chapter summarizes the ways in which the critical heritage outlined in the first chapter might now be rewritten, with a greater emphasis on recent developments in periodical studies, to reflect the subtle engagement between each author and his era. This chapter contributes to the ongoing aim of print culture studies to ensure that future studies of the journalism of literary figures take greater account of the norms of the profession at the time, and are more alert to the ways in which an author engages with those norms.

CHAPTER I

Introduction: reporting and the individual talent

The literary careers of Samuel Johnson, Samuel Taylor Coleridge, William Hazlitt and Charles Dickens encompass a diverse range of genres, periods, influences and styles. But while their literary careers might not have much in common, their careers as parliamentary reporters share some compelling attributes. All four began reporting on Parliament at a relatively young age: Hazlitt was only thirty-four, Johnson and Coleridge were not yet thirty and Dickens was not yet twenty. All were drawn to parliamentary reporting as a source of income readily available to talented writers, but also appear to have had an ongoing fascination with both politics and oratory. None of the authors had established a literary reputation at the time they began reporting, with the partial exception of Coleridge, who nevertheless still had many of his major works ahead of him. All four were ultimately prolific journalists and, perhaps more importantly, understood the role that journalism played in supporting and developing a literary career.

There is one final significant connection between them: their parliamentary journalism has been subjected to very similar scholarly critiques over the past century. These critiques typically manifest at least one of the following characteristics. They evaluate the author's reports with little or no reference to contemporary examples from other journalists. They do not take into consideration the conditions governing parliamentary reporting in the relevant period. They read the author's reports with one eye on his later literary reputation and then, perhaps predictably, find the embryo of that reputation in the parliamentary journalism. Finally, and as a result of these approaches, they conclude that the author's reports were special, memorable, transcendent.

It is a common feature of the popular conception of literary lives to enjoy the early struggles of the unappreciated genius; there is a sense in which we are quite pleased, for example, by the attacks on Keats's work

because it helps to reinforce an image of the wider world as hostile to the
fragility of talent. But this particular brand of satisfaction can only occur
if we believe that the overlooked sparks were in fact there. In the case
of poems, plays and novels, literary critics and readers tend to have the
background and the information to make these judgments; juvenilia and
promising false starts can thus be justly analyzed. As has long since been
argued within the field of periodical studies, genres such as journalism
require the same approach; they need to be read within the context of a
solid foundation of knowledge about the form in general and the conditions of composition in particular. Because this knowledge is often absent
from the critic's or biographer's repertoire in the case of parliamentary
reporting – and thus not passed on to the reader either – the template
of the literary life is superimposed instead: the sparks of genius, especially the peculiar genius of the writer in question, were there, because
they must have been. This chapter outlines the various critical heritages
that have come down to us in relation to the four authors' parliamentary reports. At its conclusion, I offer an alternative approach to these
heritages, one that involves direct engagement with the abundant source
material on normal gallery procedure, the expectations of editors, journalists and readers, and the style of reporting in each of the relevant eras.

THE CRITICAL HERITAGE: SAMUEL JOHNSON'S CREATIVE ABILITIES

Lawrence Lipking presents a common view of Samuel Johnson's collected
parliamentary reports, *Debates in the Senate of Lilliput*, when he writes
that Johnson "dedicates his hack work to the ages."[1] The implication is
that even Johnson's dreariest literary outputs are written for posterity,
moving beyond their immediate context and fitting in neatly with his
later monumental reputation. Such a view helps to generate sympathetic
readings of the debates but also contributes to a general unwillingness to
evaluate them as pieces of journalism operating within a specifically journalistic context, attributing Johnson's success as a parliamentary reporter
instead to an underlying genius that is inherently literary, in the sense that
what are considered to be the successful elements of his reports are those
which bear his stylistic signature or which manifest an attention to such

---

[1] Lipking, *Samuel Johnson*, 74.

literary devices as rhetoric and allusion, rather than those that emerge from the competitive market for magazine journalism at the time.

This interpretation began with the Stockdale edition of the *Debates*. Johnson himself had pointed out that he had only attended Parliament on one occasion and instead worked from notes supplied by others.[2] In his introduction to the collected debates, Stockdale suggested:

It is undoubtedly true, that the Parliamentary motions, which are contained in the following sheets, were made, and that they were supported and opposed by the assigned speakers: but, it must be acknowledged, that Johnson did not give so much what they respectively said as what each ought to have said. These debates, then, may be considered as so many distinct dramas, in which, on extraordinary occasions of public expectations, known characters of considerable consequence were brought forward to act their particular parts.[3]

Writing in the same year, Sir John Hawkins reserved special praise for Johnson's reports: "Never were the force of reasoning or the powers of popular eloquence more evidently displayed, or the arts of sophistry more clearly detected than in these animated compositions."[4]

Later critics have been more circumspect but remain influenced by the notion of Johnson's superior literary talent as a driving force in the success of the coverage. In particular, these scholars have noted the thematic patterns in reports, patterns that are generally attributed to Johnson's own political and intellectual interests. Edward A. Bloom argues that the success of Johnson's reports rests "not on the fact or lack of historical veracity, but rather on their literary and philosophical quality. His achievement was the reshaping of scanty facts available to him so that they became the unmistakeable expressions of his own attitudes."[5] Perhaps most excessively, W. Jackson Bate calls Johnson's reportage "one of the most remarkable feats in the entire history of journalism."[6] The latest spate of Johnson biographies, published to coincide with the 300th anniversary of his birth, repeat many of these claims.[7]

Greater caution and more reasoned analysis can be found in the work of Benjamin Beard Hoover, Donald J. Greene, James L. Clifford and Thomas Kaminski. In making his case, Hoover rightly reminded readers

---

[2] Murphy, *An Essay*, 45.   [3] S. Johnson, *Debates in Parliament*, I: vi–vii.
[4] Hawkins, *Life of Samuel Johnson*, 64.   [5] Bloom, *Samuel Johnson in Grub Street*, 59.
[6] Bate, *Samuel Johnson*, 203.
[7] See for example Meyers, *Samuel Johnson*, 141–45, and Martin, *Samuel Johnson*, 178–81. While neither biography makes especially grand claims for Johnson's reports, the standard narrative of his achievement is not challenged.

that the *Debates* are not "a magnificent *tour de force*," but even he was prone to praising Johnson's "classical eloquence."[8] Greene likewise elevates Johnson's technique by calling him "the Thucydides of the great political wars of the 1740s."[9] Clifford, meanwhile, points out that Johnson's debates

[d]espite occasional dramatic touches, with interruptions and quips as if in actual debate … are more like short essays on a particular theme. They are moral disquisitions, full of abstract reasoning, expressed in Johnson's own characteristic strong and antithetical manner.

Forced to make up a large part of his material, Johnson took the opportunity to stress many of his own dominant interests. In his imagined great arena of Parliament he could discuss what most concerned him – the power of the people, representative government, basic questions of individual liberty and civic morality. He was always intent on a larger design, on universal principles, much more, we may suspect, than were the real Parliamentary speakers in their actual orations. Here was a ready-made public forum in which he could discuss at length the major political and ethical problems of the age.[10]

Clifford's suspicion that Johnson naturally gave more thought to "universal principles" than did MPs is not substantiated, beyond an appeal to a common critical and popular bias that authors are more profound thinkers than statesmen. Even more problematically, Clifford implicitly proposes that reports that highlighted such universal principles were inherently excellent, as if the quality of parliamentary reporting in the 1730s and 1740s was undoubtedly measured in such a way. Finally, in one of the most recent and persuasive evaluations of Johnson's parliamentary work, Thomas Kaminski calls the debates neither "detailed records of fact [nor] particularly realistic fictions," positing instead that Johnson "could express [politicians'] sentiments more elegantly than they could themselves, and he could hone their reasonings and marshall [*sic*] their arguments with an eye to the overall effect of the debate."[11]

While Greene, Clifford and Kaminski provide rational readings of this aspect of Johnson's oeuvre that remind readers not only of the many flaws and limitations of the debates but also of the extent to which they were deliberate reconstructions molded by other practices, their interpretations remain centered on Johnson's personality, habits and literary talents.

---

[8] Hoover, *Samuel Johnson's Parliamentary Reports*, 55, 19.
[9] Greene, *Politics of Samuel Johnson*, 133.
[10] Clifford, *Young Samuel Johnson*, 248–49.
[11] Kaminski, *Early Career of Samuel Johnson*, 129.

Johnson himself sits at the heart of these readings, a figure whose later fame and genius inevitably color the interpretations of even such overtly contextualized scholarly titles as *Young Samuel Johnson*. In particular, the literary characteristics that so enchanted contemporaries such as Hawkins remain an important benchmark for analyzing and assigning value to the Lilliputian debates. Very few comparisons with other reports, undertaken by reporters such as those at the rival *London Magazine*, are made to support the assertion that Johnson's reports were unique or exemplary.[12] They are instead read simply as Johnsonian.

THE CRITICAL HERITAGE: SAMUEL TAYLOR COLERIDGE'S POETIC LICENSE

Coleridge's time in the gallery has not received such detailed criticism as Johnson's, in part because it resulted in a small body of work: just three reports for the *Morning Post* in the space of a few weeks in February 1800. It is not discussed, for example, in the overview of his journalism by Deirdre Coleman, and is mentioned only briefly by Richard Holmes in his biography.[13] Yet the limited critical analysis of these reports manifests some of the same characteristics as the analyses of Johnson's work, in that the author's literary pedigree and personality is front and center. Coleridge's short career in the gallery is almost inevitably discussed in terms of his poetry and his character, not the work of his fellow journalists or the nature of their reports. As I have already suggested, and as is the case for all four authors in my study, this approach is natural and understandable in studies that are concerned primarily with the life and work of a major literary figure, but it does not guarantee (and perhaps even hampers) a sound and substantiated account of his achievement as a gallery journalist. The earliest history of journalism to investigate this moment in Coleridge's career, for example, painted him as manifestly unsuitable for such work owing to an almost stereotyped notion of the

---

[12] The sections of the major critical and biographical studies that deal with Johnson's parliamentary reporting rarely offer any direct comparisons with the *London Magazine*'s coverage or other sources for the speeches. This lack can be seen, for example, in Folkenflik, "Johnson's Politics," 108–9; Greene, *Politics of Samuel Johnson*, 113–33; Bate, *Samuel Johnson*, 175–207; Lipking, *Samuel Johnson*, 74; Cannon, *Samuel Johnson and the Politics of Hanoverian England*, 279–81; Kernan, *Samuel Johnson and the Impact of Print*, 162–63; and Clifford, *Young Samuel Johnson*, 246–53.

[13] Coleman, "The Journalist," 126–41, and Holmes, *Coleridge: Early Visions*, 256.

poetic sensibility; the post of parliamentary reporter was one "the poet and philosopher was unfitted to fulfil."[14] This impression of unsuitability remained influential, and can be seen in Zachary Leader's comment, in his sparkling reassessment of the journalism, that as well as composing political articles for the *Morning Post*, Coleridge wrote "non-political essays, profiles, leading paragraphs, even parliamentary reports," that suggestive "even" implying some surprise that Coleridge would have involved himself in the work of the press gallery.[15]

In the analyses that followed Andrews's study, Coleridge emerged as a much better gallery reporter than this suggests, but the stereotype of the visionary Coleridge, familiar to fans of the major poems, persisted. Wilfrid Hindle, whose history of the *Morning Post* appeared in 1937, only mentions Coleridge's parliamentary reports in passing, but it is revealing that he titles the relevant chapter "Lake Poets in Grub Street."[16] Meanwhile, Michael Macdonagh's research in the early twentieth century praised Coleridge's achievement as a parliamentary reporter but also firmly linked it to his literary abilities. Having quoted part of another journalist's account of one particular speech, for example, Macdonagh turns to the question of "how the author of that weird and enchanting poem 'The Antient Mariner,' bent himself to the prosaic task of recording the same passages. I think it will be agreed that they were most finely rendered of all by the poet, philosopher and metaphysician."[17] It is useful to see some direct comparison made in this assessment, but the definition of what constitutes the finest passages seems inherently literary, not journalistic. Macdonagh clearly wants us to read the reports in the context of Coleridge's poetry. In that context, he is also surprised by the pleasure his subject took in some of his reports; one particularly effusive remark from Coleridge leads Macdonagh to comment that "[i]t would seem as if his wonderful poem, 'The Rime of the Antient [sic] Mariner,' gave less exaltation to Coleridge than his version of what William Pitt said on a certain night in the House of Commons."[18] The apparent incongruity of a literary luminary lowering himself to the task of reporting sits uneasily with Macdonagh, who asks: "Was it not, then, a strange and incongruous phase of his career that he with a brain so extraordinarily fertile in brilliant thoughts on all sorts of subjects ... should have set himself

---

[14] Andrews, *History of British Journalism*, ii: 6.
[15] Leader, "Coleridge and the Uses of Journalism," 23.
[16] Hindle, *Morning Post*, 86–104.   [17] Macdonagh, *Reporters' Gallery*, 304.
[18] Macdonagh, *Reporters' Gallery*, 299.

to the task of recording the reflections on politics of men of far inferior intellects?"[19] This uneasiness might be the automatic response of most fans of great literature, but it does raise an interesting question: why is it important to us to construe this period of a writer's life as either inherently demeaning or something that they are able to rise above, in preference to a sustained and substantiated analysis of how (and how well) they performed the task at hand?

David Erdman's 1960 study of Coleridge's reports is both more detailed and more balanced than these accounts, and contains an extremely important comparison of the reports with other contemporary examples, but it is also occasionally caught up in the idea that its subject's poetic talent elevated him above his fellow reporters. While making it clear that Coleridge "was not the only creative journalist in the gallery of the House," Erdman still links the evidence of creativity to the canonical poems.[20] When attempting to deduce the motives for reporting a speech in a particular way, for example, Erdman writes that "Coleridge more often makes the poet's kind of reinterpretation," suggesting a creative reportorial style that derives directly from his verse.[21] It is telling that Erdman called his article "Coleridge in Lilliput," in a clear reference to Johnson's *Debates in the Senate of Lilliput*; Coleridge's literary legacy proves to be just as inescapable as that of his forebear. Though they provide worthwhile insights into the way scholars have thought about Coleridge's parliamentary journalism, these analyses are all many years out of date and naturally do not reflect the latest thinking in periodical research.

THE CRITICAL HERITAGE: WILLIAM
HAZLITT'S CRITICAL EYE

Accounts of Hazlitt's parliamentary reporting almost invariably suggest, with palpable admiration, that he loathed the job. Catherine Macdonald Maclean noted that "[d]ay in day out he had to listen to the same things repeated over and over again. This to a man of his temperament was galling."[22] Stanley Jones believes that "we may imagine moments when the debates he was now forced to attend for long hours made him angry as well as ashamed. A man of his political views must have found it difficult to record impartially claims and assertions that filled him with

---

[19] Macdonagh, *Reporters' Gallery*, 306–7.   [20] Erdman, "Coleridge in Lilliput," 46.
[21] Erdman, "Coleridge in Lilliput," 48.   [22] Maclean, *Born Under Saturn*, 297.

irritation or disgust."[23] Reporting is variously described in these accounts as "lowly," a form of "drudgery," or a descent "from the sublime to the (comparatively) ridiculous."[24] Hazlitt is portrayed as being "confined ... to the journalists' benches in Parliament."[25] In these narratives, reporting is always something that was inflicted on Hazlitt, something he was forced to do, never something that he might have chosen, despite evidence to the contrary.

These accounts often do not acknowledge four important nuances in Hazlitt's relationship with Parliament. The first of these nuances is that, as James Mulvihill has persuasively argued, parliamentary oratory always fascinated Hazlitt, from his work on *The Eloquence of the British Senate* through to his later reflections in the essay "On the Present State of Parliamentary Eloquence" and elsewhere.[26] Listening to parliamentary speeches, whether as a reporter or as a member of the public, provided him with some important material for later reflections, and he returned again and again to the source of this material. Second, while it is true that Hazlitt was often scornful about parliamentary speech, he also drew critical strength from such instances, using his experiences as the basis for thorough meditations on the nature of speechmaking and reasoning. His consideration of the shortcomings of George Canning's addresses, for example, occupied eight pages of *The Spirit of the Age* and provided Hazlitt with important insights into the nature of oratory and rhetoric.[27] Third, his scorn was by no means universal. Parliamentarians such as Plunket and Whitbread receive a lot of praise in his work, and even less capable or more odious speakers are discussed in some analytical detail. Finally, the critical accounts often conflate Hazlitt's scorn for parliamentary speaking with scorn for the role of the reporter. In fact, he left very few comments on the work of the press gallery, and those that remain are not unequivocally damning. As A. C. Grayling has highlighted, his contemporaries did not feel that he loathed the work; Crabb Robinson described Hazlitt "in high spirits; he finds his engagement with [the *Morning Chronicle*'s

---

[23] S. Jones, *Hazlitt*, 73.
[24] Baker, *William Hazlitt*, 192 and 193; and Birrell, *William Hazlitt*, 96, respectively.
[25] Wu, ed., *New Writings*, I: 27.
[26] Mulvihill, "Hazlitt on Parliamentary Eloquence," 132.
[27] Hazlitt, *The Spirit of the Age*, XI: 150–58. There are similar insights about other politicians in "On the Difference Between Writing and Speaking," XII: 262–79, especially 265–75. For a discussion of these insights, see Mulvihill, 132–46, and Anderson and King, "William Hazlitt as a Critic of Parliamentary Speaking," 47–56.

editor James Perry] as Parliamentary reporter very easy … He seems quite happy."[28]

Duncan Wu's recent work on Hazlitt in the edition *New Writings of William Hazlitt* and the biography *William Hazlitt: The First Modern Man* avoids many of these oversimplifications. Wu points out that Hazlitt seemed to enjoy the work and that there were speakers he admired.[29] Some of Wu's language, however, reflects the older consensus about this phase of his subject's life; he describes Hazlitt's "irritation at the enforced passivity" of parliamentary journalism and, in a telling metaphor that occurs several times, refers to "the straitjacket of parliamentary reporting" that Hazlitt wished to escape.[30]

What is also striking about the existing scholarship is how little it has to say about Hazlitt's reports themselves. We are provided with images of Hazlitt undertaking (and disliking) the work, but almost no sense at all of what he produced. There seems to be virtually no interest, in fact, in establishing which reports he might have written for the *Chronicle*. This approach is particularly extraordinary given that, like Coleridge, Hazlitt left behind a notebook that he used in the gallery, containing priceless evidence about which debates he reported, and how he reported them. The notebook, which is now held in the Henry W. and Albert A. Berg Collection of the New York Public Library, belonged to Hazlitt's wife, Sarah Stoddart Hazlitt, and contains an important transcription of Coleridge's "Christabel" in her hand.[31] The existence of these parliamentary jottings is not unknown; Stanley Jones mentions them in passing in his biography, though he misdates them.[32] Surprisingly, however, the resulting reports in the *Morning Chronicle*, which are undoubtedly Hazlitt's work, do not appear in Wu's *New Writings*. This omission is not due to any apparent distaste for or disinterest in Hazlitt's parliamentary

[28] Grayling, *The Quarrel of the Age*, 153–56, and Crabb Robinson, *Henry Crabb Robinson on Books and their Writers*, I: 116.

[29] Wu, *William Hazlitt*, 149.

[30] Wu, ed., *New Writings*, II: 431. For the references to the "straitjacket," see *New Writings* II: 433; and *William Hazlitt*, 149 and 157.

[31] A typed memorandum in the notebook describes its provenance; it was passed on to Hazlitt's grandson, W. C. Hazlitt, by his grandfather's contemporary and fellow reporter John Payne Collier, who remarked, "I never knew much of your Grandfather in private; but I have a book in which he took notes of Speeches in Parliament, when he and I belonged to the Morng Chronicle."

[32] S. Jones, *Hazlitt*, 107. Jones writes that the notes place Hazlitt in the gallery in June–July 1814, but a comparison with the official record of Parliament shows that the debates covered in the notebook are clearly from late May and early June 1813.

reports; two examples are included in the volumes, with detailed and helpful notes.[33] But the attribution of these two reports is not straightforward, as I will discuss in the chapter on Hazlitt. In other words, while problematic attributions are being proposed, the best evidence of Hazlitt's abilities and habits as a parliamentary reporter is being ignored; my book contains the first full discussion of that evidence, and thus some entirely new attributions.

The Hazlitt that emerges in the existing accounts is critical, in two senses of the word. The early biographies portray him as generally critical of Parliament and thus of parliamentary reporting as a task. Wu's analysis is more subtle, proposing that Hazlitt is critical in the sense of expert, a clever observer of the nuances of a parliamentary debate. In both cases, however, it is Hazlitt's personality and his reputation as a literary critic that provide the lens for reading the reports. What he actually did, rather than what we might suppose him to have done, has not been fully explored.

THE CRITICAL HERITAGE: CHARLES DICKENS'S RENOWNED ACCURACY

Just as Johnson's friends and contemporaries set the tone for the reception of Johnson's parliamentary journalism, Charles Dickens's friend and biographer John Forster established the critical foundation for considering his reports. In his 1872–74 *Life of Charles Dickens*, Forster combined recollections from his subject with comments from his colleagues to produce an enduring image of the young reporter. Dickens's memory that he "made a great splash in the gallery" is reinforced by the opinion of his fellow reporter Thomas Beard, who remarked that "[t]here never *was* such a short-hand writer," and by the journalist James Grant, "a writer who was himself in the gallery with Dickens, and who states that among its eighty or ninety reporters he occupied the very highest rank, not merely for accuracy in reporting, but for marvellous quickness in transcribing."[34] In summary, Forster suggests that his friend's time as a reporter "was of the utmost importance in its influence on his life, in the discipline of his powers as well as of his character."[35]

---

[33] Wu, ed., *New Writings*, 1: 31–45 and 1: 94–120.
[34] Forster, *Life of Charles Dickens*, 39, 37 and 41, respectively.
[35] Forster, *Life of Charles Dickens*, 40.

Forster's evidence and analysis have formed the basis for all subsequent interpretations of Dickens's parliamentary reporting. In the decades following the publication of Forster's *Life*, scholars devoted significant attention to Dickens's early years. The late nineteenth and early twentieth centuries saw a number of publications that specifically addressed the question of the shorthand reports.[36] These studies helped to establish much of what we know about Dickens's years as a reporter and about his shorthand technique. The major biographical accounts typically relate the same anecdotes that appear in Forster and the early works on the reporting years in order to establish Dickens's credentials as the pre-eminent shorthand writer of his day, famed for his accuracy and speed.[37]

While much of the existing scholarship treats Dickens's early journalism as a single body of work without differentiating parliamentary reporting from his other reportorial tasks for the newspapers, some works of criticism have taken care to consider the parliamentary reports as a distinct genre, focusing on the ways in which the tasks of the reporter might have aided Dickens's literary development. Duane DeVries, for example, argues that

[i]n going through the process of recording in shorthand and then recopying in longhand whatever was said, Dickens constantly reproduced … in Parliament, the rhetorical patterns of sometimes educated, often officious, and frequently pompous men, surely an invaluable preparatory exercise for fictional dialogue and characterization.[38]

A similar point has been made more recently by John Bowen, who notes that parliamentary reporting shows "the roots of Dickens's industry, punctuality, reporter's eye, and his lifelong hatred for Parliament and cant."[39] Kathryn Chittick outlines the way in which Dickens's time as a reporter contributed to his understanding of the demands of the literary marketplace as he moved away from reporting and into the role of a professional author, while Lyn Pykett, Grahame Smith, Robert L. Patten and Nicola Bradbury all suggest that parliamentary reporting shaped both Dickens's later material and his mature style.[40] Matthew Bevis, meanwhile, provides

[36] See Carlton, *Charles Dickens, Shorthand Writer*, and Grubb, "Dickens's First Experience as a Parliamentary Reporter," 211–18.
[37] See for example Slater, *Charles Dickens*, 31–83; Ackroyd, *Dickens*, 157; and Kaplan, *Dickens*, 50.
[38] DeVries, *Dickens's Apprentice Years*, 23.
[39] Bowen, *Other Dickens*, 7.
[40] Chittick, "Dickens and Parliamentary Reporting," 151–60, and *Dickens and the 1830s*, 1–17; Pykett, *Charles Dickens*, 23–24; G. Smith, *Charles Dickens,*72–73 and 131–32; Patten, "From *Sketches* to *Nickleby*," 18; and Bradbury, "Dickens and the Form of the Novel," 156.

a brilliant and compelling reading of the likely effects of reporting on Dickens's notions of eloquence.[41] While attempting to uphold the significance of Dickens's parliamentary reports, however, most studies still dismiss their value as texts; Bowen, for example, calls parliamentary reporting "this writing that is not writing, endless and dull" and characterizes it as "a repetitive, secondary, painful business."[42]

There is no reason to doubt the evidence of Dickens's superior shorthand skills. Nor is it unlikely that transcribing debates helped Dickens develop an ear for dialog or exercise his creative powers. But it is difficult to test these suppositions using evidence from the journalism of the day. Out of five years' worth of parliamentary reporting, only Edward Stanley's February 27, 1833 speech on Ireland for the *Mirror of Parliament* – which will be discussed in more detail in Chapter 5 – has been connected to Dickens, and even this example is problematic since we know that he reported only part of it.

In the absence of definitive information, there has been a tendency either to pass over Dickens's parliamentary reporting, as Humphry House did with evident regret, to present only the broad outline of his work in the gallery in favor of a more detailed examination of his literary output in the same period, as Michael Slater does in his excellent recent biography, or to discuss Dickens's reporting career according to the most famous debates and orators of the time.[43] Peter Ackroyd, for example, has Dickens "listening to the words of Palmerston and O'Connell, Peel and Russell."[44] Edgar Johnson links Dickens directly to the key political events of the early and mid 1830s, as can be seen in this description of what he assumes Dickens reported:

Dickens recorded the debates on [the abolition of slavery in the colonies], saw young Mr. Gladstone leap up to deny in an indignant maiden speech that the administrator of his family estates in Demerara was a "murderer of slaves," heard Bulwer's address about keeping faith with the Negro and O'Connell's valedictory "There is nothing to add; the House must divide!" as he tore up the notes for his own speech. Dickens was in the Gallery during Macaulay's notable contributions to the passing of the Act that abolished the commercial monopoly of the East India Company … It is probable that in the previous year he witnessed the defeat of Sadler's Ten Hours Bill and the rejection of Lord Ashley's Bill to

[41] Bevis, "Temporizing Dickens," 171–91, and *Art of Eloquence*, 86–144.
[42] Bowen, *Other Dickens*, 7 and 13, respectively.
[43] House, *The Dickens World*, 37; and Slater, *Charles Dickens*, 31–83.
[44] Ackroyd, *Dickens*, 133.

limit the working hours of adults; during 1833 he certainly heard the legislators debating the recommendations of the Royal Commissions on labouring conditions in the factories and on the operations of the Poor Law.[45]

This approach does not always acknowledge the realities of the fairly systematic process of parliamentary reporting in the 1830s, however. As part of a team of reporters working in shifts, Dickens had no control over which debates he heard or which speeches he transcribed. Perhaps he did hear the famous addresses mentioned above – or perhaps he heard only the dullest complaints about procedure and the speeches of MPs whose names were little known even in their day. In either case, he would have taken down the words and transcribed them for his paper. And while there is no doubt that Dickens was an outstanding shorthand writer, the newspapers for whom he reported during this period had very different aims and the techniques that would have guaranteed successful journalism in one would not have done for the other. The standards to which he needed to work were variable and commercial; a talented journalist needed to adapt his style to suit the conditions.

Research on Dickens's parliamentary reporting thus resembles that on the earlier writers, and particularly Johnson, in that it emphasizes the way in which the experience simultaneously contributed to the development of the mature writer and demonstrated the early hints of those innate qualities for which he is known. While Johnson is praised for his ability to identify the key issues of debates and construct impressive rhetorical structures around them, Dickens is praised for the accuracy of his note-taking and, with such precise notes in hand, his ear for the distinctive or characteristic voice of his subject. Whether the subject is Johnson, Coleridge, Hazlitt or Dickens, the need to present the reporter's work as a unique combination of literary style and journalistic aptitude seems paramount.

A different, and extremely important, approach is that adopted by John M. L. Drew. Drew's *Dickens the Journalist* provides an unequalled analysis of Dickens's journalism throughout his career, without resorting to literature or literary qualities as the measure of value. Inevitably, given the breadth of his study, parliamentary reporting does not occupy much of Drew's book, but he does suggest the way forward when he mentions that most of Dickens's reports have not been recuperated.[46] Instead of

[45] E. Johnson, *Charles Dickens*, 1: 87–88.
[46] Drew, *Dickens the Journalist*, 23.

using the little information already available about Dickens the reporter to bolster an image of Dickens the novelist, it is perhaps time to consider adding to our understanding of what and how he reported.

CONCLUSION

Creative, poetic, critical, accurate: these impressions of the literary authors who worked as parliamentary reporters seem different, but they share an urge for transcendence, even in the face of well-established trends in criticism that propose a more complex notion of writing than a simple division between the literary and the journalistic, with the former ruling over the latter. They are the characteristics that are used in the critical literature to suggest that the author in question was a gifted gallery journalist. The critics who propose these readings are not necessarily wrong in this assessment; in fact, they are often right. But they are right for the wrong reasons. They assume that what makes a great gallery reporter is the ability to make reporting a literary activity or to approach it in a manner quite distinct from that of one's peers. They attempt, in Margaret Beetham's words, the "rescue of the text" in order to fit it into the more orderly world of literary publishing, an approach that has been discredited for some time in periodical studies but still seems to feature in the analysis of parliamentary journalism.[47] The assumption that gallery reporting becomes more successful as it becomes more literary fits well with the preoccupations of a biography or critical study of an author's corpus, but it is neither the only way to consider parliamentary reporting, nor an unproblematic one. By relying on the established grooves of our understanding of what makes an author special and unique, both in a general sense and in each of the instances considered here, the existing scholarship never really asks some key questions: What made a gifted reporter at each of these moments in history? Do these four men meet these criteria, if we set aside what we already know of their literary work and personalities? And, if they do, where is the contextual evidence that proves this achievement? My aim in the chapters that follow is to demonstrate that being a gifted reporter meant knowing the standards expected by editors, other reporters and readers, and thus knowing when to conform and when to innovate. The best gallery reporters interacted with these norms, delivering on them and deviating from them in compelling

[47] Beetham, "Open and Closed," 97.

ways. Johnson, Coleridge, Hazlitt and Dickens were among the best, but this cannot be demonstrated with only their own poems, novels, and literary journalism as evidence.

In pursuing this aim, I am drawing on a body of source material that ought to be incorporated into the critical and biographical studies on each of these authors, even if their days as parliamentary reporters make up a very minor part of such studies. In each case, there is considerable evidence about the way gallery journalists operated to be found in autobiographies and memoirs, the columns of contemporary magazines and newspapers, and the manuscripts and notebooks of journalists and parliamentarians. Much of this material does not appear to have been consulted at all by those writing about the respective authors' parliamentary careers, even in recent studies; some of it has been, especially where the aim of the scholarship is to examine the reports closely, but the emphasis has been on finding something exceptional about the subject's practice rather than establishing what was standard or normal. While I do not advocate giving the parliamentary reporting a greater role in studies where it is understandably a passing episode, I do propose that we should aim for the best and fullest understanding possible of this intriguing moment in the authors' lives in order to have a richer picture of each man's career as a whole. Such an understanding, as I argue in the following chapters, replaces the dated emphasis on literary genius that has dominated the scholarship with a new emphasis on journalistic genius. Johnson, Coleridge, Hazlitt and Dickens can then be seen afresh, and perhaps surprisingly, as consummate gallery journalists.

They can also be seen in a state which we might call the collaborative sublime, a state in which a writer needs to both relinquish originality and idiosyncrasy in the interests of a collective authorial voice and bring something distinctive to the collaboration. This state demands a high degree of sensitivity to form, genre, readers and their interests, one's own style and the style of one's peers. It demands a willingness to think of oneself as part of a community of writers and readers, a community that is so immersed in its norms that both conformity and innovation are welcomed as acts that uphold the significance and vitality of those norms.

Once we envisage these authors in this collaborative state, it is also necessary to ask some questions about authorial style. What does it mean to call Johnson's reporting "Johnsonian" if it is in part the product of the forces of convention? What does it mean to attribute a report to Hazlitt on the basis of style when it is in fact the work of several hands?

Parliamentary reporting, I would like to propose, provides a radical challenge to our understanding of the style of each of these authors, because it is essentially about the submersion of individual style. The following four chapters provide the specific evidence that Johnson, Coleridge, Hazlitt and Dickens were exemplars of this collaborative sublime when they worked in the press gallery and I will return to this notion in my conclusion, which considers the wider significance of their careers as reporters for our understanding of their careers as a whole and their writing styles.

CHAPTER 2

Samuel Johnson: beyond Lilliput

In the records of the British House of Commons for April 1738, sand-wiched between a debate on the bill for securing trade to America and another on the Button and Button-Hole Bill, lies an important slice of journalistic history. The Speaker informed the House that "he had in his hands a printed News Paper, which contained his Majesty's Answer to their late Address, before the same had been reported from the Chair, the only way of communicating it to the public."[1] The Speaker urged the assembled MPs to find a way to stop the publication of parliamentary business, which had for many years been tolerated as long as the publication occurred during the recess. After a short debate, the House resolved that it was a "notorious breach of the Privilege" for anyone to publish the debates.[2]

One of the London journalists affected by the new arrangements for reporting Parliament was the young Samuel Johnson. Johnson had worked for Edward Cave's *Gentleman's Magazine* since 1737 and was probably involved in establishing the new mode of parliamentary coverage that the *Gentleman's Magazine* adopted in the wake of the 1738 ban. The rival *London Magazine*, edited by Thomas Astley, had unveiled its approach in May 1738, depicting the debates as the proceedings of a political club in which speakers took the parts of the parliamentary orators. Classical pseudonyms, some invented and some implying connections with real historical figures, were used to screen the names of the speakers, with the Prime Minister Robert Walpole, for example, now appearing as "M. Tullius Cicero." The *Gentleman's Magazine* responded in the following month with "Debates in the Senate of Lilliput," a series that purported to be coverage of political speeches from Lilliput provided by Gulliver's grandson. A series of Swiftian names was devised to cover speakers, countries

---

[1] *Cobbett's Parliamentary History*, x: 801. [2] *Cobbett's Parliamentary History*, x: 812.

and regions, as well as common parliamentary terminology; thus Walpole became "Walelop," while the members of the Lords and Commons were "Hurgoes" and "Clinabs" respectively. The magazines also delayed publication of most debates and mixed up the chronological sequence in order to protect themselves from prosecution.

Oddly, Parliament appears almost at once to have either accepted the magazines' new strategy or lost interest in policing the reports. Neither Cave nor Astley was summoned to explain the fact that the parliamentary debates were still being published. While some MPs might have overlooked the breach of privilege from a reluctance to identify themselves as the figures behind the ridiculous Lilliputian names, as Thomas Kaminksi has suggested, most were probably aware that publication of the debates actually helped to raise their profile with the electorate.[3] It was, moreover, difficult for the House to react too harshly to the practice of publishing addresses when members were often making their own arrangements to circulate their orations; the *Daily Gazetteer* lampooned the decision of some MPs to "bring their *Earwigs* to carry away their *Speeches*, that they may have the Satisfaction of seeing themselves in *Print* …"[4] Parliament had flexed its muscle to reaffirm the theoretical importance of the standing order banning reporting but its practical application was of less interest. Votes for MPs and sales for editors were at stake; despite the stern words of April 13, the mutual dependence of Parliament and the press was too well established to be overthrown lightly.

Cave's method for reporting Parliament had evolved significantly since he began the magazine in 1731. His original approach had simply been to copy material from Abel Boyer's *Political State of Great Britain*, which since its founding in 1711 had carried summaries of the debates. By 1736 or 1737 Cave had developed a new plan which involved gaining entry to the Strangers' Gallery of the House of Commons for a group of reporters, who would make notes and then meet to generate a composite report based on their recollections.[5] This system in turn developed into a more specialized approach as time passed; after Johnson joined the *Gentleman's Magazine* the reporting was handled by a single reporter, William Guthrie, who would compose the reports and pass them on to his new

---

[3] Kaminski, *Early Career of Samuel Johnson*, 42.
[4] *Daily Gazetteer* (May 2, 1740): 1. Newspaper articles in this period were generally anonymous and untitled. References to periodical articles in this book will thus often include only the date and page number.
[5] Hawkins, *Life of Samuel Johnson*, 62.

colleague for editing.[6] At some stage, however, Johnson took over as the sole reporter of the debates, working from other people's notes rather than attending the House himself. James Boswell indicates that the first debate that Johnson reported on his own occurred on November 19 1740, while the last occurred on February 23 1743 and was published in March 1744, although modern critics generally date Johnson's contributions from the debate of February 13 1741.[7] He was thus involved in the coverage of some very significant political events, including war with Spain and Robert Walpole's eventual fall from grace.[8]

Johnson's installation as sole reporter was accompanied by another development in the technique of reporting Parliament. In an important and much-rehearsed anecdote, Boswell writes that Cave "resolved that [Johnson] should do the whole himself, from the scanty notes furnished by persons employed to attend in both houses of Parliament. Sometimes, however, as [Johnson] himself told me, he had nothing more communicated to him than the names of the several speakers, and the part which they had taken in the debate."[9] These remarks have proved compelling to critics, and a standard narrative has emerged from their analyses: Johnson had to invent almost all of the coverage, which he did brilliantly, not only in terms of its literary style but also in terms of its apparent authenticity. Readers were not only charmed but duped into thinking they were reading verbatim coverage. Many of these critical accounts are presented, as noted in Chapter 1, without any comparison to the norms of parliamentary reporting at the time. The major exception is Benjamin Beard Hoover's 1953 study *Samuel Johnson's Parliamentary Reporting*, to which all subsequent scholars of this aspect of Johnson's writing are heavily indebted. Hoover's chapter "The Debates as Fact" undertakes a methodical collation of most of the extant sources that contain accounts of the debates; the one important omission is the notes of Lord Hardwicke, which I will include later in this chapter. In a second, shorter chapter, "The Debates as Art: Their Place in the Career of Samuel Johnson," Hoover builds on

[6] Boswell, *Boswell's Life of Johnson*, I: 117–18.
[7] Boswell, *Boswell's Life of Johnson*, I: 150. For information about the dating of Johnson's contributions, see Hoover, *Samuel Johnson Parliamentary Reports*, 25, and Kaminski, *Early Career of Samuel Johnson*, 115–22. As Kaminski points out, much of the parliamentary coverage in the *Gentleman's Magazine* between November 1740 and July 1741 was plagiarized from the *London Magazine*; the resumption of original reports begins with the coverage of the debate on Walpole's future that occurred on February 13, 1741, suggesting a change of reporter at this point.
[8] See Cannon, *Samuel Johnson and the Politics of Hanoverian England*, 279–81.
[9] Boswell, *Boswell's Life of Johnson*, I: 118.

W. K. Wimsatt's findings by analyzing the debates for instances of three of Johnson's characteristic rhetorical techniques: parallelism, antithesis, and abstract and philosophic diction.

Hoover's findings are sound and remain an excellent source for readers hoping to gain an overview of Johnson's reports. Two related areas deserve further consideration, however. The first is the overall expectations about parliamentary reporting that magazine readers, editors and journalists in the period held. Hoover's analysis of "The Debates as Fact" tends to hold Johnson to an objective standard of accuracy rather than a historically contextualized one; in other words, the debates are tested against mid-twentieth-century, not mid-eighteenth-century, notions of factuality. Being so few, moments of clearly correct reportage, where phrases can be verified by other sources who attended the debates, are usually downplayed in Hoover's account because they are not the norm, with little attention given to the value placed on verifiable material by the magazines and their readers, for whom accurate reporting inevitably meant something less exact than it does today.

The second area that does not receive much attention in Hoover's analysis is the place of certain stylistic techniques within a general house style and a wider competitive marketplace. As the title of his chapter on style or "art" suggests, Hoover chooses to highlight examples of characteristically Johnsonian writing from the debates, examples which are occasionally compared with the *Gentleman's Magazine*'s coverage before and after Johnson's tenure, but not, in this chapter, with the most obvious point of comparison, the contemporary reporting from the *London Magazine*. As a consequence, the extent to which Johnson is shaping or being shaped by his employer's expectations and his rival's contributions is not fully examined. In its place readers are presented with compelling but perhaps not surprising evidence that Johnson's debates sound like Johnson. This information helps to elevate the writer out of the world of journalism and into the world of literature; as Hoover revealingly puts it, "Johnson can, without question, be called not simply the reporter but the *author* of all the *Debates*" (Hoover's italics).[10]

Ultimately, it is the negotiated balance between fact and fiction in contemporary reportage that does not receive sufficient scrutiny in Hoover's work. Two separate tests are applied by Hoover to establish the levels of accuracy and creativity that characterize the reports: accuracy is tested

---

[10]   Hoover, *Samuel Johnson's Parliamentary Reports*, 129.

against alternative sources but creativity is measured either against the later Johnson or against his immediate predecessor and successor using the later Johnson's style as an index. Both accuracy and creativity need to be understood, however, within the boundaries of magazine culture. Hoover tends to consider them to be opposing forces in the reports that need to be teased apart and isolated, when instead they need to be understood as interacting with each other, combining and working together as part of a publication's overall coverage. Moreover, each of the magazines developed an independent and identifiable blend of the factual and the fictional. Most modern scholars regard the *Gentleman's Magazine*'s debates as cleverly crafted recreations that are uniquely Johnsonian in simultaneously reflecting fact and creative agency. But Johnson not only worked in an environment in which magazine journalists routinely mixed the factual and fictional; he was also writing within the constraints of a specific style of reportage that had been developed in order to set the *Gentleman's Magazine* apart from the *London Magazine*, a style which demanded that creative coverage had to be generated without compromising an overall impression of accuracy.

FACT AND FICTION IN EARLY EIGHTEENTH-CENTURY PARLIAMENTARY REPORTING

The 1738 resolution was one of the most dramatic incidents in the turbulent relationship that existed between Parliament and the press throughout the seventeenth and early eighteenth centuries. While printed statutes had been available since 1484, it was not until the middle of the seventeenth century that printers and publishers began to cater to the public appetite for parliamentary news on a large scale. Although the official records of proceedings remained in manuscript form, unavailable to the general reader, newspapers began to publish collated news from Westminster regularly in the 1640s and 1650s. But while documents such as votes or orders could be published with little controversy, the publication of parliamentary debates remained a vexed issue. Members of both Houses routinely argued that it was not in the national interest to see the debates made public, and although speeches were circulated in manuscript form, printed reports were rare and often dealt with harshly by Parliament.[11] But

---

[11] Details of prosecutions for publishing the proceedings up until 1738 can be found in the Liverpool Papers, vol. CXLV, British Library Add.MS.38334, fols. 95–102.

the growing number of newspapers, the opening of the Strangers' Gallery at the House of Commons (which allowed members of the public limited access to the proceedings) and an increasing awareness among politicians of the importance of public opinion combined to create an environment in which parliamentary journalism could prosper even though it was still closely monitored by the state.[12] In the early years of the eighteenth century, Abel Boyer began publishing retrospective accounts of the previous parliamentary session. His influential monthly *The Political State of Great Britain* was the principal source for parliamentary news until the founding of the *Gentleman's Magazine* and the *London Magazine* in the early 1730s.

The 1738 ban, perhaps predictably, seemed to fuel the appetite for parliamentary reports. Alongside the versions generated by the magazines, authorized copies of speeches, which had been corrected and published by the MPs themselves, appeared in pamphlet form, as did alternative accounts and extracts.[13] There were also three major sources of parliamentary history being marketed to consumers: Richard Chandler's *History and Proceedings of the House of Commons from the Restoration to the Present Time* (1742–44); its companion publication, *The History and Proceedings of the House of Lords, From the Restoration in 1660, to the Present Time* (1742–43), edited by Ebenezer Timberland; and a rival version, *A Collection of the Parliamentary Debates in England, from the Year 1668 to the Present Time* (1741–42), produced by John Torbuck. These publications drew on the magazines' coverage to produce collected accounts that purported to be official versions of the debates. As the *London Magazine* pointed out, "nothing is received so greedily, or read with so much Attention by the People, as the Speeches that are made in Parliament upon Subjects of great Importance."[14] In such a potentially lucrative marketplace, the two magazines naturally had to devote considerable space to their parliamentary coverage and produce reports that were sufficiently accurate to be credible to an informed reader who might have known something of the proceedings or the speakers, but also sufficiently different to attract readers.[15] A blend of fact and fiction, designed to popularize one's own

---

[12] More detailed accounts of the pre-eighteenth-century situation regarding parliamentary reporting can be found in Peacey, "The Print Culture of Parliament," 2–9; and Sparrow, *Obscure Scribblers*, 7–10.

[13] See for example *The Conduct of His Grace the D—ke of Ar—le, or A Review of the Late Motion*.

[14] *London Magazine* (October 1741): 495.

[15] In the early 1740s, well over a third of the *Gentleman's Magazine* was occupied by the debates; see Cannon, *Samuel Johnson and the Politics of Hanoverian England*, 281.

parliamentary journalism while still producing a reasonably accurate record, was the obvious way to grab a share of the market.

Recognizing the complex relationship between the factual and the fictional in magazine culture in the 1730s and 1740s is crucial to making sense of Johnson's approach to parliamentary reporting. Unfortunately, a dominant theme in the scholarship on Johnson is the notion that the *Gentleman's Magazine*'s readers believed his accounts were verbatim or near-verbatim renditions of parliamentary business. Edward A. Bloom insists on "the credence usually given Johnson's accounts at the time they appeared," while W. Jackson Bate suggests that "[f]or at least twenty years, the speeches were almost universally regarded as authentic, and for long after that were still assumed to be so."[16] In a somewhat different analysis, Benjamin Beard Hoover describes two phases of the life cycle of Johnson's reports: an initial, credulous phase in which they were read as "the reflection of fact" followed by a second, more skeptical but also more admiring phase in which the reports were heralded as Johnsonian.[17] But another, much more compelling, criterion for considering the debates can be sensed in Alvin Kernan's lucid and groundbreaking study *Samuel Johnson and the Impact of Print*. Kernan complicates the existing interpretations of Johnson's parliamentary journalism, arguing that "[w]hat the *Debates* really show ... with their pattern of actual speeches transformed to notes changed to stories taken for fact by the original speakers and the author who thought he knew they were fictions, is how very tangled the whole question of fact and fiction was becoming in print culture."[18] This is a refreshing perspective because it acknowledges the most important aspect of early eighteenth-century parliamentary journalism: the way in which fact and fiction interacted.

It is difficult to be sure of eighteenth-century readers' expectations about the accuracy with which a parliamentary speech might be reported, but it seems likely that they both desired accuracy and were doubtful about its likelihood. In his seminal work *Factual Fictions*, Lennard J. Davis proposes that the early decades of the eighteenth century saw a gradual but complex teasing-out of the differences between the factual and the fictional, with the emergence of two genres, journalism and the novel, that would each be characterized by one of these notions. Kate Loveman

[16] Bloom, *Samuel Johnson in Grub Street*, 58, and Bate, *Samuel Johnson*, 203.
[17] Hoover, *Samuel Johnson's Parliamentary Reports*, 35.
[18] Kernan, *Samuel Johnson and the Impact of Print*, 163.

has described the way in which commentaries from the period put forward the concept of an ideal "sceptical reader," who understood that it was his or her "first responsibility to discern the truth-status of a work, thereby avoiding shameful misapprehension and lessening the risk of being deceived."[19] The "truth-status" of any work was also much more complex than modern ideas about accurate reporting might allow, since "[w]hen authors or readers described a work as 'true' they might mean 'factual', 'probable', 'morally correct', 'generally approved' or 'officially sanctioned'."[20] When it came to reports of speeches, readers of the 1730s and 1740s were perhaps especially wary given the practices of the previous century; during the furore of the Popish Plot, for example, falsified or doctored speeches from Parliament and testimony about the alleged plot circulated freely.[21] Numerous publications claiming to be true records of testimony, such as the last words and confessions of executed criminals, had also been exposed as politically motivated fakes.[22] While eighteenth-century readers did not have twenty-first-century expectations about recorded speech, they were nevertheless aware of the difference between fabricated accounts and accounts which attempted to meet accepted criteria of "truth-status." The reports from Parliament certainly needed to be written in such a way that they might be true; as Christopher Reid has argued, "In theory the House spoke only to itself, and it reproduced its sense of itself as a place apart, a zone of action and speech sealed from the hubbub of voices and opinions circulating outside the chamber, by means of distinctive acts of speech: more or less ceremonial pronouncements, specialized conventions of address, and styles of debate governed by parliamentary precedent and protocol."[23] These conventions needed to be reproduced in the magazines' reports if they were to be taken seriously.

The reason that many scholars believe readers accepted the *Gentleman's Magazine* coverage as entirely accurate is that Johnson's reports, along with some of those of his contemporaries, were printed quite promptly as accurate accounts of the speeches in Parliament in the collected debates of Chandler, Timberland and Torbuck. As early as 1744, not long after the last of his reports had appeared in the *Gentleman's Magazine*, a full two-thirds of Johnson's debates were being printed as the undisputed version of parliamentary proceedings in publications like these. Later in

---

[19] Loveman, *Reading Fictions*, 20.   [20] Loveman, *Reading Fictions*, 9.
[21] Loveman, *Reading Fictions*, 87–92.   [22] Loveman, *Reading Fictions*, 99.
[23] Reid, "'Community of Mind'," 321.

his life Johnson apparently claimed authorship of the debates when he heard them praised by readers who had encountered them in one of the parliamentary histories and considered them genuine. In the most famous anecdote of this sort, Johnson attended a dinner party, in the course of which the translator Philip Francis praised a particular speech given by William Pitt during Walpole's administration. The speech received "the approbation and applause of all present," before Johnson remarked, " 'That speech I wrote in a garret in Exeter-street.'" When he was asked to explain, Johnson replied:

I never had been in the gallery of the House of Commons but once. Cave had interest with the door-keepers. He, and the persons employed under him, gained admittance: they brought away the subject of discussion, the names of the speakers, the side they took, and the order in which they rose, together with notes of the arguments advanced in the course of the debate. The whole was afterwards communicated to me, and I composed the speeches in the form which they now have in the Parliamentary debates.[24]

One of the reasons that later readers such as Francis were duped into thinking they were reading verbatim accounts from the Parliaments of the day was the pronounced erasure of the original context that had informed the magazines' contemporary readers. The manner in which Chandler, Timberland and Torbuck chose to present the debates in their official histories virtually ensured that they would be accepted as fact. The editors included no citation information to indicate the original source of each debate or speech, thus making it impossible for new readers to know that there had been competing versions in the two magazines. They removed all of the nicknames and pseudonyms of the speakers. Most significantly, they omitted the hedging phrases and tentative language that had helped guide the original readers of the two magazines. In place of the magazines' typical introduction to a speech, which noted, for example, "[t]he last speaker in this debate was M. Horatius Barbatus, who spoke to this Effect," the official histories simply named the Earl of Halifax as the speaker.[25] Moreover, their prefaces and advertisements stressed the relative accuracy of their editions; Timberland informed purchasers of volume eight of his proceedings in the Lords that "where different Accounts have been given of the same Debate, such Speeches only are retain'd, as, upon

[24] Murphy, *An Essay*, 44–45.
[25] *London Magazine* (November 1741): 533; and Timberland, ed., *The History and Proceedings of the House of Lords*, VII: 730.

the strictest Examination appear'd to be genuine," the implication being that his edition conformed to the highest standards of accurately recorded speech that readers could have expected.[26]

The Stockdale edition of Johnson's *Debates in Parliament*, published in 1787, also contributed to the elision of the environment in which the speeches were originally published. Although he backed down from his original decision to remove all of the Lilliputian terminology, and included an appendix with this information, Stockdale completely reorganized the sequence of the debates, publishing them in chronological order and thus dismantling some of the competitive tension that came from the rivalry between the *Gentleman's Magazine* and the *London Magazine* as they battled to bring new and exclusive coverage to their readers.

Yet these readers, encountering Johnson's reports in their original medium and not in the later anthologies, had a great deal of information about contemporary norms for producing parliamentary reports and the mixture of fact and fiction that this process entailed. It is certainly true that the magazines sometimes suggested that their reports were close approximations of what had been said in Parliament and only posing, for legal reasons, as fictionalized accounts. This impression partly stemmed from a tradition of partisan writing with which readers would have been familiar; late seventeenth- and early eighteenth-century propaganda frequently included codes and historical allusions that were meant to be unraveled by discerning readers in order to explicate current events.[27] This tradition included not only *Gulliver's Travels* but also the more recent "Remarks upon the History of England," Viscount Bolingbroke's veiled critique of Walpole's government presented in the form of historical essays.[28] Moreover, although the speakers were usually referred to by their code names in the magazines' advertisements, Cave and Astley occasionally dispensed with the rudimentary disguises for speakers' names when the debate in question was particularly newsworthy; the *London Magazine*, for example, took delight in being able to announce publication of "the famous DEBATE on the MOTION to address his Majesty to remove Sir ROBERT WALPOLE from his Councils,

---

[26] Timberland, ed., *The History and Proceedings of the House of Lords*, VIII: i–ii.

[27] Loveman, *Reading Fictions*, 117.

[28] For a discussion of the "Remarks," see Pettit, *Illusory Consensus*, 35–57. For the best general discussion of the opposition's use of the print culture marketplace in Walpole's era, see Gerrard, *Patriot Opposition to Walpole*.

never before printed, and not to be met with in any other Magazine."[29] The disguises were, in any case, flimsy at best, especially those adopted by the *Gentleman's Magazine*, which were often simply anagrams. Readers quickly saw the parallels between the fictitious debating chambers and Britain's Houses of Parliament; a poem in the *Gentleman's Magazine* noted that readers could "Secrets veil'd from vulgar Readers, find; / With *Lilliputian* Senators debate, / And in their Contests view – the *British* State."[30]

Even in the earliest months of the new approach, when parliamentary scrutiny was presumably at its height, the magazines assisted readers further by providing keys to help decode their practices. The *Gentleman's Magazine* printed a mock advertisement for a publication called *Anagrammata Rediviva*, which used the Lilliputian names as examples of how to resolve anagrams and contained a list of the parliamentary pseudonyms that it had been using.[31] The *London Magazine*, meanwhile, included a detailed key in the collected version of its 1738 issues and a retrospective key covering all of its "Political Club" coverage in 1741.[32] From 1742, the index to the *Gentleman's Magazine* included translations of the Lilliputian terms. By July 1743, the *London Magazine* was actually including the real names of the speakers in footnotes and thus further dismantling the disguise.[33] The same impression was produced by the use of devices such as the original preface to "Debates in the Senate of Magna Lilliputia," which described the *Gentleman's Magazine*'s good fortune in allegedly receiving from Gulliver's grandson debates which demonstrated the similarities between Lilliput and Great Britain and "which the late Resolution of the House of Commons, whereby we are forbidden to insert any Account of the Proceedings of the *British Parliament*, gives us an Opportunity of communicating in their Room."[34]

The magazines took the overall credibility of their reports very seriously and bickered constantly about the relative quality of their coverage, each

---

[29]   *Universal Spectator* (May 30, 1741): 4, italics in the original.
[30]   "To Sylvanus Urban, On His Volume for 1739," *Gentleman's Magazine* (January 1739): n.p., lines 8–10. A similar point was made in a longer poem published in 1741 that used ellipsis to "name" the politicians who were covered in the Lilliputian reports; see "To Mr Urban, On His Vol. XI," *Gentleman's Magazine* (January 1741): n.p.
[31]   *Gentleman's Magazine* (Supplement 1738): 700–702. A new and more detailed key was published a few years later; see the *Gentleman's Magazine* (Supplement 1742): 699.
[32]   *London Magazine* (January 1738): n.p., and Preface (January 1741): n.p., respectively.
[33]   For the first instance of this new practice, see the *London Magazine* (July 1743): 313.
[34]   *Gentleman's Magazine* (June 1738): 283, italics in the original.

claiming to be the more accurate record. The *London Magazine* responded furiously to Cave's criticism of its reports by noting that the *Gentleman's Magazine*'s "Monthly Bundle of *Galimatias*, is neither purchased nor read by any Man of common Sense in the Kingdom."[35] The *Gentleman's Magazine*, meanwhile, noted in a self-congratulatory tone that its debates "have been so well received by our Readers in general, and so highly approved by all good Judges, that we receive Gratulations in Prose and Verse from all Quarters."[36] In a later preface, probably composed by Johnson, the *Gentleman's Magazine* likewise insisted that "[w]e have still the Satisfaction of finding, not only by the Applauses of our Friends, but by a more certain Proof, the Continuance of our Sale … that our Debates are considered as the most faithful and accurate."[37] While never claiming the status of anything approaching verbatim reports, the magazines nevertheless implied that they were engaged in the most accurate reporting that readers could expect.

During Johnson's tenure the competition became especially heated. In an introduction to a debate in the Lords he had covered, for example, Johnson noted that the *London Magazine*'s account appeared to have been composed by someone who was not acquainted with the debate, because some of the speeches had been misattributed and the order of the speakers was confused. As he triumphantly concluded:

What Confusion such an Error must make in a Learned and Political Argument, we need not inform our Readers; nor how successfully these Compilers contribute, as they have long boasted, "towards enabling the People of these Nations to form a right Judgment, with Respect to every Political Dispute that shall occur."[38]

The *London Magazine* responded angrily in its next preface:

WHAT [Cave] means by putting the Words of one Statesman into the Mouth of another, is beyond our Comprehension, for there are no Statesmen in the Club whose Debates we give an Account of; and as little do we know what he means by our being ignorant of the Number of Speakers, when in the Title Page of every one of our *Magazine* it is expressly declared, That all the Speeches made in the Club are not inserted, nor, indeed, would it be possible to afford Room

---

[35] *London Magazine* (April 1739): 171.
[36] *Gentleman's Magazine* (Supplement 1738): 699.
[37] *Gentleman's Magazine*, Preface (January 1742): n.p.
[38] *Gentleman's Magazine* (October 1742): 512. Readers were reminded of the mistake the following month; see *Gentleman's Magazine* (November 1742): 569–70.

in our *Magazine* for one Half of them, therefore we are obliged to give only the most remarkable.

IF we should shew a Contempt of our Readers by giving them such *Tittle-Tattle* as [Cave] entertains his with, in what he calls, The Debates of his *Lilliputian Senate*, we might easily give the Names, and such as he calls Speeches, of *twenty* or *thirty* Speakers in every *Magazine*; but this would not be so much as a Representation of the solemn and instructive Debates in the *Political Club*.

THE Speeches he gives, except when he steals from us, may most justly be called *Lilliputian Speeches*, and therefore, they may be proper enough for a *Lilliputian Senate*; but surely he has not the Impudence to palm his *empty and unmeaning*, or *nonsensical Stuff* upon his Readers, as the Debates of the *Political Club*, or of any other Assembly of Gentlemen in this Kingdom.[39]

A reader in the 1730s and 1740s (even one who read just one of the magazines) would thus have been aware that there was considerable controversy about the accuracy of parliamentary reporting. The constant claims about the veracity of the reports were tempered with comments designed to protect the editors against prosecution; Thomas Gordon, Johnson's counterpart at the *London Magazine*, for example, reminded readers that the use of code names and keys "has led the World into a Mistake, which is, their imagining that the Extracts of Speeches I send you, are the Speeches of the Persons whose Characters the Speakers assumed."[40] Moreover, some of the magazines' editorial practices encouraged readers to see the difference between the regular style of parliamentary reporting (embodied by the Lilliputian debates and the Gentlemen's Club) and the ideal account of a speech that came as close as possible to a verbatim record. The magazines occasionally printed much longer speeches, verified and corrected, under the full name of the original orator, as the *Gentleman's Magazine* did when it published Lord Gage's address in 1739.[41] Cave's editorial statement regarding the inclusion of authorized speeches made it clear to readers that such an approach was not the norm, since "to be so minute on every Occasion would be impossible, considering the narrow Limits of our Book."[42] Meanwhile readers of the authorized pamphlet version of Lord Limerick's address on the controversial motion to remove Robert Walpole from office, which Johnson covered for the *Gentleman's Magazine* in 1741, were advised in the pamphlet's preface that the only copies previously available were made

---

[39] *London Magazine*, Preface (January 1742): n.p.
[40] *London Magazine*, Preface (January 1743): n.p.
[41] *Gentleman's Magazine* (June 1739): 280–81 and (July 1739): 335–37.
[42] *Gentleman's Magazine* (August 1739): 411.

by "Scribblers, hired by the Publishers of *Magazines* at so much *per* Sheet … no one Member in the House can charge his Memory with a single Sentence of those palmed Speeches … which may as properly be father'd upon *Chinese* as *British* Speakers."[43]

A reader who sampled other printed sources, such as newspapers and pamphlets, would have been even more aware of the problems inherent in the magazines' reporting processes.[44] The *Daily Gazetteer*, for example, fumed over the "Pyratical Publishing" undertaken by the magazines and noted "[w]e have seen Speeches come out, that were never spoken; Meanings enforced that were not design'd; Words distorted; and the Whole mangled, and racked, and wrong applied to serve the wicked Purposes of a licentious Defamer."[45] Correspondents made the same point; one contributor to the opposition paper *The Craftsman* noted that he believed, having compared the two magazines' coverage, that "the Transactions of the present Times are … falsely deliver'd to Us."[46] This correspondent went on to note that he had been present at most of the debates in both Houses of Parliament:

there are scarce three Speeches that were spoke by the *Gentlemen*, to whom they are ascrib'd. Most of them are intirely forg'd; and if, in some others, there is a Scrap here and there, which any *Gentleman* did happen to say, it is so odly tack'd to the rest, and so spoil'd by the Way of repeating it, that the Person who said it, would have much Ado to know it again.[47]

Even novelists clarified the magazines' practices; in a direct reference to the *Gentleman's Magazine*'s Lilliputian approach in his 1743 novel *Jonathan Wild*, Henry Fielding commented that

even amongst the moderns, famous as they are for elocution, it may be doubted whether those inimitable harangues published in the monthly magazines came literally from the mouths of the HURGOS, &c., as they are there inserted, or whether we may not rather suppose some historian of great eloquence hath borrowed the matter only, and adorned it with those rhetorical flowers for which many of the said HURGOS are not so extremely eminent.[48]

---

43 *Two Speeches on the Late Famous Motion*, 2n, italics in the original.
44 An excellent and thorough overview of the metropolitan newspaper trade of the era can be found in Michael Harris, *London Newspapers in the Age of Walpole*.
45 *Daily Gazetteer* (September 23, 1738): 1.
46 *The Craftsman* (November 17, 1739): 1.
47 *The Craftsman* (November 17, 1739): 1–2.
48 Fielding, *The History of the Life of the Late Mr. Jonathan Wild*, 116. He makes a similar point in a later novel; see *Amelia*, 70.

But the most significant clue regarding the accuracy of the reports was the fact that the two magazines produced different versions. A contemporary reader who consulted both periodicals would have had to conclude that at least one of them was partly fabricating its coverage. With all of this information available to them, and the fact that they were peculiarly attuned to questions of authenticity because they had, for decades, been confronted with so many examples of deception in the texts they consumed, there is very little reason to suppose that readers in the 1730s and 1740s assumed that Johnson and his contemporaries were providing verbatim accounts, regardless of how Boswell and others portrayed the confusion around the authenticity of the debates in later years.[49] For those who remained credulous, both the fictional framework and the hedging phrases used to introduce the speeches from Parliament almost certainly made readers aware that debates were "recreated" rather than "reported," as Robert Folkenflik points out in his study of Johnson.[50]

In assuming that contemporary readers treated the debates as fact, critics are relying on a particular interpretation of Johnson's own myth-making. His feelings regarding the debates, for example, apparently led him to say on his deathbed that "the only part of his writings which then gave him any compunction, was his account of the debates in the *Magazine*; but that at the time he wrote them he did not think he was imposing on the world."[51] Scholars have interpreted this remark as confirming that the contemporary audience was deliberately duped by the way in which Johnson was "imposing on the world," but it makes more sense to read this comment as evidence that journalists working in this environment and period knew that they were *not* fooling the public and that there was no reason for Johnson, in the late 1730s and 1740s, to reproach himself until a later audience, denied the original context of publication, reacted credulously. This audience was formed as soon as the parliamentary histories began publishing the collected debates, which explains Boswell's remark that Johnson decided to stop working on the reports when he realized that some people thought they were genuine; only someone encountering the speeches in the collected debates could have thought that this was the case.[52] The same point could be made about another, much cited remark from the preface to the *Literary Magazine* in

[49] As well as Kate Loveman's work, see Lynch, *Deception and Detection in Eighteenth-Century Britain*.
[50] Folkenflik, *Johnson's Politics*, 108.   [51] Hill, ed. *Johnsonian Miscellanies*, II: 412.
[52] Boswell, *Boswell's Life of Johnson*, I: 152.

1756, in which Johnson wrote: "We shall not attempt to give any regular series of debates, or to amuse our Readers with senatorial rhetoric. The speeches inserted in other papers have been long known to be fictitious, and produced sometimes by men who never heard the debate, nor had any authentic information."[53] To read this remark as a veiled confession of his earlier deception, as Edward A. Bloom does, is to downplay the certainty with which Johnson comments that the speeches "have been long known to be fictitious." While later readers might have been confounded when they looked back over copies of the parliamentary histories, the magazines' readers in the 1730s and 1740s were alert to the mixture of fact and fiction they would encounter.

THE MAGAZINES' STYLES

This combination of the factual and the fictional was built in to the competition between the magazines. Relative accuracy was certainly one of the goals of parliamentary reporting in the period. But the second imperative governing the reporting – one that, to some extent, contradicted the attempts at accuracy – was the need to differentiate coverage from that of one's competitors, often in creative and unorthodox ways. In order to generate an audience for their reports, magazine editors had to provide something distinct and identifiably new. Advertisements for the two magazines make it clear that they were adopting such an approach in their appeals to readers; both editors routinely suggested that they had exclusive content that could not be found anywhere else, as the *London Magazine* did when it proudly announced in an advertisement for its July 1738 issue that "*[n]one of the* Speeches *in the* Debates abovemention'd *are to be met with in any other Monthly Collection.*"[54] The notions of the Lilliputian Senate and the Gentlemen's Club likewise testify to the magazines' desire for distinctive creative frameworks and distinctive brands for their reports.

There are two particularly significant differences between the parliamentary coverage that appears in the *Gentleman's Magazine* during Johnson's tenure as a reporter and that which was produced by the rival *London Magazine* at the same time, however. Both of these factors had the potential to shape Johnson's style of reporting dramatically. The first

---

[53] Samuel Johnson, *Samuel Johnson's Prefaces and Dedications*, 129.
[54] *London Evening Post* (July 27–29, 1738): 3, italics in the original. A corresponding example from the *Gentleman's Magazine* can be found in the *London Evening Post* (October 3–5, 1738): 4.

is that the *London Magazine* usually reported fewer speakers but longer speeches than the *Gentleman's Magazine*. Each magazine was explicit about its editorial strategy in this respect. In the preface to the first reports from the Political Club, the *London Magazine*'s reporter noted:

I cannot propose to send you a Copy, or even an Extract, of every Speech that is made in any Debate that happens in our Club; because upon such Occasions there must be Repetitions, which were perhaps agreeable enough to the Hearer, but might appear tedious to the Reader; and because a full Account, even of our remarkable Debates, would take up more Room than you can spare in your *Magazine*: Therefore, I shall, in every remarkable Debate, pick out some of the most remarkable Speeches that were made, and give you such full Extracts of them, that the Reader may there see all the material Arguments that were made use of upon that Occasion.[55]

The *London Magazine* was clearly engaged in an editorial selection process that aimed to reproduce the highlights of particular debates. This selective approach suited the magazine politically too, since it allowed the editor Astley to promote speeches by the anti-Walpole factions of Parliament, with whom he was sympathetic. A reader purchasing the *London Magazine* was aware that he was receiving an account that was partial in both senses of the word.

The *Gentleman's Magazine*, meanwhile, actively promoted itself in advertisements as "[c]ontaining more in Quantity and greater Variety than any Book of the Kind and Price."[56] In terms of its parliamentary coverage, this point of difference manifested itself as a plan to cover as many speakers as possible, even if it meant abbreviating the speeches. The difference in the number of speeches each periodical published was often considerable. The *Gentleman's Magazine* printed more than twice as many speakers as the *London Magazine* in the Lords' debate on removing Robert Walpole from office, and three times as many in the Lords' December 1741 debate on the address to the king. Cave was especially concerned about covering at least some of what was said by each of the speakers, particularly as it reflected on the accuracy of the magazines' respective accounts; he and Johnson gleefully attacked one particular debate composed by the

[55] *London Magazine* (May 1738): 243, italics in the original.
[56] *London Evening Post* (August 3–5, 1738): 4. The *London Magazine* occasionally inserted a similar phrase in its advertising; see for example the *Universal Spectator* (March 6, 1742): 4. In most instances, however, the *London Magazine* did not claim to include more content than the *Gentleman's Magazine*, suggesting that Astley was aware that breadth of coverage was not his magazine's strength.

London Magazine's reporters by noting that they were *"ignorant of the Number of Speakers. For, as in a former remarkable Debate they had but six Speakers instead of twenty, so in this, instead of ten, they have introduc'd but six, and those in a very confus'd Manner. It may therefore be concluded, that their Performance is founded only on Conjecture."*[57] Independent evidence, such as that recorded in the notebooks of members of Parliament during the debates, suggests that the *Gentleman's Magazine* would usually reproduce the order and identity of orators more correctly than its rival and allow at least some space to every speaker in a debate.[58]

As well as providing an identifiable point of difference for readers who were considering both sets of coverage, this editorial decision about the number of speakers to be covered radically affected the respective styles of the magazines' published debates. The *London Magazine*'s speeches were long and crammed with detail. The blend of fact and fiction that the *London Magazine* favored distorted the shape of the debate by omitting speakers but also ensured that "all the material arguments" were covered in the lengthy addresses it *did* include, and assigned to the correct side of the argument. With a greater variety of speakers and thus limited room for each individual speech, the *Gentleman's Magazine*'s versions were inevitably less dense, with the details and references to recent history either eschewed or shared across a range of speakers on either side of the argument. This lighter, less specific style helped to create a distinct brand for the *Gentleman's Magazine*; its coverage might be regarded as more factual, since more speakers were represented, but individual speeches were subject to fictionalization through abridgement and a focus on the structure and outline of an argument rather than the detail that supported it.

The *Gentleman's Magazine*'s style, and the manner in which it was achieved, were articulated in a significant 1740 editorial comment, written at a time when Johnson was away from London and not contributing to the magazine, which establishes that Cave was aiming for such a distinct brand.

It may be necessary to premise, that the Debates we have been favoured with by Mr *Gulliver*, are (as he tells us) considerably abridged. Probably he was of

---

[57] *Gentleman's Magazine* (October 1742): 512, italics in the original.
[58] See for example the debate in the Lords on the retention of the Hanover troops, which appeared in the *Gentleman's Magazine* from June to October 1743. Notes by Thomas Secker, the Bishop of Oxford, confirm that the order of speakers is entirely correct, although the *Gentleman's Magazine* makes a characteristic error in assigning Lord Carteret's final speech to the Earl of Chesterfield; a full transcription of the notes can be found in *Cobbett's Parliamentary History*, XII: 1058–68.

Opinion, that to descend to such Inferences as are evidently Consequent, is a Minuteness that would disoblige a Reader of Penetration; and perhaps in avoiding Prolixity he had some Regard to the Limits of our Book. We believe, it will be readily admitted, that the great Art of Writing consists in being concise without Obscurity, so as to leave nothing either requisite to be added or taken away. But in unstudied Speeches, especially to a publick Assembly, it is otherwise; a copiousness of Expression is there unavoidable; to enforce particular Points in Debates, Repetitions may be necessary; and where the Speakers are numerous, the same Thoughts will naturally recur, and the Argument must be protracted. Mr *Gulliver*, therefore, may be said, like a judicious Painter, to have mark'd the Outlines, to have design'd the principal Proportions, and thrown in some Characteristical Strokes of each masterly Hand, in these Pictures of *Lilliputian* Eloquence. He has thereby left to the Reader the Pleasure of supplying by his own Imagination, the circumlocutory Ornaments of Speech, and some consequential Arguments that must have arisen on the Questions that have been often disputed.[59]

This statement draws attention not only to the abridgements that were unavoidable but also to the artistry that Cave, as editor, apparently believed was necessary in producing effective parliamentary journalism. The *Gentleman's Magazine*'s reports would be stylized versions of the original controversies, written to provide readers with an overall sense of the arguments. Most importantly, its coverage was designed to avoid the "minuteness" and "copiousness of expression" that characterized the very long speeches published in the *London Magazine*. In practice this meant that the *Gentleman's Magazine* intended to ignore most of the specific evidence used in the speeches in favor of the "principal proportions" and "characteristical strokes" of each address. While not wishing to suggest that the reports were entirely inaccurate, Cave did draw readers' attention to the creative work they could expect to find in the *Gentleman's Magazine*, using the metaphor of the "judicious Painter" to suggest the imaginative reinterpretation of the debates as a particular virtue of his periodical's coverage. This is one deliberate editorial tactic, emerging out of competition with the *London Magazine*, that needs to be kept in mind when Johnson's reports are evaluated.

The second important difference between the two periodicals is that the *London Magazine* almost always presented its coverage of the debates some months before that of its rival. Readers anxious to find out about a particular parliamentary controversy were much more likely to get the

---

[59] *Gentleman's Magazine* (March 1740): 99, italics in the original. For the details of Johnson's absence, see Bloom, *Samuel Johnson in Grub Street*, 57.

news first from Cave's competitor. It is not clear from the evidence we have whether Cave expected the *Gentleman's Magazine* reporters to compile their reports immediately after the debates and then delayed publication, or whether they were afforded the months in between the debate and the eventual publication of the report to hone their offering. But even if the reports were compiled immediately, Cave's decision to delay publication could also be interpreted as a savvy business decision designed to counteract the major selling point of the *London Magazine*: its rapid production of reports. Allowing his reporters extra time to edit (if not necessarily to write) a report provided an opportunity to gather a more accurate and complete picture of the way the debate had unfolded. But it also afforded his reporters time to generate new and imaginative coverage that developed fictional elements to complement the factual basis.

Public opinion regarding the relative merits of the two sets of reports is very difficult to gauge. Hawkins suggested that the clever and distinctive presentation of the debates as Gulliver's reports from Lilliput increased the monthly sale of the *Gentleman's Magazine* from 10,000 to 15,000 copies.[60] But there is minimal evidence available and also the strong likelihood that any published comment is either a puff or a planted attack. Some enthusiasm for the *Gentleman's Magazine*'s style of coverage can perhaps be seen in a poem that appeared in the periodical in October 1738 and in *The Craftsman* in February 1739:

> Industrious *Gulliver*! our thanks receive,
> Your vary'd treats our appetites relieve;
> Tir'd with the crambe of our own Debates,
> You send us notices from foreign States;
> What *Lilliputian* senators decree ...
>   (lines 1–5)[61]

There is likewise a letter from "A Reader of Both Sides" praising the *Gentleman's Magazine*'s coverage and pointing out several mistakes and omissions in the *London Magazine*'s reports.[62] However, this praise can perhaps be balanced against the opinion of a correspondent in the *London*

---

[60] Hawkins, *Life of Samuel Johnson*, 78. He does not specify the timeframe in which this increase occurred, and Brack points out in his notes that there are no reliable circulation figures for the *Gentleman's Magazine*.

[61] *Gentleman's Magazine* (October 1738): 543, and *The Craftsman* (February 3, 1739): 2.

[62] *Gentleman's Magazine* (February 1739): 92.

Daily Post, who pointed out how much of Cave's coverage was copied from the *London Magazine*. The main difference between the two publications was that "what is clear and easily understood in the Original, is, by his *ill-judg'd Curtailings*, and by *Lilliputian Names* and *Terms*, render'd obscure and incomprehensible in the Copy. After what I have said, I need not tell you what is my Opinion, nor can I doubt what your own will be, after you have compared the two Magazines together."[63] Similar views were expressed by other writers, who noted that the *London Magazine* "is much the best of the two; but both are faulty, and the *Gentleman's Magazine* intolerable," or who criticized Cave for "the Speeches cook'd up by him in his pretended Debates."[64] It is apparent that readers, however they estimated the value of each of the two sets of coverage, recognized that they were being composed with different styles in mind.

The differences in the magazines' coverage in terms of the number of speakers and the timing of publication have been noted in earlier scholarship. However, there has been little analysis of the likely effects on Johnson's reporting, and no acknowledgment that these were primarily business decisions, not aesthetic ones, even though they affected the style of the resulting journalism. A comparison of Johnson's work with that of his competitors, based on an understanding of the marketplace conditions, is long overdue. Hoover notes Johnson's likely involvement in the reports on twenty-seven different debates in the *Gentleman's Magazine*, although he explains that the first nine of these reports are probably part of the previous phase of Johnson's work when he edited Guthrie's drafts, and thus do not provide us with a clear sense of his independent journalistic style.[65] Of the remaining eighteen debates there are eight for which the *Gentleman's Magazine* is the only source and ten which were also covered by the *London Magazine*. While it is possible to generalize about Johnson's journalism from any of his reports, the debates that generated overlapping coverage in the two magazines provide the clearest indication of the ways in which Johnson did or did not conform to contemporary norms and editorial expectations, and thus give us a much richer picture of the nature of his activity as a journalist.

[63] *London Daily Post* (May 1, 1741): 2, italics in the original.
[64] *The Craftsman* (November 17, 1739): 2, and *London Magazine* (August 1741): 390.
[65] See Hoover, *Samuel Johnson's Parliamentary Reports*, 212–14, for the chronological list, and 25–26 for the explanation of Johnson's role.

FACTUALITY AND JOHNSON'S REPORTS:
THE "SCANTY NOTES"

When Johnson told Francis and the assembled guests that the Pitt speech was composed "in a garret in Exeter-street," he set in motion a long history of assumptions about the fictionality of his reports for the *Gentleman's Magazine*.[66] But while creativity mattered in parliamentary reporting, so too did a serious attempt at accuracy. The key aspect of Johnsonian myth-making with regard to the debates – the idea that he "worked from scanty notes or none at all" – highlights the value that scholars have placed on Johnson's creative genius as the driving force in the *Gentleman's Magazine* coverage.[67] Less attention has been paid to the evidence that shows Johnson making use of the *Gentleman's Magazine*'s approach to parliamentary reporting in order to generate relatively accurate coverage. This approach provided him with not only with factual material that enhanced the debates but also, usually, with the advantage of seeing his competitor's work before he delivered his own version. Johnson was certainly expected to craft something new and inventive, in keeping with Cave's editorial demands for a creative spin on the debates, but the foundation of factuality supplied by reporters and sources, and the limitations and opportunities presented by the *London Magazine*'s versions of speeches, deserve more detailed scrutiny to establish how verifiable material was integrated into the reports.

Johnson's recollection of minimal support has significantly influenced interpretations of his parliamentary reporting, but it is important to note the language that he used when discussing this part of his life with Boswell. Boswell writes that "[s]ometimes ... [Johnson] had nothing more communicated to him than the names of the several speakers, and the part which they had taken in the debate."[68] The word "sometimes" here is crucial, and the equivocal note that it introduces into the story of Johnson's gallery career is often overlooked in the push to herald his achievement in inventing the speeches he composed from scratch. In fact, it is fairly clear that the *Gentleman's Magazine* frequently had reporters or sources at the debates. In 1737 Cave wrote to Thomas Birch, an acquaintance who sometimes attended the House of Parliament, to ask

[66] The early histories of journalism always stress this point; see for example Andrews, *History of British Journalism*, I: 149.

[67] Lipking, *Samuel Johnson*, 74.   [68] Boswell, *Boswell's Life of Johnson*, I: 118.

that "[a]s you remember the Debate so far as to perceive the Speeches already printed are not exact, I beg the favour that you will peruse the Inclosed, and in the best manner your memory will serve correct the mistaken Passages or add any thing that is omitted."[69] In another letter from the same year Cave writes, "I trouble you with the Inclosed, because you said you could easily correct what is herein given for Lord Ch—ld's Speech; I beg you will do so as soon as you can ... because the month is far advanced."[70] Cave is also likely to have had support from MPs anxious to see favorable coverage; he asked Birch to acquire an original copy of a speech for him from a member of Parliament, pointing out that "[i]t is a Method that several have been pleased to take, as I could shew, but think my Self under a Restraint. I shall say so far that I have had some by a third Hand, wch I understood well enough, to come from the first[,] others by Penny Post, & Many by the Speakers themselves, who have been pleased to visit St John's Gate."[71]

Sources such as Birch and Guthrie probably provided Johnson with more detail than the Boswell anecdote about "scanty notes" suggests. William Coxe, the early nineteenth-century biographer of the Walpole brothers, believed that "Johnson constantly received notes and heads of the speeches from persons employed by Cave, and particularly from Guthrie. The bishop of Salisbury recollects to have seen several of these notes, which Guthrie communicated to him [Johnson] on the very day on which he obtained them, which were regularly transmitted to Johnson, and formed the basis of his orations."[72] While none of these notes appears to have survived, some important conclusions can be drawn from the evidence about source material. It is clear that Johnson would have had to invent substantial portions of the speeches. It is also likely, however, that these inventions were based as much as possible on notes, which would have included the progress of the argument and also key phrases. These two imperatives – the need to be creative and the need to be accurate – were thus born out of the logistics of parliamentary reporting in the period.

[69] Birch Collection, British Library Add.MS.4302, fol. 95a.
[70] Birch Collection, British Library Add.MS.4302, fol. 97a.
[71] Birch Collection, British Library Add.MS.4302, fol. 114a.
[72] William Coxe, *Memoirs of the Life and Administration of Sir Robert Walpole*, 1: x. The bishop of Salisbury Coxe refers to is Dr. John Douglas, who held the office 1791 to 1807. Douglas had attracted the patronage of William Pulteney, the Earl of Bath and one of Walpole's fiercest opponents. Coxe writes that Douglas was in daily contact with Pulteney, who is presumably his source for the information about Guthrie's notes (1: xx).

But they also became vital components of a magazine's marketability and aesthetic style, and vital indicators of a journalist's success.

One useful example of the way these forces acted on Johnson can be found in what is likely his first sole-authored report for the *Gentleman's Magazine*: the Lords' debate on the motion to advise the king to remove Robert Walpole from office. The debate was published in the *London Magazine* from May to July 1741 and in the *Gentleman's Magazine* in July and August 1741. As Hoover points out in his detailed comparison of the magazines' reports, the significant theme in the published versions of this debate was the question of public opinion. He interprets this angle as a particularly Johnsonian one, arguing that

> [o]ne preoccupation, peculiar to Johnson's report, is worthy of note. By mass of words and emphasis of language, he lays great stress on "common fame" and the "voice of the people." Two conclusions seems obvious: Johnson is more inter-ested than Gordon [the *London Magazine*'s reporter] or the speakers themselves in the larger moral aspects of the debate, and he is highly interested in the rela-tion of the people to their government.[73]

Hoover is right to suggest that the *Gentleman's Magazine* report makes much more of the question of public opinion than does that of the *London Magazine*. Both periodicals have Lord Carteret note, in opening the debate and proposing the motion, that "common Fame," not a par-ticular crime, was an adequate basis for accusing Walpole of corruption and mismanagement, yet it is only in the *Gentleman's Magazine* that the phrase becomes central to the whole debate; the phrase does not occur again in the *London Magazine*'s report.[74] Most of Johnson's coverage in this report returns to the question of "common fame" either directly or indirectly. The Earl of Abingdon, in seconding the motion, defends the common sense of "[t]he Multitude [who] censure and praise with-out Dissimulation," and whose opinion of Walpole can thus be regarded as a reasonable gauge of the ethics of his past actions.[75] The Duke of Newcastle, a Walpole loyalist, predictably takes issue with reputation and rumour as the bases for proceeding, retorting that "[w]hen ... popu-lar Reports are alleged as the Foundation of the Address, it is probable that it is not founded in Reality upon known Crimes or attested Facts, and if the sudden Blasts of Fame may be esteemed equivalent to attested

---

[73] Hoover, *Samuel Johnson's Parliamentary Reports*, 78.
[74] *Gentleman's Magazine* (July 1741): 350, and *London Magazine* (May 1741): 210.
[75] *Gentleman's Magazine* (July 1741): 351.

Accusations, what Degree of Virtue can confer Security?"[76] The argument is picked up by all of those who speak in Walpole's defense in the *Gentleman's Magazine*. Lord Hardwicke, in Johnson's account, points out that "[c]ommon Fame, my Lords, is to every Man only what he himself commonly hears," while the Earl of Cholmondeley argues that if "the People judge for themselves on these Subjects, they must necessarily determine without Knowledge of the Questions, and their Decisions are then of small Authority."[77]

While Walpole's supporters reject "common fame" as the basis for censuring the minister in Johnson's account, his opponents continue to argue for the validity of public opinion as the basis for their case. The Duke of Argyll defends the judgment of the people, who "are far from being easily deceived" and not "Wretches whose Opinions are founded upon the Authority of seditious Scribblers."[78] The Earl of Halifax's point is similar: "My lords, Though I do not conceive the People infallible, yet I believe that in Questions like this they are seldom in the Wrong, for this is a Question not of Argument but of Fact; of Fact discoverable, not by long Deductions and accurate Ratiocinations, but by the common Powers of seeing and Feeling."[79]

Johnson may well have had private reasons for highlighting this aspect of the debate, but journalistic forces were at work too. The decision to focus on public opinion was not the creative leap of faith that it might seem. Independent notes are available for this particular debate and make it clear that "common fame" was indeed a vital feature of the arguments that day. Thomas Secker (the Bishop of Oxford, whose firsthand notes on the debates are widely cited both in William Cobbett's *Parliamentary History* and in Hoover's work) has Abingdon, Hardwicke, Carlisle and others adopt the phrase.[80] Hardwicke (who was presumably making notes in preparation for his own address but whose notebooks have not previously been considered in studies of Johnson's reporting) jotted down that "Common Fame has been held a Ground for an Impeachment. I shld be very sorry to see a Man condemned on an Impeachment ground on common Fame," and noted the phrase being used several times throughout the

[76] *Gentleman's Magazine* (July 1741): 352.
[77] *Gentleman's Magazine* (August 1741): 404 and 410 respectively.
[78] *Gentleman's Magazine* (August 1741): 396.
[79] *Gentleman's Magazine* (August 1741): 412.
[80] See British Library Add.MS.6043, fol. 76a (Abingdon), fol. 81a (Hardwicke), fol. 82b (Carlisle), and fol. 83a (Westmoreland).

debate.[81] Among Birch's papers is an account of the debate that also mentions the phrase.[82] In other words, the aspect of the report that Johnson chooses to highlight is the aspect that is *most* grounded in reality, not in the Johnsonian imagination.

More evidence of the way Johnson worked within the norms of contemporary expectations about parliamentary reporting can be found in the report on the second reading of the bill for indemnifying evidence against Robert Walpole (now Lord Orford, following his resignation as a minister and elevation to the House of Lords).[83] In his version, Johnson again appears to latch on to some particular linguistic features of the debate in order to create a coherent structure. In refusing to consent to a second reading of the bill, Carteret argues in the *Gentleman's Magazine*'s account that the standard of proof in the British justice system demanded "that there is a *Corpus Delicti*, a Crime really and visibly committed."[84] The Earl of Chesterfield later picks up on Carteret's point, suggesting that it was pointless to argue "that there is no *Corpus Delicti*; for even, though it were true, yet while there is a *Corpus Suspicionis*, then Enquiry ought to be made for our own Honour, nor can either Law or Reason be pleaded against it."[85] This same idea then gets addressed by Hardwicke, who jokes that he cannot understand the meaning of the term "*corpus suspicionis*," which he interprets as "*the Body of a Shadow*."[86]

Since "corpus delicti" and "corpus suspicionis" are not mentioned at all in the *London Magazine*'s coverage, the phrases might seem at first to be Johnson's interpolations, designed to provide a linking thread that lends shape and coherence to the debate. However, just as independent notes prove that "common fame" was not simply a Johnsonian interest but a larger parliamentary one, so extant sources support his focus on the language and phrasing in this debate. The Secker notes have Carteret

[81] Hardwicke Papers, vol. DXXVIII, British Library Add.MS.35876, fol. 92b, fol. 80b, fol. 81a, fol. 81b, fol. 83b. Edward Harley records that he mentioned the "common fame" charge in his own speech defending Walpole in the Commons; see Taylor and Jones, eds., *Tory and Whig*, 51.

[82] Birch Collection, British Library Add.MS.4107, fol. 234b.

[83] Following Walpole's move to the Lords, a secret committee of Parliament was formed to gather evidence of corruption against him. The opposition successfully guided the bill, which would have protected witnesses who could testify against Walpole, through the Commons but it was ultimately rejected by the House of Lords; see Black, *Robert Walpole*, 44–45.

[84] *Gentleman's Magazine* (October 1742): 513.

[85] *Gentleman's Magazine* (November 1742): 566. The *Gentleman's Magazine* routinely mistook Chesterfield for Carteret (although not the other way round), and this speech is thus assigned to Carteret in the magazine.

[86] *Gentleman's Magazine* (November 1742): 567.

saying that in order for the bill to be supported "[t]here must be a corpus delicti."[87] Johnson's report of Chesterfield's address is also supported by Secker, who notes that Chesterfield said "[t]here is corpus suspicionis, indeed delicti."[88] Finally, Secker confirms Johnson's information about Hardwicke's speech, recording Hardwicke's phrase as "[c]orpus suspicionis is a new Term, it is the body of a shadow."[89] The pattern that was established in Johnson's coverage of the motion in the Lords to remove Walpole is also evident here. His choice of a framing device to provide coherence to the debate is supported by independent evidence and also contributes to the success of the *Gentleman's Magazine*'s attempt to generate new and creative coverage.

In his reading of the debates, Donald J. Greene puts forward the idea that Johnson's method was "to take one important controversial topic and make of it a set piece, a formal and exhaustive dissertation in dialogue form."[90] W. Jackson Bate has proposed a similar scenario, arguing that "[w]hat Johnson did was to turn the debates into a drama of ideas, and in a way that was to become a prototype for much of his later writing. He quickly found himself using the debates to present particular points of view in counterpoint as they referred to a particular question."[91] This idea of the internal coherence of Johnson's reports can be seen in the two debates just discussed, with the phrases "common fame" and "corpus delicti" contributing to the sense of each debate as a set piece. Two elements are missing from Greene's and Bate's analysis, however. The first is that the internal coherence they perceive in the debates was considerably less obvious to the original *Gentleman's Magazine* readers, who were often encountering coverage that spanned several months, breaking off in between speeches or occasionally in the middle of an individual address. It would have been much more difficult for such readers, in contrast to those who read Johnson's contributions in the collected *Debates in the Senate of Lilliput*, to ascertain the overall thematic shape of each debate. The second, related, gap in Greene's and Bate's theory is an acknowledgment that the fictional could only thrive on a factual foundation. The

---

87 British Library Add.MS.6043, fol. 121b.
88 British Library Add.MS.6043, fol. 127a.
89 British Library Add.MS.6043, fol. 128b. Another source for the debate is Edward Harley. His notes do not include these phrases, although the general outline of the arguments is the same; see Taylor and Jones, eds., *Tory and Whig*, 60–61.
90 Greene, *Politics of Samuel Johnson*, 114.
91 Bate, *Samuel Johnson*, 207.

strongest links in these debates, links which persisted over the unfolding months of coverage, were those that were based in fact. Greene and Bate are not attentive to these points because they do not acknowledge that the source of Johnson's style can be found in the journalistic marketplace and the manner in which it shaped contemporary coverage.

This factual foundation was provided by Cave's reporters and contacts. While in the absence of their notes it is often difficult to ascertain the type of assistance they provided, there are two debates for which there is clear evidence about the help Johnson received. On February 1, 1743, the Lords examined the state of the army in light of the estimates of costs that had been presented to them by the Commons, focusing particularly on the contentious issue of pay for the Hanoverian troops. In the diary of Thomas Birch, whose input Cave sought on other occasions, there is a note for February 1, 1743 that reads, "Present at the Debates in the House of Lords."[92] Birch's help can be seen in the fact that Johnson's account covers all of the speakers from the debate, as a comparison with Harley's diary shows.[93] This is one of the rare cases in which the *Gentleman's Magazine* began publishing before the *London Magazine*'s account had appeared; Johnson's coverage was, by contemporary standards, rushed into print, appearing from June to October 1743, while the *London Magazine* did not begin to report it until November of the same year. Johnson therefore could not have consulted his competitor's version before composing his own account.

The two magazines' accounts of this debate correspond more closely than on most other occasions. Both accounts of the debate contain a reference that Lord Hervey made to the author Samuel Pufendorf, who had theorized in his writings about hereditary and elective monarchies.[94] Secker again verifies the reference; in his notes, Hervey states that "Puffendorf [*sic*] thinks it is not the interest of the Empire to have a head too powerful."[95] Both versions of the Earl of Chesterfield's address also include a distinctive reference to the war with Spain. In the *Gentleman's Magazine* Chesterfield points out:

[92] Birch Collection, British Library Add.MS.4478C, fol. 88b.
[93] Taylor and Jones, eds., *Tory and Whig*, 63. As often happened, the *Gentleman's Magazine* assigns Chesterfield's late speech to Carteret by mistake, but the list of speakers is otherwise entirely accurate. Lord Hardwicke's notes are less full, but also confirm the identity of many of the speakers; see British Library Add.MS.38161 fols. 40–47.
[94] See the *Gentleman's Magazine* (August 1743): 412; and the *London Magazine* (December 1743): 584.
[95] British Library Add.MS.6043, fol. 156b.

Before the War was declared, it is well remembered by whom, and with how great Vehemence, it was every Day repeated, that to end the War with Honour we ought to *take and hold*. What, my Lords, do we *hold*, or what have we *taken*?[96]

The corresponding section in the *London Magazine* has Chesterfield recollect:

About three or four Years since, I remember, I heard some Lords talk a great deal of our War against *Spain*, and of the mighty Feats we were to perform. We were to take: We were not only to take, but to hold. Now, after a War of three Years Continuance, in which our Trade has suffer'd extremely, what have we taken, what can we hold?[97]

Since the *London Magazine* did not routinely model its coverage on that of the *Gentleman's Magazine*, it seems likely that this close correspondence reflects a part of the debate that the editors were sure was relatively accurate.

A second instance of Birch assisting Johnson, during the Lords' debate on the Spirituous Liquors Bill, rendered similar results. A note in his diary places Birch in the House on the opening day of the debate, February 22, 1743.[98] The *London Magazine* produced the first part of its account in October 1743; the *Gentleman's Magazine* immediately responded in November and began to outstrip its rival over the ensuing months. The effect of the firsthand information is obvious. Both periodicals, for example, have Chesterfield joke that the new law might be called the "drinking fund," an allusion to Walpole's notorious misuse of the Sinking Fund, a remark which also appears in Secker's notes.[99] Both versions also include an irreverent section in which Chesterfield argues facetiously for a new preamble reflecting the government's real intentions, remarks which are verified by Secker's notes.[100]

In their coverage of Secker's own speech to the Lords in this debate, the two magazines again share a number of features. Both reports have him outlining the worst effects of the gin-shops that had appeared over recent years, including what the *London Magazine* describes as

---

[96] *Gentleman's Magazine* (September 1743): 464.
[97] *London Magazine*, Appendix (December 1743): 637.
[98] Birch Collection, British Library, Add.MS.4478C, fol. 89b.
[99] *Gentleman's Magazine* (December 1743): 627, *London Magazine* (October 1743): 488; and British Library Add.MS.6043, fol. 160a. Walpole had used the Sinking Fund to alleviate short-term financial problems facing the Ministry rather than paying off debt. The manipulation of the Sinking Fund fueled suspicions about corruption in the administration. See Black, *Robert Walpole*, 26–29.
[100] *Gentleman's Magazine* (December 1743): 627–28; *London Magazine* (October 1743): 488; and British Library Add.MS.6043, fol. 160a.

an invisible Scene still more horrible to think of; for they tell me, every one of these Gin-shops had a back Shop or Cellar, strowed every Morning with fresh Straw, where those that got drunk were thrown, Men and Women promiscuously together: Here they might commit what Wickedness they pleased, and by sleeping out the Dose they had taken, make themselves ready to take another, if they could find Money to pay for it.[101]

The same idea is rendered in Johnson's report as that which "cannot be mentioned without Horror, Back-rooms and secret Places were contrived for Receptacles of those who had drank, till they had lost their Reason and their Limbs, there they were crowded together till they recovered Strength sufficient to go away, or drink more."[102] This point was certainly raised in the debate; Hardwicke notes the Bishop's discussion of the gin-shops and Secker himself has a note that the existing law "shut up 1500 great Gin shops with places behind them for stowing drunken men & women promiscuously."[103] Another distinctive reference in Secker's speech concerns the effects of alcohol on children, with Johnson reporting that "a single Spoonful has been found sufficient to hurry two Children to the Grave" and the *London Magazine* mentioning that "the other Day, as I have been credibly informed, there were two Children murdered by giving them a Spoonful of that pernicious Liquor called Gin."[104] Again, Secker includes this remark in his own notes, which lament that "as one melancholy part of the evil is the destruction of young children, a very small quantity will do this. Two were killed with each a spoonful, but last week."[105]

The importance of factual material in the production of debates can be sensed in the examples of the debate on the army and the debate on spirituous liquors, in which every opportunity to include a phrase or reference from the House is taken by both Johnson and his competitor. This degree of firsthand information was not perhaps the norm but it was possible. Johnson was not always called upon to invent material and his inventions did not displace the facts available to him; they enhanced and elucidated them instead. The unusual publication timelines for the first debate also points to the value of accurate information; it seems likely that Birch's

[101] *London Magazine* (October 1743): 478–79.
[102] *Gentleman's Magazine* (November 1743): 581.
[103] Hardwicke Papers, vol. DXXVIII, British Library Add.MS.35876, fol. 58a; and British Library Add.MS.6043, fol. 157b, respectively.
[104] *Gentleman's Magazine* (December 1743): 621 and *London Magazine* (October 1743): 479 respectively.
[105] British Library Add.MS.6043, fol. 159a.

assistance helped Cave and Johnson to feel certain about the accuracy of their source material and thus confident about going into print first.

This publication timeline also features in another debate that both magazines covered: the Lords' consideration of an address to the king on December 4, 1741.[106] The *Gentleman's Magazine* published its account of the first of these debates between July and September 1742, while the *London Magazine* reported it from September to November the same year. The two accounts of the opening speech by Lord Milton strongly suggest that each magazine had a source at the debates. Johnson has Milton assure the king "that we will vigorously and heartily concur in all just and necessary Measures for the Defence and Support of His Majesty, the Maintenance of the Balance and Liberties of *Degulia* [Europe] and the Assistance of our Allies," a phrase which the *London Magazine* renders as an assurance "that we will vigorously and heartily concur in all just and necessary Measures for the Defence and Support of his Majesty, and the Maintenance of the Liberties of *Europe*."[107] Johnson's Milton takes the opportunity

to renew the most sincere Professions of our constant and inviolable Fidelity: And to promise His Majesty, that we will, at the Hazard of all that is dear to us, exert ourselves for the Defence and Preservation of His Sacred Person and Government, and the Maintenance of the Protestant Succession in His Imperial House, on which the Continuance of the Protestant Religion, and the Liberties of *Lilliput*, do, under God, depend.[108]

The same sentiment in the *London Magazine* is expressed rather more flatly as a desire to "give his Majesty the strongest Assurances of our inviolable Duty, Fidelity, and Affection to his Person and Government, and of our Zeal for the Preservation of the Protestant Succession in his Royal House."[109] Several key phrases show up in both accounts, such as "the common cause," "the just and necessary war" against Spain and the king's "safe and happy return."[110] It is of course possible that the *London Magazine* copied these phrases from Johnson, rather than relying on a source of its own, but such a supposition tends to reinforce the idea that

---

[106] Horace Walpole's brief account of this debate can be found in *The Yale Edition of Horace Walpole's Correspondence*, XVII: 230. Hardwicke's notes on some of the speakers can be found in British Library Add.MS.35876, fols. 133–34.

[107] *Gentleman's Magazine* (July 1742): 347; and *London Magazine* (September 1742): 433, italics in the original.

[108] *Gentleman's Magazine* (July 1742): 347, italics in the original.

[109] *London Magazine* (September 1742): 433.

[110] *Gentleman's Magazine* (July 1742): 346; *London Magazine* (September 1742): 432–33.

Gordon and Astley were confident that Johnson had accurate information about the speech.

An even more valuable source than a witness at the gallery, however, was an authorized copy of a speech submitted by an MP, which the magazines actively solicited; the *London Magazine*, for example, asked that "[a]s all the Speeches made in the abovemention'd CLUB are not inserted in their Journal Book, we are desir'd by their Secretary to advertise, that any Gentleman of the Club may send a Copy, or Extract, of what he said on any important DEBATE to the Publisher of this Magazine, and it shall be inserted in its proper Place."[111] One report which apparently attracted such contributions from the speakers themselves during Johnson's tenure as sole reporter was that of the debate on the Hanover troops, which began appearing in the *London Magazine* in May 1743 and in the *Gentleman's Magazine* in February 1744.[112] The two accounts contain identical speeches by Sir John St. Aubyn, which were almost certainly from an authorized copy that was sent to both publications; the *London Magazine* mentioned that St. Aubyn's speech was printed out of sequence since it came "too late to be inserted in its proper Place."[113] St. Aubyn was not the only politician making such contributions; the *Gentleman's Magazine* had already published Lord Perceval's speech from this debate in its April 1743 issue, as had the *London Magazine* two months later.[114] When the *Gentleman's* began to cover the debate as a whole in 1744, Johnson simply referred readers back to the issue that contained Perceval's authorized address.[115] The inclusion of authorized speeches points to the overwhelming value of factual content, a resource which naturally trumped any creative contribution that a reporter like Johnson might make.

Hoover mentions many of these examples but interprets them as minor instances of reliable source material that do not detract from the overwhelming burden to create speeches from scratch. In his discussion of the "corpus delicti" speeches of May 25, 1742, for example, he notes that Secker confirms the phrases used by Chesterfield and Hardwicke

---

[111] *London Evening Post* (June 3–6, 1738): 4.
[112] An account of this debate by William Hay, MP for Seaford, can be found in Taylor and Jones, eds., *Tory and Whig*, 186–87.
[113] *London Magazine* (June 1743): 284. For the text of this speech see the *Gentleman's Magazine* (February 1744): 68–70; *London Magazine* (June 1743): 284–86.
[114] *Gentleman's Magazine* (April 1743): 184–89; *London Magazine* (June 1743): 278–83.
[115] *Gentleman's Magazine* (March 1744): 123.

(although he does not mention that Johnson and Secker also overlap in attributing "corpus delicti" to Carteret too).[116] To Hoover these overlaps are "isolated phenomena," a reasonable assessment given how much of the coverage cannot be verified and appears to have been invented.[117] Given that journalists were supposed to know nothing of the particulars of the debates after the ban of April 1738, however, these moments of accuracy might be regarded as comprising a relative treasure-trove of information for reporters who did not expect such assistance and for readers who did not expect such veracity. The fact that reports drew on numerous sources – the magazines' staff, a friend like Birch, a member of Parliament, the account of the rival periodical, or an independent pamphlet – suggests that journalists sought and prized accurate details. Kaminski has argued that in the *Gentleman's Magazine*, "[f]or verisimilitude, the order of the speakers was followed as closely as possible and particular phrasings occasionally woven into the fabric, but for the most part, the work was subject to the invention, diction, and arrangement of the author."[118] It might be possible to modify this assessment by noting just how important details like the order of speakers and particular phrases actually were when it came to putting the debates together. They did more than lend verisimilitude: they reflected fact, enhancing the standing of the coverage. Accurate phrases were not so much threads woven into the report as the loom on which a report was constructed. These conclusions help to modify the critical consensus that has sprung up around Johnson's parliamentary journalism by tempering the emphasis on his creative powers that stems from the remarks to Francis and his friends that I have returned to throughout this chapter. This consensus invariably values the literary over the journalistic; it is revealing, for example, that scholars like Hoover regard the occasionally accurate parts of the reports as "isolated phenomena" but believe that the occasionally Johnsonian language amounts to an entirely original and identifiable personal style. While Johnson's creativity was valued, it did not overwhelm the basic journalistic imperative of providing an accurate account whenever possible. While much of what appeared in the reports was fiction, fact was an extremely marketable commodity.

[116] Hoover, *Samuel Johnson's Parliamentary Reports*, 114–15.
[117] Hoover, *Samuel Johnson's Parliamentary Reports*, 115.
[118] Kaminski, *Early Career of Samuel Johnson*, 130.

THE WALPOLE SPEECH

An understanding of the relationship between fact and fiction in the *Gentleman's Magazine*'s approach to parliamentary reporting is crucial to evaluating the speech that is usually cited by modern scholars as the epitome of Johnson's stylistic technique: Robert Walpole's address in response to the motion in the House of Commons to remove him from office.[119] The *London Magazine*'s coverage of this famous debate had appeared in installments in March and April 1742, almost a year before the *Gentleman's Magazine*'s version was published in February, March and April 1743. Johnson's account of Walpole's concluding speech on this occasion is usually held up as the masterpiece of his parliamentary reporting career. Robert Folkenflik suggests that "[m]ost scholars who have looked at his debates closely have been struck by the way in which the various speakers are enabled to put their points with dignity, especially Sir Robert Walpole at the time of the attack upon his conduct of the administration," while Donald J. Greene proposes that "[i]t is probably the most dramatic thing Johnson ever wrote."[120] This speech deserves significant attention in any study of Johnson's career as a parliamentary reporter precisely because it is so often selected as the pinnacle of his reportorial achievement. But consideration of Walpole's words often happens in isolation, or, at best, in a brief comparison with the *London Magazine*'s account of the speech itself, rather than in the context of the debate in which it occurred and of the normal editorial procedures of both magazines.[121] In the discussion which follows, I focus on the ways in which some of the most celebrated elements of the speech – its simplicity and the dramatic build-up of the debate as a whole – owe a great deal to the way the *Gentleman's Magazine* typically reported the proceedings.

One of the most impressive and easily overlooked aspects of the address is the manner in which the denouement of the debate is crafted in the *Gentleman's Magazine*. Greene isolates the "dramatic shock" provided by

---

[119] The debate had taken place on February 13, 1741, in both Houses of Parliament. The proponents of the motion failed to bring together the various strands of opposition to Walpole and mismanaged the process to such an extent that many of Walpole's enemies abstained from the vote owing to the unfairness of the proposed action against him; see Black, *Robert Walpole*, 41.

[120] Folkenflik, "Johnson's Politics," 108, and Greene, *Politics of Samuel Johnson*, 128.

[121] Hoover is of course the exception; the debates in both Houses on the motion to remove Walpole are given the fullest treatment of any of Johnson's reports. But Hoover considers Walpole's speech only in the chapter on the debates as fact, and is thus largely interested in trying to establish which parts, if any, of Johnson's account are accurate.

Walpole's final speech, but what is not acknowledged in analyses such as this is the degree to which Johnson exploits both the generic conventions of parliamentary journalism and the *Gentleman's Magazine*'s specific tactics for generating coverage to create the dramatic mood that surrounds the Minister's defense.[122] This debate, like most of those covered at the time, appeared in installments over several months in the magazines. The coverage attained a sense of drama through these delays, which encouraged readers to obtain the next month's issue in order to see the conclusion. This aspect of parliamentary reporting was, paradoxically, enhanced by the fact that the magazines held back their coverage until well after the events in question were concluded. In this case, the debate on Walpole's future was over a year old by the time it was published in the *London Magazine*, and over two years old by the time Johnson's account appeared. Readers were not drawn to the magazines to find out what had happened to Walpole but rather to see how each would report the arguments about his fate.

Beyond the effects of these shared editorial practices, the drama of Walpole's final speech in the *Gentleman's Magazine* results in part from the decision to cover as many speakers as possible. The *London Magazine*'s approach was to print only six speeches and to focus on key players in the Commons such as Samuel Sandys, Henry Pelham, William Pulteney and Walpole himself. The *Gentleman's Magazine*'s tactic was to print twenty-two speeches, thus producing a much fuller and more accurate account of the range of orators, even if it meant carrying some truncated addresses. This decision led to the inclusion of some speeches that added to the tension and anticipation around Walpole's address. While both magazines begin with Samuel Sandys's motion recommending that the king remove Walpole from office, the sequence of nine speeches that follow Sandys's in the *Gentleman's Magazine* are all ignored in the *London Magazine*. In these short addresses, a new and apparently minor motion enters the debate: Wortley proposes that Walpole should withdraw from the House according to the precedent that "every Member against whom an Accusation is brought, should retire out of this Assembly, while his Conduct is examined."[123] This topic occupies Johnson for some time, as he presents a further seven speakers who briefly address this procedural question from one or the other side.

---

[122] Greene, *Politics of Samuel Johnson*, 128. [123] *Gentleman's Magazine* (February 1743): 75.

This section of the coverage might read as an unnecessary digression from the main action, but the effect is to heighten the drama of the debate, as Walpole's brooding presence in the chamber is discussed and contested while the man himself remains silent. By including this motion and the speeches it prompted, the *Gentleman's Magazine* not only provides more comprehensive and accurate coverage of the events of that day, but also creates an appealing narrative structure for the debate, as readers are reminded that the climax of the argument will be Walpole's final defense. This impression is further reinforced by the *Gentleman's Magazine*'s decision to include the short statement, omitted by the *London Magazine*, in which Walpole requested to hear all the charges against him before he was called on to reply.[124]

The respective ways in which the two magazines reported the debate until this point inevitably shaped the coverage of the final two speakers, Pulteney and Walpole. The two accounts make it clear that Pulteney had hoped to speak after Walpole and rebut his defense; the *Gentleman's Magazine* has him note that he found himself speaking "sooner than I intended," while the *London Magazine* reports him as protesting that he "did not, at first, think of speaking so early in the Debate."[125] Instead of responding to Walpole, Pulteney would to some extent be setting the terms on which the Minister's defense would be conducted, and both magazines consequently used the former's speech as a critical counterpoint to the latter's final response. It is thus worth paying attention to the way they chose to structure Pulteney's address.

In its account of this speech, which takes up only six columns of type, the *Gentleman's Magazine* has Pulteney deal briefly with the specific charges against Walpole and instead narrow his focus to the Minister's likely defense and the manner in which he would probably speak:

That the Charge will be *answered* by the Right Hon. Gentleman I can make no doubt, because he has never wanted an Answer to any Arguments that have been alleged against the most incredible of his Assertions or the most pernicious of his Measures; but that it will be *confuted* by him, whatever my natural Candour may incline me to wish, I confess, I do not expect: Because he never yet was able to overthrow the Arguments of those who opposed him, and Time has been very far from adding to the Facility of a Vindication.

If we may guess at the Nature of the Defence which he will offer, from that which has already been advanced by his Advocates and Adherents, we

---

[124] *Gentleman's Magazine* (April 1743): 175.
[125] *Gentleman's Magazine* (April 1743): 175, and *London Magazine* (April 1742): 168.

may reasonably conclude that it will produce no remarkable effects upon this Assembly, nor persuade any Man of his Innocence who has not already determined to acquit him.[126]

In contrast, the *London Magazine* does not have Pulteney discussing Walpole's defense at all, preferring to focus instead on a long and very detailed account of the general events in recent history that contributed to the case against the minister. Occupying over twenty columns of type, this version of Pulteney's speech is full of references to specific historical occurrences – the treaties of Hanover, Utrecht and London, the establishment of the Quadruple Alliance, the marriage arrangements between the royal families of France and Spain, and changes in the balance of power in Europe.

The difference between the two accounts of Pulteney's address makes sense in the context of their respective presentations of the debate as a whole and their differing editorial strategies. The *Gentleman's Magazine* had already provided five speeches covering the general context for proceeding against Walpole, while the *London Magazine*, by selecting only a few speakers, had to leave the burden of outlining the details of the opposition's case to Pulteney. These decisions then had important consequences for the magazines' respective presentations of Walpole's address, the style, content and dramatic mood of which was determined by the way they had each chosen to report Pulteney. By the time Walpole rises to speak in the *London Magazine*, his address is inevitably concerned with rebutting the specific charges against him that have just been raised. By the time he rises to speak in the *Gentleman's Magazine*, the debate has become entirely focused on the *style* in which he will conduct his defense. Johnson's Pulteney had concerned himself with Walpole's likely rhetoric; rhetoric thus became the most important feature of Walpole's response. The lack of detail in the *Gentleman's Magazine*'s rendition of the speech is in fact what generates the drama of Walpole's words; instead of giving his account of recent history, he is allowed to deliver a dramatic monologue.

The *London Magazine*'s account of Walpole's speech begins with an outline of his initial reaction to the charges, making it clear that he intends to construct his defense around the idea that he was not, as the opposition had repeatedly alleged in Parliament, the "sole minister" responsible for every decision taken by the administration:

[126] *Gentleman's Magazine* (April 1743): 176.

I confess, I am at a Loss what to say, or how to justify myself on this Occasion. I had often heard, that some such Motion was designed against me; but I was always at a Loss to conjecture what the Hon. Gentlemen might have to say in support of their Motion … If I were to answer for myself alone, I should think my Task very easy; but as I am to answer for King, Lords and Commons, it gives me great Pain, lest their Cause should suffer thro' any Incapacity in me.[127]

Walpole goes on to say that he will deal with some of the key events that his opponents have cited as evidence of his mismanagement "in the Order of Time in which the several Transactions happened" and this account occupies much of the remainder of the *London Magazine*'s report, which has Walpole engage in detail with the specific charges, such as the botched opportunity to exploit the rupture between France and Spain, the negotiation of the Treaty of Hanover and the pursuit of the so-called "Pragmatic Sanction," which obliged Britain to intervene to help the Queen of Hungary. These details mirror the charges that Pulteney, in the *London Magazine*, had just leveled at the minister. The speech ends with Walpole's rather histrionic clinching argument:

To conclude, Sir, tho' I shall always be proud of the Honour of any Trust or Confidence from his Majesty, yet I shall always be ready to remove from his Councils and Presence, when he thinks fit I should do so; and therefore I should think myself very little concerned in the Event of the present Question, if it were not for the Incroachment that will thereby be made upon the Prerogatives of the Crown. But I must think, that an Address to his Majesty to remove one of his Servants, without so much as alledging any particular Crime against him, is one of the greatest Incroachments that was ever made upon the Prerogatives of the Crown; and therefore, for the Sake of my Master, without any Regard to my own, I hope all those that have a due Regard for our Constitution, and for the Rights and Prerogatives of the Crown, without which our Constitution cannot be preserved, will be against this Motion.[128]

Johnson's account in the *Gentleman's Magazine* is a clear move away from this methodical rendition from the *London Magazine*, and an example of the way in which he might have used the additional time afforded to him to craft a distinct product for his employer. He entirely changes the tone and emphasis of Walpole's remarks, while adhering to the main lines of argument as outlined in the *London Magazine*. Moreover, he delivers the kind of speech that readers might have expected in the wake of Pulteney's focus on the likely rhetoric of the defense. The opening of Johnson's

---

[127] *London Magazine* (April 1742): 178.
[128] *London Magazine* (April 1742): 183.

account establishes the humble aura that surrounds this account of the speech:

Having now heard the Charge against me with all the Aggravations which Suspicion has been able to form, and Eloquence to inforce; after the most fruitful Inventions have combined to multiply Crimes against me, and the most artful Rhetorick has been employed to blacken them, I stand up to offer to the House a plain unstudy'd Defence, nor do I solicite any other Favour than I shall appear to deserve, or wish to be protected in this Storm of Accusation by any other Shelter than that of Innocence.[129]

This opening paragraph not only lends dignity and grace to the address that will follow, in clear contrast to the approach taken by the *London Magazine*, which attributed a rather haughty tone to Walpole, but also reinforces for readers the importance of taking in the whole debate, in which the opposition's "artful Rhetorick" is being contrasted with Walpole's "plain unstudy'd Defence." Language itself is in many ways the subject of the speech. While Johnson makes it clear, in keeping with the *London Magazine*'s account, that Walpole's central argument revolved around shared responsibility, since "all the publick Transactions have been approved by the Legislature, which are now charged upon me as Instances of Ignorance, Negligence, or Treachery," the focus in the *Gentleman's Magazine* is on the restrained language and simple logic of the minister's defense.[130] He concludes as he began:

Having now, Sir, with due Submission offered my Defence, I shall wait the Decision of this House without any other Solicitude than for the Honour of their Counsels, which cannot but be impaired if Passion should precipitate, or Interest pervert them. For my Part, that Innocence which has supported me against the Clamour of Opposition, will establish my Happiness in Obscurity, nor shall I lose by the Censure which is now threatened any other Pleasure than that of serving my Country.[131]

As an assessment of a stand-alone piece of writing, much of the praise for Johnson's version of this concluding speech by Walpole is justified. The address is a dignified, modest response to the many declamatory attacks on him throughout the debate. It is dramatic, when read in isolation, because it does not seem especially parliamentary for Walpole to have eschewed a more specific defense of his actions. There is another layer of

---

[129] *Gentleman's Magazine* (April 1743): 179.
[130] *Gentleman's Magazine* (April 1743): 179.
[131] *Gentleman's Magazine* (April 1743): 181.

skill at work here, however, that only makes sense in the context of the coverage of this debate as a whole and of the *Gentleman's Magazine*'s typical approach to the task of reportage. The elegance of the speech owes a great deal to the lack of detail in answer to the charges; Walpole does not construct a rebuttal of the key points of the opposition's argument, noting that "[t]he Gentlemen who have already spoken in my Favour have indeed freed me from the Necessity of wearying the House with a long Defence, since their Knowledge and Abilities are so great that I can hope to add nothing to their Arguments, and their Zeal or their Friendship so Ardent, that I shall speak with less Warmth in my own Cause."[132] This point is only valid in the context of the fuller coverage provided by the *Gentleman's Magazine*, which had canvassed the specific charges against Walpole and his supporters' responses to them much earlier in the debate and had suggested, through its coverage of Pulteney's speech, that the nature, not the details, of the Minister's defense would be the key moment in the proceedings. The note of restraint in Walpole's remarks and the subsequent general discussion of his role thus stem from a key feature of the *Gentleman's Magazine*'s coverage: its technique of reporting many more speeches than the *London Magazine* and allowing the various arguments on each side to be spread among speakers. In Johnson's version, readers are constantly reminded of Walpole's presence and primed to analyze his rhetoric closely. Having established the importance of rhetoric to the debate, while simultaneously drawing on the established reportorial style for which the *Gentleman's Magazine* was known, Johnson's account of Walpole was designed to meet the expectations of both editor and reader. The report's rhetorical flair emerges from the intersection of Johnson's talent and the editorial strategies of the *Gentleman's Magazine*.

But the premium placed on fact and the availability of accurate information is also apparent in this report. Greene regarded Johnson's version of the speech to be "largely a fiction composed by Johnson for the occasion" because of the contrast between the two magazines' accounts, and Christine Gerrard reads the report of the speech as "highly fictionalized," but, while these conclusions are largely correct, there is evidence that Johnson had source material for this speech.[133] Birch's papers contain a long description of the debate, suggesting that either he or someone he was acquainted with had attended, and could provide notes about what

---

[132] *Gentleman's Magazine* (April 1743): 179.
[133] Greene, *Politics of Samuel Johnson*, 128, and Gerrard, *Patriot Opposition to Walpole*, 245.

was said.[134] There were other accounts circulating too; in a 1741 pamphlet attacking Walpole, published many months before either magazine produced coverage of the debate, several phrases are attributed to the Minister that would later form part of the *Gentleman's Magazine* account. The most notable is a reference to *"this little Ornament a-cross my Shoulders,* which might be the Envy of *another* Place; but it was impossible to imagine that it could give any Offence to the Members of this House, for restoring that Honour to Them, which some of their Ancestors had formerly worn."[135] In the *Gentleman's Magazine*, Johnson has Walpole say:

The little Ornament upon my Shoulder I had indeed forgot, but this surely cannot be mentioned as a Proof of Avarice; nor, though it may be looked on with Envy or Indignation in another Place, can it be supposed to raise any Resentment in this House, where many must be pleased to see those Honours which their Ancestors have worn restored again to the Clinabs.[136]

Johnson might have received notes from Cave's reporters or from Birch and his contacts that documented this phrase; more likely, he simply modified the language of this pamphlet, which was written by an anonymous member of Parliament and thus constituted the kind of firsthand material that the magazines delighted in including in their reports.

CONCLUSION

Most scholars have focused on the ways in which Johnson's characteristic literary strengths influenced the *Gentleman's Magazine*'s parliamentary reporting, crediting Johnson with a special ability to spin plausible fictions around scanty facts. An examination of contemporary journalism complicates this interpretation. Legal constraints and the absence of effective techniques for capturing parliamentarians' words made it inevitable that parts of the magazines' coverage would be invented, no matter who was reporting. Fictionalization, however, or the addition of aesthetic flourishes where none had existed in the original speeches, needs to be understood as a journalistic technique; that is, a journalistic technique as opposed to a literary technique, and a journalistic technique as opposed to a journalistic imperative. The literary qualities of the reports were only worthwhile to the extent that they enhanced the standing of a

---

[134] Birch Collection, British Library Add.MS.4107, fol. 234.
[135] *A Review of the Late Motion*, 28, italics in the original.
[136] *Gentleman's Magazine* (April 1743): 181.

magazine's coverage. The appealing style of a report like Johnson's version of the Walpole speech is in this light significant not as an objective measure of its quality but as an indicator of the way in which he and Cave went about differentiating their coverage from the *London Magazine*'s. Moreover, while the April 1738 ban on reporting made fictionalization inevitable, it also required the magazines to consider the ways in which creative reporting could be elevated to a technique that would separate the two publications in terms of depth and breadth of coverage, and then, inevitably, in terms of style. This technique played out differently in each magazine, as one opted to give "full extracts" from just the "remarkable speeches" and the other opted to give the "principal proportions" of every speech.

Fictionalization only flourished, however, on a factual foundation. Editors and journalists never lost sight of the important credibility to be gained from producing the most accurate report achievable. The creativity of Johnson's reporting needs to be contextualized not only within the normal creative processes of the magazines, but also within the market for facts. Numerous sources of information were available to reporters and Johnson might have later recalled only the most extreme occasions of journalistic deprivation. Kaminski suggests that "[i]t is folly to think that Johnson might have written the debates otherwise had he spent more time in the Commons gallery or been given more detailed accounts of the proceedings."[137] It might be the case, however, that wherever possible, factual information was not simply included but also highlighted in Johnson's reports, sometimes even displacing the report he might have written on those occasions when the speaker in question submitted an authorized copy to the magazine. Johnson's creative genius did not trump the real words of Parliament's orators, however much it might have augmented them. This augmentation amounted to a blend of fact and fiction, and while the particular characteristics of that blend were unique, the need to produce it was not. Nor was the *Gentleman's Magazine* blend one that Johnson himself entirely invented. It emerged from the demands of the literary marketplace.

The role of writers and writing within that literary marketplace was a consideration that Johnson understood all too well. As Alvin Kernan points out:

[137] Kaminski, *Early Career of Samuel Johnson*, 131.

Among the many who worked in the eighteenth-century print factory, Samuel Johnson stands out as perhaps the only writer of stature who fully understood, acknowledged, and consciously acted upon an awareness that print was now inescapably the primary fact of letters. He knew that his living as a man and his reputation as a writer had to be made in print terms, and he consequently accepted openly, rather than trying to conceal, the conditions of writing in print circumstances, such as his status as a paid professional writer, his need to develop a distinctive style that allowed him to write swiftly and effectively on any topic under deadlines pressures, the power of the booksellers to dictate his subjects, and the necessity of pleasing those whom he was the first to call "common readers."[138]

Johnson's reports impress later readers, but this was not the audience he had in mind when he composed them. He was instead writing for the readers of the 1730s and 1740s, readers who were alert to the blend of fact and fiction that characterized parliamentary journalism, aware of their options in terms of the two magazines' coverage and influential in convincing Cave and Astley to develop distinct styles of reportage. Read in isolation, or only in relation to what we know of the later Johnson, the *Debates in the Senate of Lilliput* feel like unusually creative, whimsical takes on the parliamentary controversies of the day, shaped by the unique talent of the young journalist. With a greater knowledge of editors' strategies, readers' expectations and reporters' techniques, Johnson's achievement moves from being a literary triumph to being a journalistic one.

[138] Kernan, *Samuel Johnson and the Impact of Print*, 17.

CHAPTER 3

Samuel Taylor Coleridge and the freedom of the gallery

At various moments throughout his career, Samuel Taylor Coleridge demonstrated an insider's knowledge of the way Parliament was reported. In an 1816 letter, he noted that "it seems epidemic among Parliament men in general to affect to look down upon & despise Newspapers, to which they owe ppp/$_{1000}$ of their influence & character, and at least $^{3}/_{5}$ths of their knowledge & phraseology."[1] In an article for the *Courier* the following year, he dismissed the reputed eloquence of the MP William Smith, saying it was "entirely owing to the Procrustes Tyranny of the Parliamentary Reporters, who had persisted in measuring his harangues by their own pocket-ruler instead of the patience of the House."[2] These were the remarks of someone who knew how parliamentary reports were generated in the early decades of the nineteenth century.

Coleridge had gained these insights in 1800, when he worked for the *Morning Post*, a paper that aligned itself with the opposition to William Pitt's government.[3] The paper's editor, Daniel Stuart, had found it difficult to hold Coleridge to his obligations since hiring him in 1799. He decided to take his recalcitrant employee to the gallery of the House of Commons, "in hopes he would assist me in parliamentary reporting, and that a near view of men and things would bring up new topics in his mind."[4] Coleridge thus became part of the parliamentary press corps in late January 1800, but he had already given some thought to the way Parliament should be covered; in his paper *The Watchman*, he had argued that "the legal disadvantages which attend the task of *reporting* the

---

[1] Coleridge, *Letters*, IV: 640.
[2] Coleridge, *Essays on His Times*, II: 467.
[3] For a detailed description of the development of the *Morning Post* in this era, see Hindle, *Morning Post*, 65–104.
[4] Stuart, "Anecdotes of the Poet Coleridge," 487.

speeches" partly contributed to the "fatiguing and colourless confusion" of contemporary parliamentary oratory.[5] The implication was not only that the reporters deserved more consideration from Parliament, but also that what citizens understood to be parliamentary oratory was inevitably mediated by the press.

Although there were still legal constraints, as Coleridge noted, the status and practices of parliamentary reporters had changed dramatically in the years since Samuel Johnson had stopped reporting for Edward Cave's *Gentleman's Magazine*. After Cave and Astley were arrested and held in custody in 1747 for printing an account of Lord Lovat's trial in the House of Lords, the magazines became much more cautious in their parliamentary journalism, and this caution remained a feature of the 1750s periodical business.[6] Complaints about the London newspapers' coverage of the debates in the early 1760s briefly stymied the embryonic development of systematic reporting, but the advent of new titles in the late 1760s and early 1770s, as well as the arrival of some pioneering figures on the London journalism scene, began to revolutionize the way parliamentary reporting was conducted and received. From 1768, John Almon composed reports for the tri-weekly *London Evening Post* based on conversations with men who had attended the debates. The *St James's Chronicle* then went one better, posting a Mr. Wall in the lobby of the House of Commons to collect news and, if possible, enter the gallery. Shortly afterwards, longer versions of Wall's reports began to appear in the *Gazetteer*. In 1769, William Woodfall established the *Morning Chronicle*, a newspaper that was to become one of the most celebrated and innovative publishers of parliamentary reporting. The accepted practice through the 1750s and 1760s of printing bare outlines of the debates now erupted into attempts at comprehensive reports.

In February 1771, Parliament responded by invoking the 1738 standing order and summoning the printers of two papers, John Wheble of the *Middlesex Journal* and Roger Thompson of the *Gazetteer*, to appear before them. The two men refused to appear and evaded arrest for a month. More printers were then summoned, and some appeared and apologized for their reports, but the *London Evening Post*'s editor, John Miller, ignored the summons. The stand-off escalated rapidly; Wheble and Thompson were apprehended in March 1771 and forced to appear

---

[5] Coleridge, *The Watchman*, 56, italics in the original.
[6] Black, *The English Press in the Eighteenth Century*, 170.

before city magistrates. One of the magistrates in Wheble's case was John Wilkes, the popular politician who had been expelled from Parliament for seditious libel and had been refused reinstatement despite winning another seat. Wilkes released Wheble, and the magistrate trying Thompson did the same. When the Commons moved to punish two of the magistrates, who, as members of the Commons, were subject to the House's disciplinary procedures, a riot ensued. Both men were sent to the Tower but the public reaction ensured that Parliament would now be forced to tolerate publication of the debates in the Commons. A similar, if less dramatic, confrontation in 1775 meant that the Lords' debates could also be printed.[7]

Parliamentarians and journalists were both forced to adjust to the new environment. As Christopher Reid has pointed out in his groundbreaking work on eighteenth-century oratory and rhetoric, the development of parliamentary reporting radically changed the way MPs thought about their speeches.

From the 1770s every parliamentarian of stature would have known as he spoke that what he said was likely to be recorded, reconstructed and textualized … Serious parliamentarians like Burke prepared their speeches thoroughly when the occasion allowed it but the ideal type of 18th-century oration was a largely extemporary effusion, the unpremeditated application of experienced eloquence to the matters brought forward in the course of debate. The cultural gulf between this image of gentlemanly ease and that of the laborious parliamentary reporter striving to channel the flow of eloquence into print was very marked.[8]

While MPs were reconsidering their oratory, journalists were rethinking their craft. The new, grudging, freedom to report gradually led to innovations in the way parliamentary speeches were gathered and presented, but effective reporting was still a challenge. Journalists were not guaranteed space in the Strangers' Gallery and were forced to queue with other interested parties and fight their way into the gallery. Once inside they were confronted with hot, noisy, crowded conditions which made the debates extremely difficult to hear, especially as reporters were required to sit in the back row of the gallery.[9] Note taking was still forbidden in the 1770s, so reporters either had to rely on their memories of the speeches or conceal notebooks and risk being caught. Any MP could order the gallery

---

[7] See Sparrow, *Obscure Scribblers*, 18–23, for a more detailed account of the events from the 1750s to 1771.
[8] Reid, "Whose Parliament?" 126.
[9] Aspinall, "Reporting and Publishing," 233–34.

cleared by invoking the rule that strangers were technically not allowed to attend the debates, and reporters could thus be removed from the House at the whim of a single member.[10]

Parliamentary reporting in such conditions required special skills and a well-organized strategy for collecting information. William Woodfall's approach was to attempt to memorize the speeches. This technique, however flawed, allowed him to produce the longest reports available in the London press and earned him the sobriquet "Memory" Woodfall. Woodfall's approach dominated as long as the papers could not take notes and relied on a single journalist to provide their parliamentary coverage.[11] But when James Perry, the new editor of the *Gazetteer*, and later Woodfall's replacement as editor of the *Morning Chronicle*, decided to set up a small parliamentary corps in 1783, after the ban on note-taking had been relaxed, the practices of the gallery changed dramatically. Coverage of the debates had always been difficult to incorporate into the morning newspapers' deadline, since each paper's reporter had to wait till the adjournment of the House, which often did not occur until the early hours of the morning, before writing up his version of the debate. Perry organized his reporters in relays; each reporter worked a two-hour "turn" in the House, before leaving to write up his section of the debate while a colleague took his place in the gallery. By the time the debate closed, the earliest part of the proceedings was already set in type.[12] Perry's approach heralded a new era of parliamentary coverage.

In the years leading up to Coleridge's time in the gallery, parliamentary reporting had again become a highly charged political issue. Newspaper reporters were extremely influential in the process of disseminating the debates, and parliamentarians were understandably concerned about the way they were presented in these accounts. In a particularly heated debate in December 1798 – and it is worth remembering here that any attempt today to cite what was said in Parliament in the eighteenth century is itself compromised by the reporting standards of the time – William Wilberforce attempted to enforce the 1738 standing order that had affected Johnson and the *Gentleman's Magazine*, arguing that recent

---

[10] See Thomas, "The Beginning of Parliamentary Reporting in Newspapers," 623–36, for a discussion of the changes in reporting in the late 1760s and early 1770s.

[11] An interesting firsthand account of the Woodfall era of parliamentary reporting can be found in Stephen, *The Memoirs of James Stephen*, 288–95.

[12] Histories of eighteenth-century journalism usually include an account of Perry's innovation; see Sparrow, *Obscure Scribblers*, 27; Escott, *Masters of English Journalism*, 157; and Macdonagh, *Reporters' Gallery*, 282–83.

reports had led to "the misrepresentation of gentlemen's speeches, tending both to pervert the public mind, and to prejudice Members in the opinion of their constituents."[13] If parliamentary reporting was to continue, he concluded, either "what passed there should be fairly stated or not at all."[14]

Wilberforce's remarks launched a series of debates about the status of reporting. A week later, George Tierney revisited the question, brandishing a copy of *The Times* that included "the most glaring and the grossest falsehoods and misrepresentations."[15] He further alleged that *The Times* had been paid to insert fabricated material into its report of the debates and moved that the paper was guilty of a breach of privilege. A few days later Tierney withdrew his complaint, and the debate might have ended there, but William Windham, the Secretary at War, insisted that, whatever the merits of the individual case, the broad principle of the right to report still needed to be discussed. In a long and intemperate speech, Windham suggested that the House ran the risk of undermining its own authority by ignoring the standing orders and of potentially contributing to the collapse of the British constitution. The practice of reporting had

contributed more to the evils of which many had complained of over the country, than any other practice he had heard of in that time; it was an evil in its nature; it was an inflammatory information at the best; it kindled over again, and spread all over the country, that heat among the lower classes, which was sometimes deprecated, even in that House, as being likely to mislead those who possessed the best means of forming correct judgments.[16]

He cited the French Revolution and the Spithead and Nore mutinies of the previous year as events directly linked to the volatile effect of parliamentary reports on ordinary readers, and memorably called the published debates "a poison which was circulated every twenty-four hours, and spread its venom down to the extremity of the kingdom."[17]

Several MPs spoke in favor of the right to report, although usually in the context of criticism of specific reportorial practices. When introducing his complaint, Wilberforce had said that he "was far from objecting, nay he was willing and desirous that every thing transacted within that House should be fairly represented."[18] Likewise, when Tierney attempted

---

[13] *Parliamentary Register*, VII: 319–20.   [14] *Parliamentary Register*, VII: 320–21.
[15] *Parliamentary Register*, VII: 428.   [16] *Parliamentary Register*, VII: 473.
[17] *Parliamentary Register*, VII: 474, VII: 471 and VII: 475 respectively.
[18] *Parliamentary Register*, VII: 320.

to bring a motion against *The Times'*s coverage, he nevertheless declared that "there is no gentleman in this House who would be less desirous than myself to curtail or abridge the liberty which the House has allowed to the printers and editors of newspapers, of gratifying the curiosity of the public, by publishing the debates of the House."[19] In the same debate, Prime Minister William Pitt added that be "should be very sorry ... to be obliged to interpose the authority of the House in restricting what has long been permitted, as a medium of communication between this House and the Public."[20] But Windham's remarks pointed to an under-current of uncertainty about the effects of parliamentary reporting and the power wielded by newspaper editors. It was in this tense environment that Coleridge worked.[21]

The qualities of a good reporter in this era are illustrated in an adver-tisement from 1796:

A Gentleman capable of Reporting the DEBATES in PARLIAMENT is wanted for a London Newspaper, a business of no such great difficulty as is gen-erally imagined by those unacquainted with it. A tolerably good style, and facil-ity of composition, as well as a facility of writing, together with a good memory (not an extraordinary one), are all the necessary requisites. If a Gentleman writes SHORT HAND it is an advantage; but Memory and Composition are more important ... A Gentleman who has never tried Parliamentary Reporting will be preferred by the Advertiser, because he has observed that those who have least attempted it, are now the best Reporters.[22]

The advertisement implicitly gives insights into what readers were expect-ing in terms of reportage. Some degree of creative style needed to be combined with the accuracy of one's memory to create a report that was both correct and interesting, but in neither case did one need excep-tional skills.[23] Perhaps the most startling part of the advertisement is the preference for novices, suggesting that editors were looking for fresh

---

[19] *Parliamentary Register*, VII: 426.
[20] *Parliamentary Register*, VII: 433. Pitt was a very astute manager of the press; see Werkmeister, *The London Daily Press 1772–1792*, 317–79.
[21] For an account of the debates about parliamentary reporting in the late eighteenth century more generally, see Barker, *Newspapers, Politics, and Public Opinion*, 15–19, and Aspinall, *Politics and the Press*, 35–36.
[22] *Star* (21 September 1796): 1.
[23] In a compelling reading of one of William Wilberforce's anti-slavery speeches from 1789, Brycchan Carey makes the point that the rhetoric of sensibility in the address might have been enhanced by reporters familiar with the tropes of sentimental literature; similar kinds of literary skill or attention to popular tastes could no doubt be found in other close readings of the sort Carey undertakes. See Carey, *British Abolitionism*, 156–73.

perspectives on the practice of reporting at around the time Coleridge joined the gallery.

The survival of Coleridge's notebook from the period means that attempts have already been made to identify his exact contributions to the *Morning Post*'s parliamentary coverage. Kathleen Coburn identifies three sets of notes that ultimately led to reports of three speeches in 1800: the second half of William Pitt's major address of February 3, a short oration by Richard Brinsley Sheridan on 10 February, and another Pitt speech on February 17.[24] These reports have been the subject of limited but extremely valuable scholarly interest. In 1960, David V. Erdman undertook a collation of the extant coverage of the speeches in the major London daily papers in order to evaluate Coleridge's technique. In a detailed analysis, Erdman demonstrated the moments at which Coleridge seems either to capture accurate phrasing or to interpolate his own language, ultimately concluding that "he was making the kind of notes and writing the kind of reports that rank his work with that of the best professional practicers of the art."[25] Erdman's collation provides extremely important information about the way Coleridge reported. By focusing on the notes and texts of the speeches themselves, however, he does not directly address the wider question of Coleridge's role within the *Morning Post*'s gallery corps at this time, or the general expectations about parliamentary reporting, questions which are vitally important to appreciating his approach. Erdman concludes that there are, progressively, "three degrees of originality" in Coleridge's three reports.[26] In the course of outlining the way Coleridge's practices as a reporter compare with those of his peers, I would like to suggest that we might instead consider that there are three degrees of autonomy, as he becomes less and less bound by the norms of gallery journalism as February 1800 unfolds.

In the preface to this book I proposed that Dror Wahrman's idea of parliamentary reports as "distinct reconstructions" was an appropriate theory to use for considering the authors in question. This theory is especially applicable to Coleridge, however, as it was the coverage of the late 1790s that Wahrman was examining when he expounded this idea. He argued that these "distinct reconstructions" were "mediated through rhetorical practices specific to each newspaper and dependent on its political

[24] Coleridge, *The Notebooks of Samuel Taylor Coleridge*, 651–53.
[25] Erdman, "Coleridge in Lilliput," 33–62, 34.
[26] Erdman, "Coleridge in Lilliput," 33.

convictions. Therefore, as far as the public in Britain was concerned, there was no single image of parliament available to and shared by everyone. Instead the public was confronted with a plurality of representations."[27] Wahrman's reading of late 1790s reporting is a reminder of the import-ance of understanding the ways in which the reporters of this era inter-acted with editorial and readerly expectations. These interactions shaped the role that a reporter was asked to play, in turn shaping his reports. In most cases, the role of the reporter did not differ much from paper to paper or person to person. But the nature of Coleridge's role, and how it was constructed, needs further elucidation.

COLERIDGE'S ROLE

In his 1838 biography, James Gillman passed on an anecdote about Coleridge in the gallery.

Coleridge was requested by the proprietor and editor to report a speech of Pitt's, which at this time was expected to be one of great éclat.

Accordingly, early in the morning off Coleridge set, carrying with him his supplies for the campaign: those who are acquainted with the gallery of the house on a press night, when a man can scarcely find elbow room, will better understand how incompetent Coleridge was for such an undertaking; he, how-ever, started by seven in the morning, but was exhausted long before night. Mr. Pitt, for the first quarter of an hour spoke fluently, and in his usual manner, and sufficiently to give a notion of his best style; this was followed by a repeti-tion of words, and words only; he appeared to "talk against time," as the phrase is. Coleridge fell asleep, and listened occasionally only to the speeches that fol-lowed. On his return, the proprietor being anxious for the report, Coleridge informed him of the result, and finding his anxiety great, immediately *volun-teered* a speech for Mr. Pitt, which he wrote off-hand … The following day, and for days after the publication, the proprietor received complimentary letters announcing the pleasure received at the report, and wishing to know who was the reporter. The secret was, however, kept, and the real author of the speech concealed; but one day Mr. Canning calling on business, made similar inquir-ies, and received the same answer. Canning replied, "It does more credit to the author's head than to his memory."[28]

Although the details of this anecdote seem highly suspect – Stuart later referred to them as "a romance" of Coleridge's invention and they clearly conflate at least two different occasions – the overall picture that emerges

[27] Wahrman, "Virtual Representation," 85.
[28] Gillman, *The Life of Samuel Taylor Coleridge*, 207–8.

of a journalist operating outside the system is worth considering.[29] Coleridge also conveyed this impression to his friends while he worked in the gallery; when he sent a copy of one of his reports to Josiah Wedgwood, for example, he noted that he did not report "ex officio; but Curiosity having led me there, I did Stuart a service by taking a few Notes."[30] The comment is disingenuous, since he was certainly under more of an obligation to Stuart than the word "curiosity" suggests, but it is nevertheless the case that in his own mind he had no official role within the *Morning Post*'s gallery corps.

Coleridge's amateur status is further reinforced by the fact that he reported so few of the debates that occurred during his tenure in the gallery. Between January 27, 1800, the first day on which we can be certain that he was at the House, and February 17, the date of the last speech reported in his notebook, the *Morning Post* covered proceedings in the Commons on thirteen occasions. On four of those days the House conducted almost no business before adjourning, but the remaining nine produced quite long reports, of which Coleridge apparently contributed to only three. If he had been acting as a regular member of the corps, he would surely have been expected to take a turn in the gallery during all of these debates.

And yet some evidence does point to Coleridge's integration in to the gallery system. I have elsewhere argued that the freedom afforded to him amounted to the ability to choose which speeches he covered, hence the focus on important speakers such as Pitt and Sheridan and speeches that were either highly anticipated (Pitt's February 3, speech) or highly effective (Sheridan's February 10 and Pitt's February 17 speeches).[31] Yet reconsidering this material with the benefit of a much better understanding of gallery practices, it seems to me that, on the first two occasions at least, Coleridge was simply taking a turn like any other reporter. On February 3, for example, his notes begin about halfway through Pitt's speech. Erdman suggests very tentatively that Coleridge might have been relieving another reporter, but this conclusion deserves more credence than he or I have allowed.[32] Erdman has nothing to say about the reasons why Coleridge ended up reporting the February 10 and 17 addresses, and I have made a case for considering their impact on the night as the main

[29] Stuart, "Anecdotes of the Poet Coleridge," 488.
[30] Coleridge, *Letters*, I: 568.
[31] Hessell, "Coleridge and Column Inches," par. VI.
[32] Erdman, "Coleridge in Lilliput," 42–43.

motivation for Coleridge's attention, but the prosaic answer is much more likely: these speeches simply fell to him as part of his turn. This conclusion is supported by a closer look at the notebook, since the notes for February 10 actually complicate the idea that he was reporting individual speeches. The February 10 jottings conclude with a short note about Michael Angelo Taylor's reply to Sheridan, which Coleridge must also have reported.[33] This reply was brief and unimportant, but it got recorded in the notebook nevertheless because it occurred during Coleridge's turn.

To reconcile this evidence about Coleridge's complicated relationship with the other gallery reporters – sometimes their colleague, sometimes not – it is helpful to turn to the testimony of other journalists. William Jerdan, who began work as a parliamentary reporter for the *Aurora* newspaper just a few years after Coleridge's time in the gallery, provides an invaluable insight into the routines of the parliamentary press corps in the first decade of the nineteenth century.

> [N]early the whole staff of every paper, on great occasions, had to wait with the crowd till the doors were opened at noon, force their way with great struggle into the gallery, and secure as well as they could the back seat, not only as the best for hearing but as having no neighbours behind them to help the motion of their pencils with their knees and elbows. From twelve o'clock till four when the business began, the position thus occupied had to be secured; and it was only when the outer gallery door was locked against farther admissions, that those who had not the first two hours' … duty to discharge, could venture to steal up stairs to the coffee-room and recruit the physical man for his turn at the wheel.[34]

It is implicit in these remarks that two broadly different approaches to the coverage were in operation at the time. On the days that Jerdan calls "great occasions," editors tried to get as many reporters into the gallery as possible, in order to ensure that they had the manpower to cover the debates in detail and at length. This recollection is verified by John (later Lord) Campbell, who joined the *Morning Chronicle*'s reporting team the same month that Coleridge entered the gallery; Campbell wrote that he went to the gallery "when any debate of importance was expected."[35] This arrangement was presumably not the case on other occasions, when no important business was expected, and Campbell draws a revealing distinction between the newspapers' attitude to the major debates and to the

---

[33] Although Erdman does not discuss this fact in "Coleridge in Lilliput," he does include the Taylor speech as Coleridge's in *Essays on His Times* (1: 176).

[34] Jerdan, *The Autobiography of William Jerdan*, 1: 84–85.

[35] Hardcastle, ed., *Life of John, Lord Campbell*, 1: 105.

rest of the House's deliberations when he remarks that "debates were very rare, and to the ordinary routine business of Parliament hardly any attention was paid."[36]

This two-fold approach to parliamentary reporting explains much of Coleridge's role and the way in which he portrayed it to others. Although the first speech he reported occurred on February 3, 1800, the first day that he went to the gallery was actually January 27, the day that Pitt intended to discuss Napoleon Bonaparte's overtures for peace. The subject of the debate, and the fact that Charles James Fox intended to return from his self-imposed exile from the Commons to join the fray, meant that public interest was extremely high. The newspapers were consequently very anxious to provide comprehensive coverage on this occasion; on the day of the debate, the *Morning Chronicle* begged for "the indulgence of our advertising friends for to-morrow, as it will require the whole space of the paper to do justice to the important proceedings which are expected this day in the House of Commons."[37] Much to the papers' disappointment, Pitt pleaded illness, and the debate was postponed till January 29. It was then put off for a second time, before finally taking place on February 3.

Coleridge was present in the heaving crowd on both the night of the debate and the two earlier abortive occasions; after he had finally covered the debate, he told Josiah Wedgwood, "I have been three times to the House of Commons, each time earlier than the former, & each time hideously crowded – the two first Day[s] the Debate was put off."[38] The *Morning Chronicle* likewise noted the incredible interest in the debate, pointing out that on January 27 the promise of the event brought out "a croud unprecedented in the most eager period of Parliamentary Debate."[39] Even newspapers that did not usually provide very detailed coverage of the debates produced relatively long reports of this one.[40] Coleridge's first three trips to the Commons, in other words, were explicitly related to the peace debate, one of those great occasions on which the editors ensured that all available journalists were in attendance.

Coleridge's presence was not required on the next three days that the House sat. On February 5 and 6, very little business was conducted, and the *Morning Post*'s coverage amounted to less than a column. On

[36] Hardcastle, ed., *Life of John, Lord Campbell*, 1: 107.
[37] *Morning Chronicle* (January 27, 1800): 2.   [38] Coleridge, *Letters*, 1: 568.
[39] *Morning Chronicle* (January 30, 1800): 2. See also *Oracle* (January 28, 1800): 2; *Whitehall Evening Post* (February 4–6, 1800): 2.
[40] See for example *E. Johnson's London Gazette* (February 9, 1800): 3–4.

February 7, a long debate on supply ensued, but it was not one of the highly anticipated moments where Stuart would have needed to marshal his forces, and Coleridge was presumably excused. When he returned on February 10, it was again to cover a prominent debate. On January 30, Sheridan had informed the House that his motion on the expedition to Holland would not be forthcoming until the 10th. The debate again drew the attention of newspapers that did not normally cover the proceedings in any detail.[41] Stuart would have needed a large team in the gallery; as on February 4, the *Morning Post*'s February 11 issue was entirely composed of the parliamentary report and Coleridge's letters mention the fact that he had gone to the House at 10 a.m. on the morning of the 10th to try to get a seat.[42]

Another hiatus in Coleridge's reporting followed. The *Morning Post* covered the deliberations of February 11, 12 and 13 fairly briefly; none of the debates occupied more than a page of the *Post*'s coverage, and there is no evidence that Coleridge contributed to them. But then we reach an intriguing day. On February 14, Coleridge wrote to Thomas Poole that he was trying to extricate himself from the *Morning Post*, "but [Stuart] is importunate against it – to night I must go with him to the House of Commons."[43] There are, however, no notes in his notebook for this evening. The *Morning Post*'s coverage of the debate is very brief – less than two columns – and it is evident that little of interest occurred. Why then did Stuart insist that Coleridge go to the House? Perhaps because Pitt had made two announcements the previous evening. Having tabled a message from the king regarding funding for troops, Pitt moved that the message be debated on the 14th, "and gave notice, that on Monday next [i.e. the 17th], in the Committee of Supply, he should move that 500,000l. be granted to His Majesty towards defraying the expences of the troops to be employed agreeable to the Message."[44] Stuart might have anticipated that the debate on the 14th would thus be a significant one; as it turned out, the House promptly agreed to Pitt's request to refer the king's message to the Committee of Supply and, after a little more business, adjourned. In such a short debate, Coleridge probably had no opportunity to take a turn.

[41] See for example *E. Johnson's London Gazette* (February 16, 1800): 3–4.
[42] Coleridge, *Letters*, 1: 569.   [43] Coleridge, *Letters*, 1: 572.
[44] *Morning Post* (February 14, 1800): 1.

The events of February 17 also seem anomalous. Although it turned out to be a sensational debate, the report of which encompassed all but the last column and a half of the following day's *Morning Post*, the February 17 debate was not, in fact, expected to be a dramatic one. Stuart remembered that Pitt had said previously that "he did not suppose there would be any opposition to this vote of money; and hence, I think, there was no crowd at the gallery, no early hour for seats, as no debate was expected."[45] This was not one of the obvious great occasions, then, but it was related to the debate of the 14th, to which Stuart had also brought Coleridge. On February 14, the brevity of the debate had meant that Coleridge's services were not required; on February 17, however, the fact that the debate became more newsworthy than expected would have led Stuart to make use of all of the reporters at his disposal, and he may have been rather short-staffed on this occasion, given that nothing substantial was anticipated at the House that night. The significance of the occasions on which Coleridge went to the Commons thus squares with Stuart's memory that he asked Coleridge to assist with the report; such assistance would have been very necessary on these days. Coleridge's sense that he was not part of the regular corps likewise seems to be justified when his contributions are considered as part of the *Morning Post's* parliamentary coverage for these three weeks.

These impressions are further reinforced by an examination of Coleridge's place within the system of turns. He appears to have heard whole debates, rather than waiting in the coffee-room until his turn, as Jerdan describes, and then leaving the gallery after his turn to write up his section of the report. On February 3, he not only heard Pitt and Fox, but also those who spoke before them, informing Wedgwood that

Pitt & Fox completely answered my pre-formed Ideas of them. The elegance, & high-finish of Pitt's Periods even in the most sudden replies, is *curious*; but that is all. He *argues* but so so; & does not *reason* at all. Nothing is rememberable in what he says. Fox possesses all the full & overflowing Eloquence of a man of clear head, clean heart, & impetuous feelings. He is to my mind a great orator. All the rest that spoke were mere creatures. I could make a better speech myself than any that I heard, excepting Pitt's & Fox's.[46]

[45] Stuart, "Anecdotes of the Poet Coleridge," 487.
[46] Coleridge, *Letters*, 1: 568, italics in the original.

Coleridge did not leave until the debate ended, complaining that "I went at a quarter before 8, and remained till 3 this morning."[47] His movements were similar on February 10, when he went to the House early in the morning but did not end up reporting until close to the 1 a.m. adjournment.[48]

Stuart's two objectives in bringing Coleridge to the gallery also deserve further scrutiny in relation to the question of Coleridge's role. The editor recalled that he hoped Coleridge "would assist me in parliamentary reporting, and that a near view of men and things would bring up new topics in his mind."[49] The first goal, to obtain assistance, might simply mean that Coleridge reported part of the debates. But it also appears to have involved him in other work. On each of the three occasions that he attended the House, Coleridge corrected the *Morning Post*'s report. After leaving the Commons around 3 a.m. on February 4, he "sate writing, & correcting other men's writing till 8"; on February 11, after the House adjourned at 1 a.m., he continued working till 4 a.m., and again till 5 a.m. on February 18.[50] If correcting the report meant ensuring that it was a fair reflection of the proceedings, it would have been necessary to have heard the whole debate, perhaps explaining the divergence between his practice and that described by Jerdan, although it seems more likely that Coleridge was expected to correct the style of the report. Stuart's second objective was also much more likely to be achieved if Coleridge could witness whole debates rather than the randomly occurring chunks that fell to each reporter during his turn. The editor's tactic was largely successful in this regard; throughout February, Coleridge provided leaders and commentaries on his experiences in the House, culminating in a celebrated character sketch of Pitt that drew directly on the speech of February 17 that he had reported.[51]

Jerdan's autobiography is again useful for understanding the circumstances in which editors encouraged journalists to step outside the boundaries of normal reporting. Describing his own later work for the *Morning Post*, when he was required to write leaders about the Duke of York and his mistress Mary Anne Clarke, who had been involved in a corruption scandal, Jerdan noted that he

remained in the House of Commons every night during the whole debates. Thence I went to the office and did my best and worst for the next morning's

[47] Coleridge, *Letters*, 1: 568.   [48] Coleridge, *Letters*, 1: 569.
[49] Stuart, "Anecdotes of the Poet Coleridge," 487.
[50] Coleridge, *Letters*, 1: 568, 1: 569, and 1: 573 respectively.
[51] See Coleridge, *Essays on His Times*, 1: 219–27.

publication; and then, generally about three o'clock in the morning, I walked from the Strand to Old Brompton, a fair three miles. One way and another I had my mind engaged, and my pen in my hand, above nineteen hours in the twenty-four; and let me say, the exertion was extraordinary.[52]

It was apparently possible, albeit in exceptional circumstances, for the journalists who were expected to write leaders and other political articles to listen to entire debates in order to familiarize themselves with the major arguments being advanced in the House of Commons.

The unconventionality of Coleridge's role in the gallery makes more sense if it is considered in the context of the competition between the newspapers in 1800. In its first issue of the year, *The Times* had noted that its reports were "relied upon for their precision and truth," and were composed by "Gentlemen of integrity and talents."[53] Stuart delayed making a similar statement until January 27, the date that the *Morning Post*'s new typeface was unveiled. The announcement, in which Coleridge might have had a hand, declared:

To the Readers of this Paper, we hope, that our habitual vigilance renders unnecessary any assurances of attention to every customary department. But as some Journalists have stepped forward to pledge themselves more particularly on the score of their Parliamentary Reports, we may be permitted to say, that we are prepared to give them with the same copiousness and accuracy, which on former occasions added much to the reputation of THE MORNING POST.[54]

The timing of this statement is important. On the date it was published, Stuart, like all of the newspaper editors, was expecting that Pitt would be introducing the debate on the peace negotiations that night. It was thus a critical day in the world of parliamentary reporting. It was also, not coincidentally, the first day on which Coleridge went to the House. By drawing attention to his paper's gallery reporting on this date, Stuart was perhaps signaling that he intended to put new energy into parliamentary journalism.

Coleridge's role in the gallery is thus best understood as a patchwork one: a combination of reporter, editor and political correspondent. The unconventionality of this role needs to be foregrounded when considering his parliamentary reports, which were not being composed under the same conditions as those of many of the other journalists. On the occasions when he sat in the gallery, Coleridge potentially exercised

[52] Jerdan, *The Autobiography of William Jerdan*, I: 112.
[53] *The Times* (January 1, 1800): 2.   [54] *Morning Post* (January 27, 1800): 2.

considerable influence over the way the debates were reported the following day. Unlike most of his fellow reporters, the decision about the way in which his contribution to the coverage was to be presented lay somewhat within his own power. Moreover, he was engaged in reporting partly as a tactic to stimulate his thinking about politics and thus stimulate his journalism for the *Morning Post*. Erdman proposed that the three reports represent "three degrees of originality," as Coleridge's texts vary more and more from what the other reporters were producing.[55] This finding could be reconfigured to focus instead on the way that the reports demonstrate Coleridge taking more and more advantage of his ability to shape the coverage. His reporting was original, but it was created in an environment that, in some circumstances, permitted originality to flourish.

PITT AND THE DEBATE ON PEACE: FEBRUARY 3, 1800

February 3 was a testing day for the newspapers; the long-awaited debate on peace ran for nearly twelve hours, and Coleridge only finished working on the coverage at 8 a.m. The pressure to gain a seat in the gallery was intense; the *Oracle* reported that the crowd of people waiting for admission had assembled

almost as early as the day broke, and kept continually augmenting till the doors were thrown open. The bustle then became prodigious between the Parties presenting their different claims and titles to admission.

Here their situation was far from being enviable – opposed by the bars and bolts of the door-keepers in front, and dreadfully compressed by the irresistible pressure of the multitudes in their rear. Under such circumstances as these, it was painful to observe one unfortunate Gentleman whose arm was fractured in the struggle, notwithstanding which some time elapsed before it was possible to disengage him from the crowd. In the end it was found that the Gallery was insufficient to contain one-sixth of the Candidates for Seats; and the remainder, panting and half fainting, were obliged to return.[56]

The major morning papers gave over their entire issue of February 4 to the parliamentary report and attempted to cram in as much coverage as possible: the *Morning Post* added a fifth column to each page; the *True Briton* and *The Times* switched to a more densely printed type on their final page; and the *Morning Chronicle* and the *Oracle* abbreviated earlier

---

[55] Erdman, "Coleridge in Lilliput," 33.
[56] *Oracle* (February 5, 1800): 2.

speeches in order to fit in Fox's concluding remarks. The process was clearly draining; Stuart had to apologize to his audience the following day, asking that "Readers and Correspondents will excuse the omission of many valuable articles this day: our Printers, &c. being quite exhausted by the fatigue of preparing yesterday's paper."[57]

Coleridge's turn that evening, as noted earlier, fell during Pitt's speech, which had run for nearly three hours when he finally concluded around 1 a.m.[58] Pitt began by outlining the history of the conflict between Britain and France, before moving to more recent events in the continental war, including the French invasion of Switzerland. He stressed the ambition and rapacity of post-Revolutionary France, and described Bonaparte as the epitome of the Revolution's corruptions. He then went on to address the recent coup in France and the subsequent peace negotiations. Dismissing the validity of the Bonaparte government, and placing the French Consul's character at the center of the debate, he rehearsed the history of Bonaparte's military leadership, which he portrayed as a vicious and bloodthirsty catalog of crimes. Considering the instability of the new French Constitution, Pitt urged caution on the question of peace.

Erdman's collation assesses the section of the report that Coleridge produced against six other sources: the reports in *The Times*, the *Morning Herald*, the *Morning Chronicle*, the *True Briton* and the *Oracle*, and a published pamphlet of Pitt's speech, later republished in the *Parliamentary Register* as the official text, which Erdman uses as the most trustworthy version owing to its length. As he points out, this report is a particularly significant example for scholars of Coleridge's parliamentary reporting, because it is the only one of the three instances for which such a comprehensive independent source as the pamphlet exists. In an extremely detailed and thorough consideration of the report, using rules of attribution designed to assess whether phrases are accurate or invented, Erdman concludes that Coleridge is both more accurate and more creative than his peers. The implication is that Coleridge succeeds magnificently, in both literary and journalistic terms.

The freedom afforded to Coleridge in the gallery helps to contextualize some of these findings, however, starting with the question of where his contribution to the report begins. Coleridge's notes on this occasion are

---

[57] *Morning Post* (February 5, 1800): 2.
[58] The *Morning Chronicle* informed its readers of the length of the speech before commencing to report it (February 4, 1800): 3.

difficult to decipher.[59] The first note that can be clearly made out is the phrase "Now let us see what this change has been," which was translated into the start of a new paragraph in the *Morning Post*'s report.[60] There are some notes before this phrase, however, which are almost entirely illegible. Coleridge's turn clearly began earlier than the phrase quoted above would suggest, and Erdman identifies two moments in the section preceding this phrase that he regards as potentially Coleridgean. The first of these moments begins with Pitt's reference to Tipu Sultan, the leader of Mysore who had fought against the British, as "Citizen Tippoo." Most of the reporters caught this remark in one form or another. As Erdman points out, however, only in the *Morning Post* is this description subsequently applied to Bonaparte himself, when the *Post* has Pitt say that the French had been "fitly rewarded for their perfidy by having now no other Sovereign on the throne of France, than a rank Citizen Tippoo."[61] Shortly after this remark in the *Post*, there is an entirely unique passage praising General Suvorov in comparison with Bonaparte.

Erdman explains these two moments in separate ways. He points out that Pitt's original mention of "Citizen Tippoo" was greeted by laughter, as recorded by *The Times*'s reporter, who informed his readers "[h]ere a loud laugh," and that it is possible that whatever Pitt said next was not heard.[62] He also suggests that the Suvorov passage potentially supports, in part, the Gillman anecdote about Coleridge writing an imaginary speech for Pitt, putting forward "the hypothesis that Coleridge did have to 'volunteer' a portion of Pitt's remarks at the point where the preceding reporter stopped and an obvious gap was to be bridged. Perhaps he had indeed been dozing when Stuart called on him to take over."[63] In both cases, he suggests that Coleridge's literary skill allowed him to embellish Pitt's words.

An examination of the other newspaper accounts suggests a more straightforward explanation for both of these examples, however. It seems likely that Pitt's remark about "Citizen Tippoo" coincided with the end of one two-hour shift in the gallery and the beginning of a new one. The *Morning Chronicle*, for example, notes immediately after this remark that "[f]or want of room we find it necessary to state only the heads of the

---

[59] Coburn provides a good description of this notebook entry; see Coleridge, *Notebooks*, 651n.
[60] Coleridge, *Notebooks*, 651.
[61] Erdman, "Coleridge in Lilliput," 43; *Morning Post* (February 4, 1800): 3.
[62] Erdman, "Coleridge in Lilliput," 43; *The Times* (February 4, 1800): 3.
[63] Erdman, "Coleridge in Lilliput," 42–43.

remainder of the Chancellor of the Exchequer's Speech."[64] The *Oracle* continues for a few lines beyond that, but then stops reporting Pitt altogether, informing its readers that "[t]o-morrow we shall resume our Report of this able and important Speech, being now obliged to leave off, in order to make room for a Sketch of the Reply to it by Mr. Fox."[65] The change of shifts was a natural place at which to make such a break; the earlier turn would be written up and set in type, but once the next reporter returned to his office, and it became clear that Pitt had continued talking for such a long time that to report him in full would eliminate any space for Fox, the papers would decide to compress or omit the first section of the new reporter's turn in favor of giving room to Fox's address. It is revealing that it is at precisely this moment, immediately after the reference to Citizen Tippoo, that the evening *Star* switches from its initial source of coverage to using the *Morning Post*'s text instead, which implies that there was a change of reportorial approach at this moment.[66] Although there is no such mention in the other papers, including the *Morning Post*, they operated on largely the same timetable and would have made this change at approximately the same time. In other words, in addition to the laughter that might have prevented anyone hearing what Pitt said about "Citizen Tippoo," there was also a great deal of activity in the crowded gallery at this moment, as one group of reporters left and another entered.[67]

The change of shifts helps to clarify a number of questions about this report. First, it suggests that Coleridge began reporting at around the moment Pitt mentioned "Citizen Tippoo," and that his illegible notes might cover this section. Second, it offers a possible explanation for the *Morning Post*'s unique reference to Bonaparte himself as a "Citizen Tippoo." Not only would it have been difficult to hear this remark at that moment, but there might have been no one directly on duty for some of the papers when Pitt said it. Coleridge was in an unusual position, in that he began his shift having heard everything that came before and without

---

[64] *Morning Chronicle* (February 4, 1800): 3.

[65] *Oracle* (February 4, 1800): 4.

[66] *Star* (February 4, 1800): 4. The evening papers did not have their own gallery teams and instead relied on their morning counterparts, with whom they often shared owners. The *Star* generally relied on the *Morning Chronicle* for coverage, but since the *Chronicle* had chosen this moment to begin abbreviating Pitt's speech, the *Star* presumably looked elsewhere for a full account and found Coleridge's. For the relationship between the *Star* and the *Chronicle*, see Werkmeister, *The London Daily Press*, 366.

[67] The comings and goings from the gallery were noisy and disruptive, especially as the reporters sat at the back; see Aspinall, "Reporting and Publishing," 235.

having to change seats with another *Post* reporter, with all the confusion and loss of sustained reportage that that involved. Erdman calls the *Post*'s version of Pitt's witticism "a giant step and probably the reporter's own … I assume that if Pitt had said [that Bonaparte was "a rank Citizen Tippoo"], the other reporters would hardly have taken a step backward from it."[68] Perhaps not, under normal circumstances, but this moment represented one of the inevitable ruptures in the process of parliamentary reporting, one from which Coleridge was largely protected by his role. The assumption of poetic license here might be a giant step in itself.

The reporters who began their shift with Coleridge were thus operating in a manner quite different from the way in which he operated. Although probably unbeknown to them as they sat in the gallery, the report that they might have produced for the second half of Pitt's speech was going to be heavily abbreviated when the spatial constraints became clear. Whether or not they took full notes – of which we cannot be sure – they certainly did not have the opportunity to produce a full report. Coleridge was in a different position, however. As the de facto subeditor of the parliamentary report, and as someone who had been brought in that day specifically to enhance the *Post*'s coverage, he had the opportunity to produce a full account of his notes, and the *Post*'s report is consequently much longer than the others. The inclusion of passages such as the remarks about Suvorov fell somewhat within Coleridge's control. It is possible that he invented them but also possible that he was simply granted the room to include them.[69]

This difference in roles is very important in clarifying the existing conclusions about the relative accuracy and creativity of Coleridge's report. At first glance, the evidence that Erdman produces on these questions seems extremely compelling. Testing accuracy by making "a list, for each newspaper, of all the salient words and phrases in it which are matched in one or more other newspapers" and then checking this list against the pamphlet version of the speech, Erdman finds that Coleridge's account has the highest number of phrases confirmed by other accounts

[68] Erdman, "Coleridge in Lilliput," 43.
[69] As Erdman points out, there is significant evidence that Pitt did say something about Suvorov, including Fox's reference to a comment from Pitt and a later editorial by Coleridge in which the comment is mentioned; see Erdman, "Coleridge in Lilliput," 44; and Coleridge, *Essays on His Times*, 1: 170. Erdman does not mention it, but the reference also seems to be supported by the *Morning Post*'s "Analysis or Skeleton of the Debate in the House of Commons, Monday, February 3, 1800," which was certainly Coleridge's work; see Coleridge, *Essays on His Times*, 1: 165.

(fifteen) and the highest number confirmed by a comparison with the *Parliamentary Register* text (twelve).[70] When testing creativity by making a list of phrases unique to each newspaper when compared with the other papers, and then comparing that list with the *Parliamentary Register*, Coleridge again scores very high; twenty-eight phrases appear which are not in any other newspaper account, nineteen of which are also not in the *Register*.[71] The next highest number comes from the *True Briton*, which has thirteen unique phrases (eleven of which are not in the *Register*), well behind Coleridge's totals. Erdman concludes that the evidence of this speech showed that, while this was the least original of the three speeches under consideration, "Coleridge's stands out, both as capturing more of the memorable phrases of Pitt and as adorning his report with more of his own."[72]

Erdman's sense that Coleridge "stands out" is typical of the scholarship in this area of writers' working lives. The criteria for standing out seem almost paradoxical: one must include more examples of accurate content from the speakers' lips but also stamp one's own creative sensibility on the final product. This odd conjunction of skills seems plausible, in light of the similarly paradoxical expectation at the time, particularly among MPs, that reporters would attempt to capture the debates faithfully despite being hampered by their working conditions and Parliament's reluctance to recognize them formally, and editors' attempts to differentiate their coverage from that of their competitors. In fact, it seems that these two seemingly incompatible motives are what drove Stuart to hire Coleridge in the first place. But Erdman does not propose that there is any reason why Coleridge should have succeeded in this task, beyond his natural ability as a writer, and in taking that approach, he adheres to the scholarly orthodoxy that great writers must, in their early writings, have manifested the characteristics that would later mark them out as great.

A footnote to Erdman's analysis also makes his findings problematic. When explaining his method, Erdman notes at the bottom of the page that "[a]ll these counts are limited to passages that have some parallels in Coleridge's portion of the *Morning Post* report."[73] Two weaknesses in the method consequently become apparent. The first is that, while not treating it as a copy-text, Erdman is using Coleridge's account as a guideline

[70] Erdman, "Coleridge in Lilliput," 52.
[71] Erdman, "Coleridge in Lilliput," 52–53.
[72] Erdman, "Coleridge in Lilliput," 53.
[73] Erdman, "Coleridge in Lilliput," 52n.

to reporting standards. Anything Coleridge ignored, whether from boredom, inaudibility, incomprehension or fatigue, is not being factored in to the analysis. It is quite possible that many phrases (and perhaps even large chunks) of Pitt's speech are much better reported, by Erdman's own standards, in other newspapers; these sections simply would not show up in the analysis if Coleridge did not attempt them. Moreover, it is clear that Coleridge had the opportunity to produce much fuller reports than his peers, making his contribution atypical. The analysis is being undertaken with Coleridge at the center, and while this might be understandable, given his prominence in literary history, in light of the notion of distinct reconstructions and the unconventionality of his role this approach seems potentially flawed.

The second, more significant problem is that Erdman does not consider in any detail the style of reporting adopted by the other *Morning Post* reporters, as opposed to the reporters from other papers. This point is particularly relevant to the February 3 coverage; since Coleridge only reported part of Pitt's speech, the whole text of the address reflects the work of at least two hands and provides an excellent opportunity for considering his technique alongside not only that of his rivals on other papers, but that of his own colleagues. Erdman remarks that "[o]f the first half of Pitt's speech little need be said" and provides a short collation of the section just before the "Citizen Tippoo" passage in order to establish the "characteristic differences" between the papers' reporters.[74] The *Morning Post*'s other reporter does not come out well from this brief comparison, but what would be the result of applying Erdman's method of testing accuracy and creativity to the section of Pitt's speech that was reported by Coleridge's colleague?

Such a test complicates the findings about Coleridge's contribution. His accuracy actually appears to have fallen somewhat below the standards of the *Morning Post*'s team. The application of Erdman's method, in which he includes variant phrases that do not quite match in terms of syntax, reveals that the *Post*'s version of the early part of Pitt's speech includes at least thirty phrases or words that are verified by one or more of the other newspaper sources, compared with fifteen phrases in Coleridge's section.[75] Virtually all of these phrases are further confirmed, sometimes in

---

[74] Erdman, "Coleridge in Lilliput," 40.
[75] Erdman does not mention which phrases he counted, so it is difficult to be sure whether we are applying exactly the same standards. The phrases to which I am referring in the *Morning Post*

a slightly different form, in the *Parliamentary Register*. Coleridge's report does have a higher ratio of creative phrases; Erdman's finding of twenty-eight phrases that are not in any other newspaper account, nineteen of which are also not in the *Parliamentary Register*, can be compared with twenty-two phrases in the early section of the report, seventeen of which are also not in the *Register*.[76] It might be expected that he would come out ahead of his fellow *Morning Post* reporter on the counts of both accurate and original phrases. In fact, his efforts on this occasion seem to be roughly in line with those of his *Morning Post* colleagues.

The balance between accuracy and creativity was as important for the newspapers in 1800 as it had been for the magazines in 1740, albeit under very different circumstances. Readers were again being confronted with complex signals about the reliability of the reports they read. Stuart argued in the *Morning Post*, for example, that

report are "inevitable destinies of the world," "controuled by any human exertions," "the most dreadful visitation with which Heaven had ever afflicted mankind," "impossible to separate the question now before the House from the antecedent causes of the French Revolution," "arguments contained in the pamphlet he had written," "exhibit those circumstances of danger arising out of the situation," "an inadequate security," "men of their great genius," "a love of peace and respect for other nations," "one of the blackest and most atrocious murders ever committed," "all regular and civilized Governments," "they had waged war with all the nations of Europe, save two," "It had been proposed that this decree should be confined to those nations with whom France was actually at war, but that proposal had by a great majority been rejected," "There was enclosed to every General a blank, to be filled up with the name of the nation requiring the aid of the Republic," "we are almost ashamed to own it," "the Brissotines and Robespierres," "the Treaties of Pavia and Pilnitz were spurious," "forgery," "durance," "conducted him to the scaffold," "desiring, on the part of Russia, to have an explanation on the subject of war with France," "two leading points," "plan of conduct," "withdrawing of their armies, restoring the conquests they had made," "fraternal embraces," "dismembering France," "mistress of the sea, had collected the wealth of the world, had annihilated the commerce of France, and had doubled her own," "asylum," "a people proverbial for the innocence of their lives," "not confined to Europe alone," "The only subject that remained to speak on was, the expedition to Egypt," "the all-searching eye of the French Revolution," "except their good ally, Citizen Tippoo." See *Morning Post* (February 4, 1800): 3–4.

[76] Again, it is not clear that we are applying exactly the same standards, but the phrases to which I refer are "patiently to resign themselves to a passive endurance of a system," "origin and continuance," "productive of every possible evil," "barrier to its farther progress," "the original conduct of the French," "inadequate to impart security to the negotiations," "future discussion between the two countries impossible," "she would consider our rejection as a declaration of war," "unlawfully murdered," "in his former capacity," "the new destroyers of thrones," "had the English government sought to make the war unavoidable?," "preserve the relations of peace and amity," "did not manifest the least spirit," "pre-eminent as was her situation," "new moulding her code of laws," "unrelenting hostility," "the name of Bonaparte appeared as the principal personage," "dreadful scene of carnage and horror," "unmasked the conduct of the French to those who were previously blind to their deformity," "the picture of French cruelty," "the machinations of Russia." See *Morning Post* (February 4, 1800): 3–4.

Proprietors of Newspapers pay too highly for Parliamentary Reports to be indifferent about their accuracy. The expence of Reporters is an enormous burthen on every Paper, and often renders them incapable of other exertions. The Proprietors struggle for pre-eminence in their reports as eagerly as Candidates struggle for success in a General Election.[77]

Yet it was also made clear to readers that the reporters routinely altered what was said in Parliament; when introducing its version of Pitt's speech of February 3, the *Morning Chronicle* noted, "of course we can only give a very faint outline of the topics upon which he insisted."[78] Readers sometimes found this infuriating; Sheridan crowed about the success of a particular debate in July 1800 but told a correspondent: "I don't send you the Papers – for there is not one of them that gives an idea of the Debate, which the Citizens who have been with me this morning are outrageous at."[79]

Coleridge's work on February 3 reflects both the wider complexity of balancing accuracy and creativity and the specific demands of this debate. The newspapers' coverage on this occasion was always going to be subject to close scrutiny, since public interest was high in advance of the debate; as one newspaper pointed out, "[t]he edge of Public Curiosity did not seem in any degree blunted by the former Disappointments in hearing the Debate."[80] This was particularly true in regard to the speeches of Pitt and Fox. Some newspapers printed only these two speeches.[81] In an attempt to extend what Christopher Reid has called the "rhetorical afterlife" of a speech, booksellers moved quickly to produce pamphlet versions of the Pitt and Fox addresses, meaning that readers had the rare opportunity to compare the newspapers' handiwork with an authorized text.[82] As Lord Campbell recollected, Pitt's addresses were notoriously difficult to report effectively because so much of their impact was in the manner of delivery, not the words themselves, which presented a significant challenge on a night when his speech was likely to be of widespread interest to the public.[83] The *Morning Post*'s position was perhaps especially sensitive, given that it had recently (and in the context of this very debate) alluded to the

[77] *Morning Post* (March 8, 1800): 2.
[78] *Morning Chronicle* (February 4, 1800): 3.
[79] Sheridan, *The Letters of Richard Brinsley Sheridan*, 2: 135.
[80] *Oracle* (February 5, 1800): 2.
[81] *E. Johnson's London Gazette* (February 9, 1800): 3–4.
[82] Reid, "Whose Parliament?" 127. An advertisement for Fox's speech, for example, appeared in the *Morning Chronicle* on February 10 (2).
[83] Hardcastle, ed, *The Life of John, Lord Campbell*, 1: 107.

strength of its parliamentary reporting, although Stuart would no doubt have been pleased that, as he had hoped, the experience of attending the House prompted some new political journalism from Coleridge.[84]

This example is thus a case not so much of less originality as of the least degree of autonomy of the three that Coleridge composed. His contribution helped to sustain the paper's report, by approximately meeting the standards that his fellow reporters had established. The newspapers needed to produce an extremely accurate version where possible, and the emphasis on accuracy can be seen not only in Coleridge's section of the report but also in that of the *Morning Post* journalist he relieved. But there was likewise a need to differentiate the paper's coverage. Coleridge is again largely in step with the norms of the *Morning Post* in the number of original phrases that he inserted into his report, thereby giving it a flavour that would not be evident in the other papers' coverage, although his superiority on that score perhaps reflects his own control over the final report. If he had the inclination to interpret Pitt's words more creatively, it was no doubt kept in check by his relative inexperience as a reporter, the importance of covering this particular debate as carefully as possible, and the fact that the style for reporting Pitt had already been established by the preceding journalist. What he was able to do was to generate a much longer text than his peers, and thus not only differentiate the *Post*'s reporting, but also influence the coverage published in papers like the *Star*, which did not have their own gallery reporters. These factors contributed to the circumscribed autonomy with which he produced his text.

SHERIDAN'S CANDOUR: FEBRUARY 10, 1800

Coleridge was again required at the House on February 10, when Sheridan introduced his motion on an inquiry into the Dutch expedition, which he had signaled on January 30. Sheridan's initial speech that night was covered at length by all the morning papers, but only the *Morning Post* gave much room to his later, impromptu speech towards the end of the debate, in which he responded to Michael Angelo Taylor, who had referred to him earlier in the debate as "meally-mouthed" and made comments about

---

[84] Coleridge produced the "Analysis or Skeleton of the Debate in the House of Commons, Monday, February 3, 1800" and the leader of February 6, which dealt with Pitt's and Fox's relative performances in the debate; see Coleridge, *Essays on His Times*, 1: 162–71.

his candour. It was this later address that Coleridge reported as he took the final turn for the *Post* in the gallery that evening.

The space allotted to this speech is a very interesting indicator of Coleridge's technique for generating speeches. For the first three and a half pages of its coverage, the *Morning Post* printed the addresses with normal spacing between the lines of type. But at the end of Tierney's long address, which brought the coverage to the bottom third of its penultimate column, the *Post* switched to a smaller, more closely spaced font. This decision was not unusual; the papers often made this change as their pages filled in order to ensure that they included as much coverage as possible. What is unusual is that, after printing speeches by Spencer Perceval, Taylor, Henry Addington, Sir James Murray Pulteney and Colonel Hope in this form, the *Post* reverted to normal type for Sheridan's reply, which took up most of the final column.

This speech did not attract as much attention in the other papers. *The Times* gave it only thirty lines, the *Oracle* forty-two, the *True Briton* sixty-five and the *Morning Chronicle* over seventy. At around a hundred lines, the *Morning Post*'s coverage of the speech is certainly the most extensive, and it is not surprising to find that the *Star* again chose to reproduce Coleridge's version of the speech.[85] The fact that Sheridan spoke near the end of the day's debate is perhaps one explanation for the relative brevity of the other reports; under Perry's system, as each reporter filed an account and it was set in type, the space remaining for subsequent speeches naturally shrank. But this conclusion still raises the question as to why the *Morning Post* decided to print Sheridan's fairly insignificant speech at some length on a day when space was tight.

There are three likely factors in the decision. The first is that the speech was clearly very funny. None of the versions conveys the true humor of Sheridan's remarks, yet they were obviously amusing; Coleridge included one "loud and continued laugh," *The Times* recorded three instances of laughter, the *Oracle* included several laughs including some "loud and reiterated bursts of laughter," and the *True Briton* noted that Sheridan displayed "that delicate vein of humour so peculiar to him."[86] Erdman notes that Coleridge seems to have had a better grasp of this aspect of the speech, using the example of the phrase "a lie of candour," which

[85] *Star* (February 11, 1800): 4.
[86] *Morning Post* (February 11, 1800): 4; *The Times* (February 11, 1800): 3; *Oracle* (February 11, 1800): 4; *True Briton* (February 11, 1800): 4.

other reporters recorded as "a line of candour," as possible evidence that Coleridge caught a witticism that others missed.[87]

A second factor was the place that this particular orator occupied in the esteem of reporters and in the public imagination. Campbell called Sheridan "the most brilliant speaker in the House," and was particularly proud of an occasion in December 1800 on which he wrote "six columns of Sheridan" for the *Morning Chronicle*.[88] Others were less impressed by the gallery's regard. In a later pamphlet, William Cobbett attacked Sheridan, alleging that he received favorable treatment from the reporters. Citing the coverage of one particular debate which he had observed from the Strangers' Gallery, Cobbett noted that while Sheridan had spoken for about as long as the other MPs, his speech was granted at least four columns in the following day's papers, more than the rest of the speakers combined.[89] Cobbett also provided some interesting insights into how the reporters conceived of their task; when one of them missed a passage of Sheridan's speech, he asked for Cobbett's help, "'for,' said he, 'you cannot imagine, Sir, how fond the public are of Sherry's little jokes.'"[90] Reporters obviously tried to be alert to Sheridan's speeches and their witticisms whenever possible. On February 10 this was a difficult task, given the limited space available for Sheridan's last address, but Coleridge was in step with the general practices of the gallery on other occasions in anticipating potential public interest in the speech.

The third factor in the decision to report Sheridan in this way is that Coleridge had some control over the *Morning Post*'s coverage. As the de facto editor of the debates, he had the opportunity to ensure that this address was reported at length, presumably with Stuart's blessing. But this was not simply a matter of elevating his own reporting by highlighting everything that he heard; he was also responsible for the final comments of the night from Taylor, whose remarks feature briefly in the notebook. This brief speech was not printed in the extravagantly spaced type afforded to Sheridan, but instead given four lines in small type at the end of the *Post*'s report.[91] Coleridge clearly differentiated between the two speeches he had heard and presented their relative significance accordingly.

---

[87] Erdman, "Coleridge in Lilliput," 54.

[88] Hardcastle, ed., *The Life of John, Lord Campbell*, 1: 107 and 1: 62, respectively.

[89] Cobbett, *The Political Proteus*, 209–10. Sheridan was, in turn, a great supporter of the gallery journalists and had championed their cause during a bitter debate on excluding strangers in December 1810; see *Parliamentary Debates*, 1st ser., vol. XV (1810): 324–25.

[90] Cobbett, *The Political Proteus*, 214.

[91] Coleridge, *Notebooks*, 652; *Morning Post* (February 11, 1800): 4.

The decision to report Sheridan's speech in this way demonstrates Coleridge's understanding of what appealed to readers and the use he made of his role in the gallery. Much more autonomy is evident here when compared with the earlier Pitt speech, where it appears Coleridge simply took a turn and largely fitted in with what the *Morning Post*, and indeed many of its competitors, decided to do on that occasion. The coverage of Sheridan's February 10 speech is instead quite distinct from that of the other papers and involves a special allowance of space being made towards the end of the issue. The humor of this address from one of the House's most popular orators made it a perfect selection for inclusion. Coleridge generally abhorred the references to laughter in contemporary reports, and he later condemned the "*laughs, loud laughs, and very loud laughs*: (which, carefully marked by italics, form most conspicuous and strange parentheses in the newspaper reports)."[92] The Sheridan speech represents the only occasion on which he included one of these interpolations, suggesting that it was perhaps a moment of genuine mirth rather than either political grandstanding or journalistic favoritism. Otherwise, Coleridge eschewed this shorthand in favor of a full report of those parts of the speech that were most amusing, particularly its opening.

This second example of Coleridge's reporting shows not only how his vision of the debates could influence the *Post*'s coverage, but also how well-attuned he was to the world of gallery journalism. The attention given to the Pitt speech on February 3 was largely in line with the newspapers' practices, and particularly with the practices of the *Morning Post* that night. It served more as a springboard for other journalism than as a canvas on which to display an impressive reportorial style. The Sheridan speech shows Coleridge using his position in the gallery to produce a fuller, more comprehensive report, and Stuart highlighting it to readers through the use of larger, more widely spaced type. But while Coleridge had the freedom to shape the report in this way, he relied on some of the same indicators of significance that all good gallery journalists were using at the time.

PITT'S "SECURITY" SPEECH: FEBRUARY 17, 1800

The final speech covered in Coleridge's notebook, and the most significant in terms of his reportorial career, is Pitt's address of February 17. Unlike the earlier Pitt speech, which had been widely anticipated as part

---

[92] Coleridge, *The Friend*, 1: 109.

of the debate on the terms of peace, this oration was impromptu. The House had dealt with a number of minor matters in the early part of the evening, before it resolved itself into a Committee of Supply to consider the king's request for more funding for foreign troops, as Pitt had indicated on February 13. Following several short opening speeches, Tierney launched an attack on the government and its policies in relation to the war, specifically querying the object of the conflict. At the end of this speech, he asked Pitt, according to the *Parliamentary Register*, "in one sentence to state, if he can, without his *ifs* and *buts*, and special pleading ambiguity, what this object is."[93] Pitt immediately stood to answer the question, and it was at this point that Coleridge's turn began. As Coleridge rendered it in the *Morning Post's* version, Pitt said dramatically: "The Hon. Gentleman calls upon Ministers to state the object of the war in one sentence. I can state it in one word. It is security."[94]

Erdman's collation is again extremely thorough. He points out that the *Morning Post's* coverage of the speech, at over four thousand words, was the longest of any of the dailies.[95] He also produces another statistical analysis on the relative accuracy and creativity of Coleridge's report, which demonstrates once more an apparently superlative performance; the *Morning Post's* report has twenty-five phrases supported by other reports, while the next highest is seventeen, but also forty-three phrases that appear to be completely original, compared with only eleven in the next highest newspaper tally.[96] Of these forty-three phrases, thirty-nine do not appear in Coleridge's notebook, suggesting that they might have been completely invented. This finding squares with Coleridge's own comments about the report. He urged Robert Southey to "[r]ead Pitt's Speech in the Morning Post of today (Tuesday Feb. 18.) I reported the whole with notes so scanty, that – Mr Pitt is much obliged to me. For by heaven he never talked half as eloquently in his Life time. He is a *stupid insipid* Charlatan, that *Pitt*."[97]

This speech marks the climax, then, of Erdman's "three degrees of originality," and the comprehensive list of unique phrases that he produces,

---

[93] *Parliamentary Register*, x: 567, italics in the original.
[94] *Morning Post* (February 18, 1800): 2.
[95] Erdman, "Coleridge in Lilliput," 55. The lengths of the other reports, as recorded by Erdman, were 3,450 words (*Morning Chronicle*), 3,300 words (*Oracle*), 3,150 words (*True Briton*), 2,800 words (*The Times*), 1,550 words (*Morning Herald*) and 820 words (*London Chronicle*).
[96] Erdman, "Coleridge in Lilliput," 59–60.
[97] Coleridge, *Letters*, i: 573, italics in the original.

combined with the obvious lack of firsthand notes and Coleridge's own testimony, suggests that this was a highly original report. The phrases that Erdman isolates as Coleridge's creative contributions are certainly evocative ones. Coleridge has Pitt call Bonaparte the "gaudiest puppet" of Jacobinism's folly, assert that there are in France "mere spectators, who have but sympathized in the distance, and have caught disease [of Jacobinism] only by *looking on*," and praise Britain as the only nation that has "pierced with so stedfast an eye through the disguises of Jacobinical hypocrisy," none of which phrases appears in other texts of the speech or in the notebook.[98] But several questions remain unanswered in Erdman's account. Why did Coleridge want to make this "stupid insipid charlatan" speak so eloquently? Why did he deviate from the pattern he had established on February 3 and 10, where he apparently produced relatively accurate versions of the speeches in question? And did such creative material necessarily enhance the report?

The question of Pitt's eloquence in this speech is an important one, because it speaks to the nature of Coleridge's role and his journalistic vision. From the time of its publication, readers have struggled to understand this report. Thomas Poole called it called it "the finest manufacture from the worst materials," but asked Coleridge "wherefore deck out the minister in this way?"[99] Michael Macdonagh, meanwhile, felt that the speech was "most finely rendered of all by the poet, philosopher and metaphysician," but was surprised by Coleridge's letter to Southey about the report in which "[i]t would seem as if his wonderful poem, 'The Rime of the Antient [sic] Mariner,' gave less exaltation to Coleridge than his version of what William Pitt said on a certain night in the House of Commons."[100]

The answer perhaps lies in a letter that Coleridge wrote to Poole a week after the speech. In a short aside, he commented that "[m]y report of Pitt's Speech made a great noise here – What a degraded Animal Man is to see any thing to admire in that wretched Rant – !"[101] In the context of his comment about the effect of his report, and given that readers had no access to the actual texts of the addresses, the rant to which he refers is his own version of the speech, not the speech itself. As Erdman points out in relation to the depiction of Jacobinism in this report, Coleridge

[98] *Morning Post* (February 18, 1800): 2, italics in the original. See also Erdman, "Coleridge in Lilliput," 60.

[99] Sandford, *Thomas Poole and His Friends*, ii: 6.

[100] Macdonagh, *Reporters' Gallery*, 304 and 299 respectively.

[101] Coleridge, *Letters*, i: 574–75.

does not simply give more space than other reporters to this subject in the speech, but also a "greater intensity of revulsion."[102] Pitt is made to sound almost obsessively concerned with Jacobinism. Erdman attributes this to "the reporter's own fascinated interest in the subject," while John Colmer proposes that Coleridge "seized the opportunity to demonstrate what a fine piece of writing such a report could be," but these conclusions again place Coleridge himself and his literary talents at the center of the analysis.[103]

In fact, rendering Pitt's ideas about Jacobinism in vibrant, memorable language achieved several important journalistic purposes. First, it created the *Morning Post's* own distinct reconstruction of the debate, emphasizing to the point of distortion an image of Pitt that suited the paper's anti-government politics. This in turn fueled Coleridge's other journalism for the paper; he wrote leaders that drew on the speech and ultimately made it the basis of his celebrated sketch of Pitt's character on March 19, 1800, which Stuart called "a masterly production" that led to several hundred extra sales.[104] In this sketch, Coleridge criticized Pitt's easy eloquence:

Mr. Pitt proceeds in an endless repetition of the same *general phrases*. This is his element; deprive him of general and abstract phrases, and you reduce him to silence. But you cannot deprive him of them. Press him to specify an *individual* fact of advantage to be derived from a war – and he answers, SECURITY! Call upon him to particularise a crime, and he exclaims – JACOBINISM! Abstractions defined by abstractions! Generalities defined by generalities![105]

By building up the speech, Coleridge transformed it into a springboard for later work, just as Stuart had hoped he would when he brought him to the gallery.

It is also likely that Coleridge's journalistic antenna was at work on this occasion as it had been on 10 February when he covered Sheridan. Philip Henry Stanhope later noted that on February 17

[t]he speech of Pitt, thus suddenly called upon to rise, may deserve to rank among the most successful instances of a ready reply … Many years afterwards I have heard divers persons congratulate themselves on their good fortune at being present as spectators in the Gallery or as members of the House that evening, more

---

[102] Erdman, "Coleridge in Lilliput," 57.
[103] Erdman, "Coleridge in Lilliput," 57, and Colmer, *Coleridge*, 75.
[104] Stuart, "Anecdotes of the Poet Coleridge," 488.
[105] Coleridge, *Essays on His Times*, 1: 223, italics in the original.

especially as regarded the speech of Mr. Pitt. They spoke in the highest terms of the general impression which that speech produced.[106]

Just as Coleridge probably anticipated readerly interest in a witty riposte from Sheridan, he might also have seen the likely appeal of this speech for readers.

Finally, Coleridge's take on the speech exemplified the standards of the best reports of the time, as Campbell later described:

> To have a good report of a speech, the reporter must thoroughly understand the subject discussed, and be qualified to follow the reasoning, to feel the pathos, to relish the wit, and to be warmed by the eloquence of the speaker. He must apprehend the whole scope of the speech, as well as attend to the happy phraseology in which the ideas of the speaker are expressed. He should take down notes as abbreviated long-hand as rapidly as he can for aids to his memory. He must then retire to his room, and, looking at these, recollect the speech as it was delivered, and give it with all fidelity, point, and spirit, as the speaker would write it out if preparing it for the press.[107]

Although Campbell stressed that "[f]idelity is the first and indispensible requisite," the balance of "fidelity, point, and spirit" suggests that the best reports blended accuracy with a recreated feel for the atmosphere and tone of the speeches.[108]

Coleridge's approach to the Pitt address brought together this mixture of accuracy and creativity in fascinating ways. A critical moment in the speech occurred when Pitt called Bonaparte "the child and champion" of Jacobinism.[109] Four of the other six reporters covering the speech caught this phrase exactly.[110] Coleridge rendered it as "nursling & champion" in his notes, and Stuart recollected that "it was with difficulty I could prevail on him to adopt my reading."[111] If the *Morning Post* had gone ahead with Coleridge's rendition, its mistake would have been quickly exposed; as Stanhope pointed out in his biography of Pitt, the phrase "'the child and champion of Jacobinism,' became for many months a popular watchword in England."[112] But while the decision to use the exact phrase here was wise, there were other instances of wholly invented language in Coleridge's report. Stuart recalled questioning the phrase "breasted the

[106] Stanhope, *Life of the Right Honourable William Pitt*, III: 216–18.
[107] Hardcastle, ed., *The Life of John, Lord Campbell*, I: 106.
[108] Hardcastle, ed., *The Life of John, Lord Campbell*, I: 106–7.
[109] *Parliamentary Register*, X: 568.   [110] Erdman, "Coleridge in Lilliput," 58.
[111] Coleridge, *Notebooks*, 653; Stuart, "Anecdotes of the Poet Coleridge," 488.
[112] Stanhope, *Life of the Right Honourable William Pitt*, III: 218.

tide of Jacobinism": "I recollect objecting that Pitt did not say so, but it passed as Coleridge wished."[113]

Coleridge's instincts were again in step with the gallery's, however, since complete accuracy, which was never really achievable in any case, was certainly not the aim when covering Pitt. Campbell recalled that "if Pitt could have been taken down *verbatim*, all his sentences, however long and involved, would have been found complete and grammatical, and the whole oration methodical and finished, but it would have been sometimes stiff and cumbrous and vapid, although, animated by his delivery, it electrified the House."[114] In order to capture the effect of Pitt's words, it was necessary to deviate from them, to exercise the final degree of autonomy available by representing the impression that Pitt's speech made on its listeners, more than its actual content. This approach is perhaps Coleridge's version of Wahrman's "distinct reconstruction": a politically motivated report, but also one that reconstructed the experience of being in the House when the Prime Minister spoke. By composing it in this fashion, Coleridge displayed the qualities of many of his peers, who were also alert to the sort of speeches that would interest readers. But he also had more opportunities than other reporters to shape his coverage into a form that would serve the purpose of his editor and stoke the flames of his own political journalism.

CONCLUSION

There is clearly a progression in these three reports, a progression that Erdman has labeled "three degrees of originality." But was this emerging originality the work of a poet, who "managed to outdo other newspaper reporters by being simultaneously more faithful and more splendidly creative"?[115] Or did it have its roots in the fluid gallery procedures that allowed some journalists to step outside the normal boundaries? It is clear that two different methods for assigning work operated within the overall system established by Perry and copied by his rivals. While Jerdan speaks of the system of turns, with each journalist reporting for two hours, Campbell recollected that "it was usual for one reporter to take the whole of a long speech extending to five or six columns of a newspaper,"

---

[113] Stuart, "Anecdotes of the Poet Coleridge," 488.

[114] Hardcastle, ed., *The Life of John, Lord Campbell*, 1: 106, italics in the original.

[115] Erdman, "Coleridge in Lilliput," 62.

and that his own developing prowess meant that "the best speakers were assigned to me."[116] However, Campbell's suggestion that individual speeches, not set periods of time, determined what one reported is undermined somewhat by a letter he wrote while he worked in the gallery in which he informed his father that he had "to take a considerable part of Mr. Pitt's budget speech."[117] The contradictions between these accounts, and within Campbell's own account, imply that reporters were utilized in different ways, perhaps even graduating from working a set turn to being called upon to cover specific speeches or speakers as their competence increased.

This contradiction might help to explain what happened between February 3 and February 17. Coleridge's first two attempts at reporting seem to fit into the model of turns, as he simply covers the part of the debate that falls to him, whether it be a section of a speech, as in the case of Pitt on February 3, or the tail end of a debate encompassing a couple of short speeches, as in the case of Sheridan and Taylor on February 10. Perhaps these two examples, particularly the difficult case of covering Pitt on February 3 convinced Stuart to assign an address, rather than a turn, directly to Coleridge, so that on February 17, when Pitt burst into his "security" speech, the editor saw an opportunity to make use of his reporter's skills, as Campbell's skills were used on some occasions by Perry at the *Morning Chronicle*.

If we want a way to evaluate Coleridge's suitability for the role of reporter, we might usefully measure him against the 1796 advertisement for a reporter that was cited near the start of this chapter. He certainly possessed more than the minimum level of style and facility of composition. He was also, crucially, a novice, someone who could join the ranks of new reporters who were taking over from the old hands. As the newspapers struggled for supremacy in their coverage of the debates, new perspectives and new ways of interpreting the role of the reporter were clearly desirable. Coleridge's reinterpretation of that role is creative but also part of the contemporary trend in parliamentary reporting, and his style, while naturally containing elements that we associate with his later career, nevertheless emerges out of this trend.

Instead of Erdman's three degrees of originality, which tends to project originality, a literary quality, as an automatic virtue in journalism,

---

[116] Hardcastle, ed., *The Life of John, Lord Campbell*, 1: 107 and 1: 105.
[117] Hardcastle, ed., *The Life of John, Lord Campbell*, 1: 64.

we might consider three degrees of autonomy. Coleridge's approach to reporting the debates becomes progressively more independent, as he uses the freedom granted to him by Stuart to develop the reports in the way he sees fit. Such freedom, however, was not unique to him, nor representative of the outmoded idea of a literary resistance to the task of reporting, but rather built in to the competition between papers, the need to cover certain debates and certain speakers with both fidelity and flair, and the desire to produce a distinct reconstruction of the proceedings in ways that would flow into further articles. Coleridge demonstrates his fitness for his role in the way that he exploits these possibilities, manifesting a shrewd sense of the gallery journalism of the time.

CHAPTER 4

William Hazlitt and the real eloquence
of the British Senate

When the words "Hazlitt" and "gallery" are used in the same sentence, one would usually think of William Hazlitt's visits to the Louvre or his extraordinary art criticism. But Hazlitt was also involved in the affairs of a different kind of gallery. In October 1812, Charles Lamb asked the journalist John Dyer Collier if he would be able to secure Hazlitt some work as a reporter for the *Morning Chronicle*.[1] The *Chronicle*'s editor, James Perry, hired Hazlitt a week later to join his paper's renowned parliamentary corps, which would resume covering the debates when the House met again on November 30. If one wanted to work in the gallery, the *Morning Chronicle* was the best paper to join; as Hazlitt later recalled, "[f]rom the time of Woodfall, the Morning Chronicle was distinguished by its superior excellence in reporting the proceedings of Parliament."[2]

Hazlitt thus became part of the highly successful press gallery system that Perry had established in the last decades of the eighteenth century, which he described in an essay for the *Edinburgh Review*:

At present, several Reporters take the different speeches in succession – (each remaining an hour at a time) – go immediately, and transcribe their notes for the press; and, by this means, all the early part of a debate is actually printed before the last speaker had risen upon his legs. The public read the next day at breakfast-time (perhaps), what would make a hundred octavo pages, every word of which has been spoken, written out, and printed within the last twelve or fourteen hours![3]

He stayed in this role until at least the end of 1813, by which time he had begun to contribute dramatic criticism and other writing to the *Morning*

---

[1] Charles and Mary Anne Lamb, *The Letters of Charles and Mary Anne Lamb*, III: 85–86. Hazlitt also approached *The Times*; see Crabb Robinson, *Henry Crabb Robinson on Books and their Writers*, I: 110.
[2] Hazlitt, "The Periodical Press," 224.
[3] Hazlitt, "The Periodical Press," 224.

Chronicle.[4] The work also left him comfortable financially; Crabb Robinson commented that he had visited Hazlitt "in a handsome room, and his supper was comfortably set out, – enjoyments which have sprung out of an unmeaning chat with Mrs. Clarkson at Lamb's."[5]

But while Perry's system was still the norm, some aspects of the process of parliamentary reporting that was in operation when Coleridge came to the gallery in 1800 had altered. First, as Hazlitt noted, the turns had shortened from two hours to one hour. Second, there had been a reconsideration of the status of reporters. On May 23, 1803, a delay in opening the Strangers' Gallery meant that no journalists were able to get in before the seats were filled by members of the public. An important speech by William Pitt was thus not reported. The unhappiness of the newspapers was matched by frustration among some MPs, who, as was evident in the late 1790s debates about reporting mentioned in the previous chapter, had become aware of the need to protect the right to report and the publicity to be gained through the papers. This combination of forces led to a crucial change in the treatment of parliamentary reporters.[6] The Speaker ruled that the back row of the Strangers' Gallery must now be reserved for journalists, so that they would not need to take their chances with members of the public and MPs' guests. Although it was some time before a dedicated press gallery would be established, journalists now had a sanctified space from which to work.[7]

The conditions for reporting were still extremely challenging, however. A source from the 1820s notes that there were no desks or other writing surfaces available to reporters in the Commons gallery and very little light. The speakers themselves were difficult to see because of the position of the gallery and a large chandelier in the chamber, which blocked journalists' lines of sight. Journalists could be ejected for whispering or consulting books or newspapers. Despite all of these obstacles, it was "in this small, dark, mat-covered, and inconvenient corner, called the Gallery of the British House of Commons [that] the caterers of the newspaper Press *steal* the speeches of our modern Ciceros."[8]

[4] For an account of this period of Hazlitt's life, see Wu, *William Hazlitt*, 149–61.
[5] Crabb Robinson, *Henry Crabb Robinson on Books and Their Writers*, 1: 116.
[6] For contemporary reactions, see the *Morning Herald* (May 24, 1803): 3, and the *Morning Post* (May 24, 1803): 4.
[7] The full details of these developments can be found in Sparrow, *Obscure Scribblers*, 30–31.
[8] *The Periodical Press of Great Britain and Ireland*, 132–36.

Hazlitt had already shown himself to be very interested in the question of how these modern Ciceros compared to orators of the past. In 1808 he had published *The Eloquence of the British Senate*, a two-volume collection of speeches taken from official records and supplemented with short pieces of commentary. The advertisement provides some fascinating insights into his thinking about oratory in the House. It is often noted that he said in this advertisement that "a very small volume indeed, would contain all the recorded eloquence of both houses of parliament," as if he was generally dismissive of the speeches in Parliament.[9] In fact, the advertisement makes the case for taking parliamentary speechmaking seriously, even when it is not eloquent; the context in which Hazlitt makes this remark is by way of an explanation of his inclusion of many speeches that were chosen for reasons other than eloquence, reasons such as the historical significance of the speech, the important subject under discussion or the status of the speaker. It was not to be a guide to the very best speeches, but rather "an abridged parliamentary history."[10] As the advertisement makes clear, Hazlitt saw great merit in becoming familiar with these speeches, eloquent or otherwise; he wrote that he was concerned that of the politicians of the past "who filled the columns of the newspapers with their speeches ... all of them are now silent and forgotten; all that remains of them is consigned to oblivion in the musty records of Parliament, or lives only in the shadow of a name."[11]

It is true that Hazlitt was damning about contemporary orators in the advertisement, but these comments also deserve further scrutiny. After explaining the scope of the volumes, he wrote:

It is possible that some of that numerous race of orators, who have sprung up within the last ten years, to whom I should certainly have first paid my compliments, may not be satisfied with the space allotted them in these volumes. But I cannot help it. My object was to revive what was forgotten, and embody what was permanent; and not to echo the loquacious babblings of these accomplished persons, who, if all their words were written in a book, the world would not contain them. Besides, living speakers may, and are in the habit of printing their own speeches. Or even if this were not the case, there is no danger, while they have breath and lungs left, that they will ever suffer the public to be at a loss for daily specimens of their polished eloquence and profound wisdom.[12]

[9] Hazlitt, *Eloquence of the British Senate*, I: vii. For the use of this remark in the critical literature on Hazlitt, see for example, Baker, *William Hazlitt*, 160.
[10] Hazlitt, *Eloquence of the British Senate*, I: vi.
[11] Hazlitt, *Eloquence of the British Senate*, I: iv–v.
[12] Hazlitt, *Eloquence of the British Senate*, I: v–vi.

As Hazlitt points out here, while his compilation was not the place for a consideration of modern speeches, there were other outlets that served this purpose, such as pamphlets and the newspapers that ran "daily specimens" of such addresses. Hazlitt is clearly mocking contemporary parliamentarians in his sarcastic reference to their "polished eloquence and profound wisdom," but he is not mocking the process of parliamentary reporting in the newspapers per se. In fact, he is suggesting that this process serves an entirely different, and not unworthy, purpose.

Opinion is divided on the effect that compiling *The Eloquence of the British Senate* might have had on Hazlitt's career as a parliamentary reporter. In an early biography, P. P. Howe noted that "[t]he cheerfulness with which the author of *The Eloquence of the British Senate* took his seat in the Press Gallery as a reporter is to his credit," suggesting that the experience with the volume had only soured him on parliamentary oratory.[13] This opinion is also held by Herschel Baker, who believes that the speeches were "a type of oratory that his work on *The Eloquence of the British Senate* had made him wary of."[14] The opposite view is put forward by Stanley Jones, who argues that Hazlitt's "familiarity with the best speeches of two centuries may have done him the disservice of arousing the forlorn hope of some inspired departure from the hackneyed arguments, the threadbare metaphors, the appeals to established maxims he was now obliged to endure night after night."[15] These arguments each focus on one aspect of *The Eloquence of the British Senate*: either its suggestion that sparkling oratory was a novelty in the House, or its attempt to reproduce some of the great speeches of the past. The fact is that the book supports both of these views, not because it is inconsistent but because it is complex. It recognizes how little of what happens in Parliament is timeless and transcendent, but argues for its importance all the same.

This sophisticated understanding of the nature of parliamentary speechmaking is a crucial element of Hazlitt's reporting. He was aware that the process of producing parliamentary reports for the newspapers was quite different from his task in *The Eloquence of the British Senate*. Newspapers could only report what happened on the night, and that could include moments of brilliance and moments of boredom, prominent speakers and obscure speakers, debates that were historically significant and debates that were utterly transitory. Being an effective compiler

---

[13] P. P. Howe, *Life of William Hazlitt*, 134.
[14] Baker, *William Hazlitt*, 192.   [15] S. Jones, *Hazlitt*, 81–82.

of past speeches and an effective reporter of present ones were two quite different things, but it is clear that Hazlitt knew the difference when he joined the *Morning Chronicle* in 1812.

PARLIAMENTARY JOURNALISM AND PARLIAMENTARY ORATORY IN 1812–1813

There was considerable public interest in the business of Parliament in the 1812–13 session. A new ministry was in place, following Spencer Perceval's assassination in May 1812. The future of the East India Company, questions about the Princess of Wales's conduct, the Peninsular War, and agitation for Catholic rights dominated the House's time and generated much controversy. The evidence in the newspapers suggests that readers paid close attention to the reported debates; the *Morning Chronicle* frequently mentioned that there was "lively interest" in the coverage, and letters to the editor and satirical poems often drew on the exact words of the reports.[16]

Readers had a number of places to turn for their parliamentary coverage. The daily London papers all carried the debates, as did periodicals like the *Examiner*. In 1812, William Cobbett sold to the Hansard family his *Parliamentary Debates*, which he had begun publishing in 1802 and which was the fullest record available, although it still relied on exemplars from the newspapers rather than producing its own coverage. One contemporary reader referred to "this age of oratory and politics, when we have so many volumes of parliamentary debates."[17] Multiple versions of the proceedings abounded, with readers selecting between publications and sometimes constructing their knowledge of a particular debate from several accounts.[18]

In such an environment, the *Morning Chronicle* jealously guarded its reputation for excellent parliamentary coverage. During Hazlitt's time in the gallery, the paper was quick both to celebrate its achievements and to correct any mistakes. On one occasion, for example, the paper drew attention to the fullness of its report, remarking that "[o]ur statement of

---

[16] For the suggestion of "lively interest," see for example the *Morning Chronicle* (December 2, 1812): 3. For examples of readers responding to the speeches, see the *Morning Chronicle* (December 12, 1812): 3, and the *Morning Post* (May 10, 1813): 2.

[17] "Investigator," "Civic Consistency and Justice," 234.

[18] See for example "Investigator," "Civic Consistency and Justice," 235–36, in which the author consults texts from *The Times* and the *Morning Chronicle*.

the course of proceeding was correct; and we have no space left for any observations on what passed this day."[19] On another occasion the paper mentioned that part of a speech by Whitbread "was not correctly given in our hasty report."[20] The *Chronicle* likewise highlighted moments when their reporters had been excluded from the gallery, so that readers were aware that the account might be faulty or abbreviated.[21]

There were concerns, however, about the way the newspapers approached the task of reporting Parliament. In February 1813, the MP M. A. Taylor told the Commons that

[h]e had no objection to the publication of the debates in the House; but in these debates false accounts ought not to be suffered to go out to the public, nor false insinuations allowed to be thrown out, which might have a tendency to lower the character of any member of that House in the public estimation … In the account of the debate on the Vice-Chancellor's Bill on Thursday night, he was described as having been assailed with loud noise in the course of his speech. He appealed to the House if this was the case. In the paper in question [the *British Press*] he was described also as having, with a degree of arrogance, said he would not waste his valuable time in answering lord Redesdale's book. Such was the vicious and unfounded mode of attack resorted to by the Editor of this paper.[22]

While the newspapers did not admit to publishing deliberately misleading reports, they did accept that their coverage was not full. Commenting on the extraordinary eloquence of the speeches on Catholic emancipation in February 1813, some of which Hazlitt covered, the *Morning Chronicle* hoped

that it will not be left to the public memorial of the periodical Reports. We sincerely hope that steps were taken to procure a faithful narrative of the most important Debates, and that they will be speedily presented to the public – not only the incomparable speech of Mr. PLUNKETT, the influence of which on the ultimate division, was so remarkable, but the admirable and conciliatory reasoning of Mr. CANNING are almost wholly lost to the world, since the sketches of what they said were so imperfectly given.[23]

While MPs attacked the press, some journalists attacked the House. Thomas Barnes, the future editor of *The Times*, began a column called "Parliamentary Criticism" for the *Examiner* under the pseudonym

[19] *Morning Chronicle* (December 1, 1812): 1.
[20] *Morning Chronicle* (June 12, 1813): 3.
[21] *Morning Chronicle* (March 6, 1813): 2.
[22] *Parliamentary Debates*, 1st ser., vol. XXIV (1812–13): 518.
[23] *Morning Chronicle* (March 8, 1813): 2.

Criticus in the summer of 1813. The column consisted of critiques of the current crop of parliamentary orators, and might be imagined as a project complementary to *The Eloquence of the British Senate*. In the prefatory essay, Barnes noted that when considering the performance of the House, "all whose transactions appear at least to be conducted through the medium of speech, it is impossible not to be struck with the dearth of dexterity and excellence in the management of the chief instrument of its operations."[24] In a setting that should inspire outstanding oratory, Barnes believed that

about half a dozen speakers who have acquired a certain fluent mediocrity, are allowed to settle the disputed proposition with little knowledge and less spirit, while the rest remain idle and almost unconcerned hearers, sometimes yawning, sometimes sleeping, and sometimes to evince their claims to sit in a speaking assembly, shouting in a style to be envied only by a Stentor or a whipper-in.[25]

The columns which followed examined around forty parliamentarians, with largely unfavorable results.

Hazlitt would have been aware that parliamentary speechmaking and reporting were under immense scrutiny from politicians, journalists and the public in this period. It is possible that he heard Taylor deliver the speech attacking the press in February 1813, and he certainly would have been aware of such an attack. He was also friendly with the *Examiner*'s editor, Leigh Hunt, so would no doubt have known about Barnes's pieces. The competitive nature of parliamentary reporting and the *Chronicle*'s attempts to maintain its reputation in that area would have been conveyed to him by Perry and obvious every night as reporters crowded into the gallery. The question is how he responded to this environment.

In his recent biography, Duncan Wu suggests that the main drawback of parliamentary reporting for Hazlitt was that "the job lacked challenge. It was basically a memory test."[26] Wu focuses his discussion of Hazlitt's time in the gallery on the ways in which he tried to get out of "the straitjacket of parliamentary reporting" by turning his hand to other kinds of writing for the *Morning Chronicle*.[27] But there is an important piece of evidence about Hazlitt's approach to reporting that does not feature in this biography, one which complicates the idea of the inflexibility of the genre.

---

[24] "Criticus," "Parliamentary Criticism," 525.
[25] "Criticus," "Parliamentary Criticism," 525.
[26] Wu, *William Hazlitt*, 149.   [27] Wu, *William Hazlitt*, 149.

THE EVIDENCE OF THE NOTEBOOK

Hazlitt's body of parliamentary reports will probably never be fully established, but there is indisputable evidence of his work on several occasions.
Later references in his works make it clear that he heard William Plunket's
speech on Catholic emancipation on February 25, 1813, the Marquis of
Wellesley's address in the Lords on April 9, 1813 and James Mackintosh's
maiden speech on December 20, 1813.[28] Additionally, his wife's notebook
for the period, which he briefly used for taking longhand notes and which
has not been the subject of any sustained critical attention, places him in
the gallery at the Commons for the debates of May 24, 25 and 31 and June
1, 2 and 3, 1813.[29] Part of the *Morning Chronicle*'s report in these instances
can thus be confidently attributed to Hazlitt, despite the fact that only
two examples from different occasions, the speeches of Wellesley, and of
Mackintosh and the speakers that followed him, have so far been published under his name.[30]

The six reports covered in the notebook are in many ways the most
interesting of the examples that can be attributed to Hazlitt, partly
because they have been unaccountably overlooked by scholars, but also
because his notebook allows us to trace his method from gallery to page;
it is one of the rare examples of the survival of the notes of any gallery
reporter, let alone one who was well known in later life.[31] This method can
be divided into three approaches. The first shows Hazlitt taking detailed
notes which become a full report of certain speakers. The second shows
him taking scanty notes that contribute to an abbreviated report. The
third shows him inventing content to make up for lapses in his note-
taking. Within an individual report, these approaches often coalesce and
overlap. The notebook thus tells us a great deal about the world of the
contemporary reporter and Hazlitt's place within it.

---

[28] Hazlitt also mentions hearing Samuel Whitbread speak on the Princess of Wales in 1813. A likely
contender is the long address of March 17, but since Whitbread gave numerous speeches on this
subject it is not possible to be certain which one Hazlitt means. See Hazlitt, "On the Present
State of Parliamentary Eloquence," 10.

[29] As I noted earlier, Stanley Jones is the only scholar to have mentioned these notes, and he does so
only in passing, misdating them as belonging to June–July 1814 (107). Although he did not use it
in this notebook, Hazlitt knew shorthand; see his *Letters*, 70.

[30] Wu, ed., *New Writings*, 1: 31–45 and 1: 94–120 respectively.

[31] Wu mentions another manuscript, the whereabouts of which is unknown since it was sold at
auction, which might contain more of Hazlitt's gallery notes; see Wu, ed., *New Writings*, 1:
xxxiii.

The first debate in the notebook, which covers the House of Commons' deliberations on the Roman Catholic Relief Bill on May 24, 1813, illustrates the way Hazlitt's first two techniques manifested themselves. His notes, which become progressively more chaotic and sprawling as the debate wears on, cover the speeches by George Ponsonby and Sir John Cox Hippisley, before he is apparently relieved by a colleague. The first step in analyzing Hazlitt's report on this occasion is to consider the ways in which these fifteen pages of scribbled and often illegible notes become translated into one and a half columns of uniform type in the *Chronicle* of the following morning. The notebook demonstrates that he certainly did not produce full sentences in his notes. The notes that cover Ponsonby's speech, for example, begin: "With all deference to member," who has "mistaken the nature of resolution."[32] Such notes were then translated into the version that appears in the *Chronicle*, which has Ponsonby say "that with all his deference to the Honourable Member who opened the debate (the Speaker), he could not help observing that he seemed to have mistaken the nature of the Resolution under which the Committee acted."[33] A great deal of what appears in the notebook finds it way, with some editorial embellishment, into the final text, and all of Ponsonby's material arguments are outlined, largely in the language that he seems to have used in the House. For example, his question, as taken down by Hazlitt, "who knows upon whose head crown rest in 20 years," appears as the more elegant "who knows upon what head the Crown of this kingdom will rest in twenty years?"[34]

The second step in making sense of Hazlitt's technique is to compare his account with those produced by other reporters. A comparison with *The Times*'s report, which was the one the *Parliamentary Debates* used on this occasion, and with that of the *Morning Post*, shows that while the ideas are expressed very differently, as was to be expected when reporters supplied much of the language themselves, Hazlitt's account clearly outlined Ponsonby's key arguments. Certain phrases are also echoed. *The Times*, for example, has Ponsonby ridicule the suggestion that if Catholics were admitted to Parliament they would "quietly, gently, imperceptibly, hardly knowing it themselves, become masters of the country, and overturn the Crown. Quiet advancement to the first offices

---

[32] Sarah Stoddart Hazlitt Poetry Commonplace Book, fol. 6a. Hereafter referred to as the "Commonplace Book."
[33] *Morning Chronicle* (May 25, 1813): 2.
[34] Commonplace Book, fol. 7b; and *Morning Chronicle* (May 25, 1813): 2.

in the State, unknown to any person, was rather difficult to conceive. If a Roman Catholic was advanced to be Lord High Admiral, would it not be known?"[35] The *Morning Post* records Ponsonby saying that his opponents seemed to imagine that Catholics would "quietly and gently be brought into all the great offices ... quite unperceived by any one."[36] Hazlitt's version of this passage likewise has Ponsonby attack the idea that Catholics

would quietly and gently, and by imperceptible degrees introduce themselves into all the seats in that House, and into all the great offices of the State. A gentle and quiet introduction to all the great offices of the State! Nobody was to know of it – the change was to be silent and imperceptible. Nobody would be able to learn whether a Catholic was appointed First Lord of the Treasury, or First Lord of the Admiralty.[37]

The coverage of Sir John Cox Hippisley, who spoke after Ponsonby, allows us to see the other side of Hazlitt's reporting. His notes begin with Hippisley saying that the first clause of the bill "had his most cordial support," before clarifying that "[t]hough the clause in itself had his approbation, yet in the form in which it stood he could not."[38] This phrase appears, largely unchanged, in the *Chronicle* as "though the clause in itself had his most cordial approbation, yet in the order in which it stood he could not support it."[39] Up to this point, the coverage of Hippisley resembles that of Ponsonby in fullness. Other parts of Hippisley's speech have clearly been abbreviated, however, both in the notes and in the report. The notes include the word "consistent," while in the *Chronicle*'s report Hazlitt records that "[t]he Honourable Member at some length defended his own consistency," without including any of Hippisley's arguments on this point.[40] Moreover, the sequence of these remarks about Hippisley's support for the clause and his consistency has been altered from how it appears in the notebook, suggesting a reshaping of the speech by the reporter before it reached the page.

On this occasion, Hazlitt's approach differed markedly from that of his fellow reporters. Hazlitt chose to summarize Hippisley's defense of his own position and focus instead on his comments about the haste with which the Bill was being pushed through the House. *The Times* and the *Morning Post* chose the opposite approach; much of their coverage involves

[35] *The Times* (May 25, 1813): 2.   [36] *Morning Post* (May 25, 1813): 2.
[37] *Morning Chronicle* (May 25, 1813): 2.   [38] Commonplace Book, fols. 11a-b.
[39] *Morning Chronicle* (May 25, 1813): 2.
[40] Commonplace Book, fol. 11b; *Morning Chronicle* (May 25, 1813): 2.

Hippisley's response to attacks on his stance.[41] Certain phrases still link the examples: *The Times* has Hippisley mention the "indecent precipitation" of the bill, which Hazlitt renders as "indecent precipitancy," but the emphasis has been placed on different aspects of the speech.[42]

Hazlitt's coverage of Ponsonby's speech demonstrates one possible approach to reporting: capturing as much of the language as possible but supplying the syntactical structure oneself when transcribing. Another possibility, demonstrated in the Hippisley coverage, was to truncate parts of the speech and reshape it into a coherent whole. While they could and did ultimately produce quite different results, both techniques appear to be part of the normal range of approaches used by Hazlitt's colleagues, such as those at *The Times* and the *Morning Post*. Another *Morning Chronicle* reporter, Walter Coulson, later commented that "[t]he space which can be allotted to a report in a newspaper is contingent upon the greater or less quantity of other matter of superior interest that presents itself. An abridgement, sometimes a very condensed one, is necessary ..."[43]

A second example of this combination of techniques can be seen in the report of the debates for May 31, 1813. Hazlitt's turn on this occasion again encompassed just two speeches: all of the speech by Richard Hart Davies, and most of that by George Phillips.[44] He appears to have taken quite detailed notes, although they are only the outlines of the report as it appears in print. The opening of his notes, for example, reads "delusion, I must say gross delusion."[45] This idea is amplified as he begins his final report to record that Hart Davies "considered the opinions entertained on the subject of the East India Charter as a delusion, a gross delusion."[46] One note reads "East India company must keep their accounts distinct. Interest of E. I. C. insuperable, whereas it was not."[47] In the *Chronicle*, this passage appears as follows: "One cause which contributed to produce this effect was the confusion in which the accounts of their civil and commercial establishments were kept. It was the interest of the Directors to represent this intricacy as insuperable, but it was by no means so in

---

[41] *The Times* (May 25, 1813): 3; *Morning Post* (May 25, 1813): 2.
[42] *The Times* (May 25, 1813): 3; *Morning Chronicle* (May 25, 1813): 2.
[43] [Coulson], "Review of *The Periodical Press of Great Britain*," 204.
[44] Commonplace Book, fols. 15a–23b. It is clear that Hazlitt was relieved before Phillips finished speaking, as his notes do not encompass the whole speech, and he rules off his page with a line. There is a change to a larger, more widely spaced type in the same place in *The Times*, which suggests that one reportorial turn ended at that moment; see *The Times* (June 1, 1813): 2.
[45] Commonplace Book, fol. 15a.   [46] *Morning Chronicle* (June 1, 1813): 2.
[47] Commonplace Book, fol. 15a.

fact."[48] Details from Phillips's speech, such as the story of someone who had gone to India "with a bulldog and attacked a cow, another of a monkey," likewise become rather fuller anecdotes in the published report.[49] At the same time as he was expanding the speeches, however, Hazlitt was also sometimes truncating them when it came time to transcribe. In his notebook, for example, Hazlitt recorded that Phillips used the phrase "guardian angel," but omitted this part of the speech in his report. In *The Times*, this striking phrase was rendered as the question: "Was this the Paradise which the Company as a guardian angel with a flaming sword, watched, in order to keep out the British Traders?"[50]

Hazlitt's report on Hart Davies and Phillips is a particularly important example of his efficacy as a reporter. On this occasion, the *Parliamentary Debates* chose to use the *Morning Chronicle*'s report verbatim for its coverage of these two speeches.[51] It is clear that his reporting was very good on this occasion, but also that he was part of a strong reporting team; the *Parliamentary Debates* reproduced the whole of Phillips's speech as given in the *Morning Chronicle*, only the first part of which was Hazlitt's work. This selection is an endorsement of his skill, but also of his adherence to the standards upheld by his paper.

The Ponsonby, Hippisley, Hart Davies and Phillips examples show Hazlitt selecting speakers or parts of speeches for very detailed treatment, while also abbreviating or summarizing other parts of his report. He was also capable, however, of severely curtailing his coverage, at both the note-taking and the reporting stages. His turn on May 25, 1813, for example, encompassed fifteen short addresses during the debate on the Irish Firearms Bill.[52] The orthography of Hazlitt's notes suggests a rapid debate; the clear, neat hand of the early notes deteriorates markedly as speaker after speaker rises to his feet. His notebook shows that a journalistic selection process was clearly at work even while he sat in the gallery, although it is difficult to be certain what criteria he used. There does not appear to be any particular prejudice at work on Hazlitt's part, except perhaps a sense that some of the speeches were dull or too brief to offer much to readers. It might be the case, as often occurred, that some speakers were difficult to hear or spoke too quickly. Six of the fifteen speakers

[48] *Morning Chronicle* (June 1, 1813): 2.
[49] Commonplace Book, fol. 18a; and *Morning Chronicle* (June 1, 1813): 2.
[50] Commonplace Book, fol. 20a; *The Times* (June 1, 1813): 2.
[51] See *Parliamentary Debates*, 1st ser., vol. XXVI (1813): 457–63.
[52] Commonplace Book, fols. 13b–14b.

are simply mentioned by name in the notebook in order to record the sequence of who spoke, with no notes at all being taken of what they said. Four of the remaining nine speakers are recorded as offering very short statements that simply summarize their views; General Hart, for example, "thought the measure insufficiently strong," while next to another speaker's name Hazlitt has simply written "necessary."[53] Even the fullest notes, which are jotted down for five of the speakers, are extremely brief when compared with those taken when Ponsonby spoke the day before.

If these notes seem brutally short, Hazlitt's report of the debate is even more ruthless. His one-hour turn produces a contribution that amounts to only sixteen lines, compared to over a column of reporting on Hart Davies and Phillips. Sir John Newport's short speech, which was one of the few that had prompted him to take notes, is further abbreviated in its printed form; his assessment that "no ground had been stated" to support the decision to control firearms in Ireland and his observation that the suggestion showed "a peculiar ill grace" both found their way from Hazlitt's notebook to the newspaper, but his references to habeas corpus did not.[54] Sir Frederick Flood and Sir Henry Parnell, the next two speakers, both of whose speeches Hazlitt had briefly recorded, end up simply speaking "on the same side of the question."[55] A further eight speakers are lumped together, in some instances out of sequence, with a summary statement about what they said. Two are left out completely, and the final two have their views toned down; Hazlitt's note that C. W. Wynn "thought that a rather paltry account had been given" does not quite square with the final section of his report, in which Wynn declared himself "perfectly satisfied with the grounds which had been stated."[56]

Hazlitt's approach might seem far from satisfactory, but it was in keeping with the needs of his employer and the general approach taken by the gallery. Perry and his reporters had clearly decided that the parliamentary report for this day's paper would need to be curtailed; the *Morning Chronicle*'s coverage of the debates of both Houses on this occasion occupies less than a column, an unusually small section. Moreover, other reporters had similarly deemed the speeches Hazlitt covered to be

---

[53] Commonplace Book, fol. 14a.
[54] Commonplace Book, fol. 13b; *Morning Chronicle* (May 26, 1813): 2.
[55] *Morning Chronicle* (May 26, 1813): 2.
[56] Commonplace Book, fol. 14b; *Morning Chronicle* (May 26, 1813): 2. Wynn was famously difficult to report because of his quiet voice; see "Criticus," "Parliamentary Criticism: Mr. C. W. Wynne [*sic*] and Mr. Bankes," 636.

unworthy of many column inches; the corresponding sections of *The Times* and the *Morning Post* are longer than the *Chronicle*'s, but their reporters choose, like Hazlitt, to reduce many of the speeches to notes that an MP "spoke on the same side," or "said a few words."[57] Hazlitt's abbreviated report is thus in keeping with his colleagues' coverage that day.

He was also following the norms of the press gallery in his note-taking and reporting of the debate of June 2, 1813. Some interesting issues were discussed that night, including the East India Company's affairs, but Hazlitt's turn fell during a section of the debate that was heavy on procedure, as various MPs introduced bills. Hazlitt took only one page of notes, covering an initial comment by Lord Palmerston, a response from Ponsonby and a reply from Palmerston.[58] These brief notes produced a brief report, which read:

Lord PALMERSTON brought up a Bill for the more speedy punishment of Soldiers serving in Spain. Read a first time.

Mr. PONSONBY wished the Bill to be printed before it was read a second time. It might be necessary and wise, but it was certainly novel.

Lord PALMERSTON wished every satisfaction to be given to Members on the subject. The Bill was ordered to be printed, and read a second time this se'nnight.[59]

Despite seeming like a severely abbreviated account of an hour's parliamentary business, Hazlitt's account here is actually rather generous, within the strictures of press gallery norms. Much of this turn would have been consumed by the reading of the bill, which the newspapers never reported in full, focusing their attention instead on the speeches. Hazlitt's report compares favorably with the other extant accounts. The *Morning Post* omitted Ponsonby altogether, but provided some detail about the bill that was missing from Hazlitt's report.

Lord PALMERSTON having obtained leave, brought in a Bill to provide for the Punishment of Soldiers detached from head-quarters in the Peninsula, and guilty of excesses; it was read a first time, second reading on Wednesday next.[60]

The Times, meanwhile, recorded this part of the debate as follows:

---

[57] *Morning Post* (May 26, 1813): 3; *The Times* (May 26, 1813): 3.
[58] Commonplace Book, fol. 25a.   [59] *Morning Chronicle* (June 3, 1813): 2.
[60] *Morning Post* (June 3, 1813): 2.

Lord PALMERSTON's Bill, of which he had given notice, respecting the punishment of officers in Spain and Portugal, was brought up, read a first time, and, on the proceeding for its second reading,

Mr. PONSONBY suggested, that considering both its novelty and its importance, it ought to be first printed.

Lord PALMERSTON acquiesced in the suggestion; and it was accordingly ordered to be printed, and to be read a second time this day se'nnight.[61]

Although there are weaknesses in Hazlitt's account in comparison with these versions, such as the omission of Portugal, there are also strengths. More of the speakers' voices are conveyed, not only in comparison with the *Morning Post*'s very brief account, but also with *The Times*'s. Placing Ponsonby's comment about the novelty and necessity of the bill into a separate sentence, for example, captured some of the pithiness of the remark and made it appear almost as if it was written in the first person. Likewise, more of Palmerston's courtesy is captured in Hazlitt's phrase that the MP "wished every satisfaction to be given to Members on the subject" than in *The Times*'s report that he "acquiesced in the suggestion." Hazlitt's approach is distinctive but sound, conforming with the newspapers' routines while attempting to capture what was said and enhance the *Morning Chronicle*'s coverage.

However, another approach to reporting, one that is potentially more problematic, can be seen when the debate on the Irish Firearms Bill resumed on June 1. Hazlitt's notes cover five speakers and are extremely brief. The first speech by Charles Bathurst, which Hazlitt evidently began reporting near its conclusion, is covered in a little detail in the notebook, as is that of Phillips, the final speaker in this sequence, but those in between barely register.[62] Alexander Baring's name is recorded, with no additional information, while another speaker (presumably Bathurst again, as this is how Hazlitt reports the debate the following day) is indicated simply by the word "Mr."[63] Ponsonby's speech, meanwhile, is reduced to the note

---

[61] *The Times* (June 3, 1813): 2. The *Parliamentary Debates* did not provide any coverage of the introduction of bills, so there is no way to compare Hazlitt's account with the official record.

[62] Commonplace Book, fols. 23b–24b. Hazlitt's notes begin with a reference to "5, or 600" thousand pounds, a figure that Bathurst did not use until he had nearly finished speaking. There is also an unusual transition in the *Chronicle*'s coverage at this point. Although there is no suggestion that anyone else would be speaking, the *Chronicle* records that "Mr Bathurst continued," the phrase probably suggesting that a new reporter was beginning to cover a speech that was already in progress. See the Commonplace Book, fol. 23b; *Morning Chronicle* (June 2, 1813): 2.

[63] Commonplace Book, fols. 24a

"Mr Ponsonby applauded."[64] From these jottings, Hazlitt constructed a report of thirty-three lines for the *Morning Chronicle*. Ponsonby's applause is transformed into six lines of speech, and Bathurst's brief response to him is likewise concocted from scratch. Baring does not feature at all.

Some of these decisions are borne out by other sources. Hazlitt clearly had the correct sequence of speakers; the *Parliamentary Debates* also records the order of speaking as Bathurst, Ponsonby, Bathurst and Phillips. Hazlitt was probably right to omit any reference to Baring speaking; the *Parliamentary Debates*, which usually aimed to recreate the fullest report possible, did not mention Baring, while the *Morning Post* recorded only that he "explained," suggesting a short, perhaps inaudible, remark.[65] It is also clear from both the *Parliamentary Debates* and the *Morning Post* that Ponsonby did give a short speech, and that Bathurst responded to it.[66] Moreover, Hazlitt's coverage of Ponsonby appears to reflect accurately the sentiments of the speech. The full text of his account reads:

Mr. PONSONBY contended, that the argument of the Right Honourable Gentleman who spoke last, reduced it to the single circumstance of the danger to be apprehended from the misconduct of the private trader, which he could not concede to exist, as it would be the interest of the private trader to behave with the utmost possible circumspection and propriety.[67]

This rendition is a fair reflection of the text in the *Parliamentary Debates*, which records Ponsonby saying in conclusion that Bathurst's argument "resolved itself into this, that great danger would arise from the misconduct of the private traders. Now, he never could admit the proposition, that the private traders were likely to conduct themselves in such a manner as would ruin their own interests."[68]

Hazlitt's coverage is among the best of that in the major papers. It is slightly less comprehensive than the coverage in the *Morning Post*, but it compares very favorably with that provided by *The Times*. Of the four speeches to appear in Hazlitt's report for the *Chronicle*, only Bathurst's first address is covered in any detail in *The Times*. Ponsonby's response, and Bathurst's rejoinder, do not feature at all, and Phillips's is only recorded as "Mr. G. PHILLIPS opposed the Resolution."[69] On the basis of these published reports, Hazlitt's technique again seems to be in keeping with

[64] Commonplace Book, fols. 24a.   [65] *Morning Post* (June 2, 1813): 2.

[66] *Parliamentary Debates*, 1st ser., vol. XXVI (1813): 498; *Morning Post* (June 2, 1813): 2.

[67] *Morning Chronicle* (June 2, 1813): 2.

[68] *Parliamentary Debates*, 1st ser., vol. XXVI (1813): 498.

[69] *The Times* (June 2, 1813): 3.

the normal practice of his colleagues. But what are we to make of the fact that Hazlitt produced two of the speeches (Ponsonby's and the second one delivered by Bathurst) without having taken down any notes? Both were clearly constructed from memory, but with very different results. Hazlitt's version of Bathurst's speech is dissimilar to the other accounts, but his version of Ponsonby's is supported by the *Debates*. Was he reliant on his memory in some instances, even when he had a notebook in front of him? Did he sometimes collaborate with other journalists to discover details that he'd missed?

Charles Lamb's impressions can shed some light on this question. Lamb had recommended Hazlitt to John Dyer Collier for the role of parliamentary reporter in part because of "his singular facility in retaining all conversations at which he has ever been present."[70] The specifics of this remark might be exaggerated to help his friend find work, but it was presumably true in a general sense that Hazlitt had a remarkable memory. He was also working in the gallery at a time when some reporters still followed the old practice, instituted by William Woodfall, of attempting to memorize the debates without the use of a notebook; one of these practitioners, a Mr. Proby, worked for the *Chronicle*.[71] So too did Walter Coulson, who later wrote that a reporter's job involved writing "from his notes with the aid of a practised memory the speech or speeches he has heard."[72] It does not seem too farfetched to suggest that Hazlitt created both Bathurst's second speech and Ponsonby's remarks from scratch, relying on his recollections and perhaps the notes of some of his colleagues, as both examples were short and the former is not actually substantiated by other sources.

Hazlitt's memory is also an issue in his report of the debate of June 3. The entirety of his legible notes for this turn reads:

Mr. G Smith – was against the [resolution]
Mr. Protheroe –
Mr. Baring[73]

It is possible that Hazlitt did not hear much of Baring's speech before being relieved, but the implication of these notes is that he did at least have responsibility for reporting George Smith and Edward Protheroe.

---

[70] Lamb, *Letters*, III: 85–86.   [71] Andrews, *History of British Journalism*, II: 70.
[72] [Coulson], "Review of *The Periodical Press of Great Britain*," 204.
[73] Commonplace Book, fol. 25b. The final word of the Smith note is almost illegible; "resolution" seems likely, however. There are also some illegible words at the beginning of the note.

Hazlitt's account of Smith's speech appeared in the *Morning Chronicle* as a single summarized line: "George Smith spoke in favour of the continuance of the Charter."[74] This account is shorter even than the brief account provided by the *Morning Post*, which was only three lines long, and considerably shorter than that of *The Times*, which covered Smith in twenty-two lines and predictably formed the basis of the speech recorded in the *Parliamentary Debates*.[75] But the other accounts make it clear that this was an extremely difficult speech to report. The *Morning Post*, for example, noted that Smith spoke "in a low voice."[76] *The Times*, meanwhile, was clearly summarizing Smith when it recorded that he "recapitulated a variety of arguments, and stated a series of strong facts."[77] It is quite possible that Hazlitt heard very little of what was said, perhaps because he was sitting in part of the gallery that made hearing difficult, and was unable to provide anything more detailed.

Hazlitt's account of Protheroe's speech, however, presents the same kind of interpretative challenge posed by the Ponsonby and Bathurst speeches of June 1. He took no notes at all, but produced a report of fifteen lines. Some of the language in the report made it clear that he was summarizing the speech. He began by noting that Protheroe "remarked at some length" on Tierney's address of the previous evening and "vindicated the conduct of the Petitioners from the outports."[78] Such a summary would have been entirely possible to construct from memory. Other parts of the speech, however, seem to have been remembered in rather precise detail. Hazlitt noted, for example, that Protheroe characterized Tierney's speech "as more remarkable for a vein of sarcastic observation, than for closeness or strength of argument."[79] The same ideas were captured by *The Times*, which noted that Protheroe had said that Tierney's speech was "more remarkable for sarcasm than for argument," and appeared in the report in the *Parliamentary Debates*, which had Protheroe say that Tierney's argument had "dwelt more largely in sarcasm than argument."[80] Hazlitt also wrote that Protheroe had reminded the House of "the language used by the French merchants, when asked by Colbert what the Government should do for them, 'Let us alone.' This short sentence ... contained more

74 *Morning Chronicle* (June 4, 1813): 2.
75 See the *Morning Post* (June 4, 1813): 2; *The Times* (June 4, 1813): 2; and *Parliamentary Debates*, 1st ser., vol. XXVI (1813): 534–35.
76 *Morning Post* (June 4, 1813): 2.   77 *The Times* (June 4, 1813): 2.
78 *Morning Chronicle* (June 4, 1813): 2.   79 *Morning Chronicle* (June 4, 1813): 2.
80 *The Times* (June 4, 1813): 2; *Parliamentary Debates*, 1st ser., vol. XXVI (1813): 535.

sound commercial wisdom than the 591 pages of the evidence brought forward by the East India Company."[81] This remark is corroborated by the *Parliamentary Debates*, which has Protheroe use the phrase "Let us alone" before noting that "there was more practical commercial knowledge, and political wisdom, displayed in that short sentence, than in the 590 pages of evidence in favour of the East India Company."[82] While these are very close matches, they largely rely on remembering some key details, not an unlikely feat for someone with a very good memory.

The notebook demonstrates that Hazlitt was not the aloof, skeptical reporter of the standard biographies and critical accounts. It points instead to an effective gallery journalist who deployed a range of contemporary techniques, many of them standard weapons in the journalistic arsenal, to produce his reports. A new vision of Hazlitt the reporter thus emerges from the evidence in the notebook: someone who was well versed in the routines and norms of newspaper journalism, who immersed himself in the task of reporting both while sitting in the gallery and while preparing his finished report, and whose contributions were good enough but also, it must be pointed out, sufficiently generic in style to be integrated into both his own paper's coverage and that of the collected debates. There is no obvious Hazlittian voice in these reports, no sense of him as the scourge of parliamentarians. In place of the critical Hazlitt, there is the competent Hazlitt, less compelling, perhaps, but no less skillful.

REPORTING PLUNKET

The insights into Hazlitt's technique that the notebook provides are useful when considering his versions of some of the speeches he specifically recalled reporting, speeches that were especially memorable after he had left the gallery. One oration that we can be sure Hazlitt covered was William Plunket's address on February 25, 1813, about the rights of Roman Catholics, during a debate which brought a huge and noisy crowd to the gallery.[83] The Plunket speech is a particularly important one in the context of Hazlitt's work as a reporter. Among the occasions on which we can be sure he was in the gallery, this address is certainly the most celebrated. The *Chronicle* noted that "[t]he speech of Mr. PLUNKETT

---

[81] *Morning Chronicle* (June 4, 1813): 2.
[82] *Parliamentary Debates*, 1st ser., vol. XXVI (1813): 536.
[83] Aspinall, "Reporting and Publishing," 236.

in particular made a deep sensation on both sides of the House, and is deservedly considered as ranking among the most brilliant and success-ful displays of parliamentary eloquence."[84] Hazlitt later recalled that

[its] effect was extraordinary: the impression grew stronger from first to last. No one stirred the whole time, and, at the end, the lobbies were crowded with members going up stairs and saying, "Well this is a speech worth going without one's dinner to hear," (Oh, unequivocal testimony of applause!) "there has been nothing like this since the time of Fox," &c.[85]

Hazlitt left a detailed account of his experience of listening to Plunket that night; his essay "On the Present State of Parliamentary Eloquence" contains two pages of analysis of Plunket's style on this occasion. He admired Plunket generally, calling him "[t]he best Irish speaker I ever heard (indeed the best speaker without any exception whatever)," but he especially admired this address, commenting that "I never heard any other speech that I would have given three farthings to have made."[86] Although he did not claim this report directly, Hazlitt's discussion of the way Plunket was reported makes it clear that he was one of the journalists charged with taking down the speech.

[Plunket's speech] did not make the same figure in the newspapers the next day; for it was but indifferently reported, owing to the extreme fluency with which it was delivered. There was no boggling, no straggling, irrelevant matter; – you could not wait for him at the end of a long parenthesis, and go on with your report as if nothing had happened in the interval, as is sometimes the case … [I]t was a speech better calculated to strike in the hearing than in the perusal.[87]

These were clearly the observations of someone who had tried to capture Plunket's words. Hazlitt's recollections of this debate help us to attribute at least part of the *Morning Chronicle*'s report to him, but also provide priceless evidence of the way he thought about the relationship between speech-making and speech-taking.[88]

84 *Morning Chronicle* (March 4, 1813): 2.
85 Hazlitt, "On the Present State of Parliamentary Eloquence," 14.
86 Hazlitt, "On the Present State of Parliamentary Eloquence," 13–14.
87 Hazlitt, "On the Present State of Parliamentary Eloquence," 14.
88 There are issues of attribution to be resolved in this instance. Plunket's speech occupied nearly three columns in the *Chronicle*, and is thus too long to be the work of a single reporter. Later sources suggest that an hour's speaking translated into roughly two columns of type; see "Parliamentary Reporting," 20; Grant, *The Great Metropolis*, II: 223; *The Times* (March 30, 1831): 5. Moreover, there is a noticeable change of technique in the reporting of the speech. The first two columns contain no reportorial interpolations. At the beginning of the third col-umn, however, an initial "hear!" is included (*Morning Chronicle* [February 26, 1813]: 3). Several

Given the challenging combination of the gallery's crowd, the speaker's fluency and the journalist's admiration, how did Hazlitt report Plunket? It is useful to take note of his recollections of the way in which the speech was structured and its rhetorical effect, before turning to the report itself. Hazlitt wrote that Plunket

went strait forward to his end with a force equal to his rapidity. He removed all obstacles, as he advanced ... No part of the subject could come amiss to him – history, law, constitutional principle, common feeling, local prejudices, general theory, – all was alike within his reach and his controul. Having settled one point, he passed on to another, carrying his hearers with him: – it was as if he knew all that could be said on the question, and was anxious to impart his knowledge without any desire of shining. There was no affectation, no effort, but equal ease and earnestness. Every thing was brought to bear that could answer his purpose, and there was nothing superfluous. His eloquence swept along like a river, "Without o'erflowing, full." Every step told: every sentence went to account. I cannot say that there was any thing very profound or original in argument, imposing in imagination, or impassioned in sentiment, in any part of his address – but it was throughout impregnated with as much thought, imagination and passion as the House would be likely to understand or sympathise with.[89]

The *Morning Chronicle*'s coverage, unsurprisingly, bears out this estimation of the speech. Plunket used Bankes's speech attacking Grattan, who had moved that a committee be established to consider the claims of Catholics, as a framework for defending the principles of equality and compassion. He dismantled each of Bankes's objections in turn, using

more instances follow, including "loud cries of hear!" at one point later on the same page in the *Chronicle*'s coverage of Plunket's speech. The speeches immediately preceding Plunket's are likewise scattered with comments like the "hear, hear, from the Opposition benches" that appears in the coverage of Bankes's speech, also on page three of the *Chronicle*. It is clear from reading the *Morning Post*'s and *The Times*'s report that there were many of these interjections from the House early in Plunket's speech, suggesting that the *Chronicle* reporter who covered the first part of the speech deliberately omitted them. Hazlitt's other verified reports are characterized by the lack of these interjections; his coverage of Ponsonby and Hippisley, for example, contains none of this interpolated material, while the coverage of Sir John Nicholl, who spoke before Ponsonby, which was produced by a different reporter, is filled with notes like "hear, hear!" and "a laugh" (*Morning Chronicle* [February 26, 1813]: 2). The point at which these interjections begin to appear in the *Chronicle*'s report of Plunket also marks a change in the report of *The Times*, which switches to a smaller type, suggesting that there was a wholesale change of reporters at this point, as one turn ended and another began (*The Times* [February 26, 1813]: 3). It seems likely, therefore, that Hazlitt reported the first part of Plunket's speech, up to roughly the beginning of the final paragraph in the first column on p. 3 of the *Morning Chronicle*, perhaps staying in the gallery to listen to the conclusion once he had been relieved.

89 Hazlitt, "On the Present State of Parliamentary Eloquence," 13–14.

effective rhetorical questions to challenge the assumptions that had underpinned the debate and to introduce relevant historical detail and precedents. In questioning Bankes's analysis of the situation, for example, Plunket asked "[i]f the Honourable Gentleman meant to intimate that he must at all times think the Claims of the Catholics inadmissible, then what came of his vote of last year in their favour?"[90] Having established the inconsistency of Bankes's principles, Plunket went on to question the consistency of his arguments against the proposal. Since Bankes had "agreed that something must be done ... why not go into a Committee?"[91] As Hazlitt suggested, each obstacle was removed by Plunket's reasoning.

Plunket drew the House (and the gallery) to his side with both subtle and blunt appeals to their reasoning. In discussing the unfairness of excluding Catholics from office, Plunket asked, according to Hazlitt: "Would any man deny that even such an exclusion as this was sufficient to irritate?"[92] Having established through detailed examples that the historical trend had been to allow Catholics rights under the Constitution, Plunket put the following choice to the House:

Part of the load which had been heaped on the backs of those sons of earth, they had already removed; were they prepared to replace it again on their shoulders, or to grant them a fair participation in the advantages of the Constitution? Either the one or the other they must do: if the former, he must be excused for saying, he must be a madman who would advise it, and an ideot who would attend to the recommendation.[93]

A familiarity with Hazlitt's general approach to reporting is helpful in instances such as this one, in which his notes have not survived. The Plunket speech demonstrates the hallmarks of Hazlitt's technique when confronted with a long and important speech. It is clear, first of all, that there is quite a lot of accurate reporting. According to the *Parliamentary Debates*, Plunket did use the words "madman" and "ideot" to characterize those who would support exclusion.[94] He did suggest that refusing to accept the sincerity of Catholics' oaths of allegiance was "worse than transubstantiation" in its lack of logic.[95] According to the *Morning Post*,

---

[90] *Morning Chronicle* (February 26, 1813): 2.
[91] *Morning Chronicle* (February 26, 1813): 2.
[92] *Morning Chronicle* (February 26, 1813): 2.
[93] *Morning Chronicle* (February 26, 1813): 3.
[94] *Parliamentary Debates*, 1st ser., vol. xxiv (1813): 798.
[95] *Morning Chronicle* (February 26, 1813): 3; *Parliamentary Debates*, 1st ser., vol. xxiv (1813): 803. Other reporters also caught this remark; see, for example, *The Times* (February 26, 1813): 3.

he did use a phrase very similar Hazlitt's suggestion that "[i]t was to bur-lesque the Revolution to hold [the Test and Corporation Acts] up as the bulwarks of it."[96]

But it is also clear that some aspects of the speech were altered, not simply by the process of turning notes into a full report, but by what appear to be conscious omissions. Hazlitt recalled later that one of the strengths of the speech was that Plunket "overturned Mr. Banks [*sic*] with his right hand, and Mr. Charles Yorke with his left – the one on a chronological question of the Concordat, and the other as to the ori-gin of the Corporation and Test Acts."[97] The version of the speech in the *Parliamentary Debates* does indeed include Plunket's attack on Yorke. However, Hazlitt's report makes no mention of Yorke, and simply blends Plunket's comments about Yorke's opinions into his overall criticisms of the opponents of the motion. As with so many of his reportorial decisions, this one mirrored that of his fellow reporters. Neither *The Times* nor the *Morning Post* mentioned Yorke directly, choosing instead to have Plunket move on to consideration of the issues Yorke had mentioned without indi-cating that he was responding to him.

The Plunket speech thus allows us to see how Hazlitt's technique oper-ated when he was confronted with a speech that he admired and that attracted widespread attention. The evidence, important to our under-standing of his career, is that he reported this significant address using the techniques that he would use on other occasions when he decided to generate a full report, such as his coverage of Hart Davies and Phillips. But it is also the case that this approach largely followed that undertaken by his fellow reporters, who would likewise have seen the value in grant-ing extensive coverage to this speech.

The Plunket speech has further significance for spawning a popular anecdote about Hazlitt. Augustine Birrell recorded, in his 1902 biography, that "[t]radition says Hazlitt was so excited by [Plunket's speech] that he quite forgot he was in the gallery for a purpose, and sat motionless and entranced."[98] The anecdote has the hallmarks of much of the critical lit-erature on Hazlitt's time as a gallery reporter (and has echoes of Coleridge too), in that it implies not only a general disgust with Parliament that is briefly alleviated by Plunket, but also Hazlitt's apparent unsuitability for

---

[96] *Morning Chronicle* (February 26, 1813): 3. The *Morning Post*'s report has Plunket say that "[i]t was a burlesque on the Revolution to call these its bulwarks" (February 26, 1813): 3.
[97] Hazlitt, "On the Present State of Parliamentary Eloquence," 13.
[98] Birrell, *William Hazlitt*, 99.

the task of reporting, as he neglects the task at hand in a reverie of delight. However, nothing about his general approach to reporting suggests that he would have stopped taking notes during a speech that he intended to report in full. A comparable occasion, when he reported Hart Davies and Phillips, shows him producing very detailed notes while the speeches progressed. His published report of Plunket is approximately the same length as that in *The Times*, and longer than that in the *Morning Post*; while there is always the possibility that he was working from memory, having put down his notebook as Birrell suggested, the other occasions on which this appears to have happened involved short speeches and equally short reports. Finally, Hazlitt himself makes no mention of such an event in his recollections; if anything, they point to a concerted attempt to keep up with Plunket in his notebook.

In a similar vein, the Plunket speech is also important for provoking one of Hazlitt's few direct comments about parliamentary reporting. In a footnote to his remarks about the struggles of capturing Plunket on the page, Hazlitt wrote that "[t]he best speeches are the worst reported, the worst are made better than they are. They both find a convenient newspaper level."[99] This comment is appealingly self-deprecating, since one of the best speeches in question was Plunket's and thus one of the worst attempts at reporting was his own. His appreciation of the limits of parliamentary reporting and his sense that the reports, regardless of who composed them, generally met a level suitable for publication in a newspaper, paint him as someone entirely at ease with the norms of the profession and the uniformity that those norms inevitably provoked, even in "a philosopher employed at so much a week to take down the words of ordinary mortals."[100]

WELLESLEY AND MACINTOSH: THE CHALLENGES OF ATTRIBUTION AND ANALYSIS

There are only two reports that have been previously attributed to Hazlitt: the Marquis of Wellesley's speech to the House of Lords on April 9, 1813 and James Mackintosh's maiden address, and the responses to it, in the House of Commons on December 20, 1813, which Duncan Wu included in *New Writings of William Hazlitt* in 2007. In general terms,

---

[99] Hazlitt, "On the Present State of Parliamentary Eloquence," 14n.
[100] Birrell, *William Hazlitt*, 99.

these attributions are sound. Wellesley's speech was the subject of a squib that Hazlitt later claimed, making it fairly certain that he reported the speech originally, and in his later writings Hazlitt also mentioned hearing Mackintosh's maiden address.[101] But Wu's approach to attribution and thus to subsequent analysis manifests some of the problems with critical readings of parliamentary reports by literary figures.

Wu is no doubt correct, for example, based on the comprehensive evidence he provides, that Hazlitt was present for Wellesley's speech. But it is impossible that he would have been responsible for reporting the entire address. Occupying four columns in the following day's paper, the final report is far too long to have been one man's work. There is also the evidence of other turns from which Hazlitt produced a very full report, such as that of Hart Davies's and Phillips's speeches on May 31; based on the length of the published version on this occasion, he would, at most, have been responsible for around half of the Wellesley report. Moreover, Henry Crabb Robinson, who has present during the address, noted that he left after an hour and a half, at which time Wellesley was still speaking.[102] Coverage of the speech would thus have fallen to at least two reporters, each working the standard one-hour shift.

This is an important point for a number of reasons. First, it casts significant doubt on Wu's attribution of the entire report to Hazlitt. Second, it complicates the conclusions that Wu draws from the *Morning Chronicle*'s text of the speech. He notes that the subsequent satirical squib on Wellesley's speech that he can definitely attribute to Hazlitt

makes no secret of the irritation he must have felt at having to turn a lengthy, rambling performance into coherent prose. He did his best, constructing sentences which carried their meaning through to a logical conclusion which, if he is to be believed, was sorely lacking from the original. All the same, evidence of the difficulties he had is scattered throughout the text.[103]

If there are sentences that manifest this translation into coherent prose all through the report, and if examples of the reporter's difficulties are really scattered throughout the text, then only some of that evidence actually relates to Hazlitt. And if the whole performance manifests this evidence, in what sense are these characteristics Hazlittian? Might it not be more

---

[101] See Wu, ed., *New Writings*, II: 431 and I: 94–95.
[102] Crabb Robinson, *Diary, Reminiscences, and Correspondence*, I: 216.
[103] Wu, ed., *New Writings*, I: 31. Wu makes the same point in his biography; see *William Hazlitt*, 150.

accurate to say that Hazlitt approaches the task of reporting Wellesley in much the same way as his fellow reporters?

Wellesley's speech on this occasion was certainly disappointing. Crabb Robinson

discerned in the speech (evidently a prepared and elaborate one) not one of the great qualities of an orator or statesman. His person is small, and his animation has in it nothing of dignity and weighty energy. He put himself into a sort of artificial passion, and was in a state of cold inflammation. He began with a parade of first principles, and made a fuss about general ideas, which were, I thought, after all very commonplace.[104]

Hazlitt's thoughts were almost identical. In his damning squib on the Marquis, he called Wellesley's speeches

lamentably deficient, particularly his opening speech on India affairs ... We confess, his last two speeches which we have heard appear to us prodigies of physical vigour and intellectual imbecility. The excess of his natural temperament, stimulating and irritating the ordinary faculties of his mind, the exuberance of his animal spirits, combining with the barrenness of his genius, produced a degree of dull vivacity, of pointed insignificance, of impotent energy, which was without example. It was curious, though somewhat painful, to see this lively Nobleman always in the full career of his argument, and never advancing one jot the nearer; seeming to utter volumes in every word, and yet saying nothing; retaining the same unabated vehemence of voice and gesture, without any thing to require it; still keeping alive the hope and expectation of genius without once satisfying it; soaring into mediocrity with adventurous enthusiasm, harrowed up with some plain matter of fact, writhing with agony under a truism, and launching a common-place with all the fury of a thunderbolt.[105]

These remarks suggest a speech that was unintentionally amusing, frustrating, and disappointing, but do they imply that it was a difficult speech to report?

Wu infers the difficulties Hazlitt faced on this occasion from three reportorial techniques. The first is that much of the speech is related in the third person. Wu assumes that this means that the original address was clumsy, noting that this was "a technique Hazlitt does not, for instance, use with the more competent performance given by Macintosh several months later."[106] But it is precisely the technique he used with Plunket's speech, the one that he most admired. Second, Wu notes that much of

[104] Crabb Robinson, *Diary, Reminiscences, and Correspondence*, I: 216.
[105] Wu, ed., *New Writings*, II: 432–33.   [106] Wu, ed., *New Writings*, I: 31.

the Wellesley speech was given in summary form. It is not absolutely clear what is meant by summary form; if it means that the account is at times paraphrased, then that was the normal practice in the gallery at the time, as several of Hazlitt's verified reports, discussed earlier in this chapter, can attest. Finally, Wu comments that "parts of the speech are composed in such a manner as to leave little doubt that it had been necessary to correct a number of solecisms for which the speaker was responsible."[107] This is no doubt true, but tidying up speeches in order to translate them into reports was a standard part of the job of a reporter.

There is, moreover, evidence to suggest that, while poorly delivered, the *Morning Chronicle*'s reporters did not find this speech especially difficult to report. The *Parliamentary Debates* text of the speech draws very heavily on the *Chronicle*'s account; of the approximately 580 lines of print encompassing Wellesley's address in the paper, nearly 300 made it into the *Debates* text, marking another occasion in which some of Hazlitt's work found its way into the official record.[108] The editors of the *Debates* clearly regarded the *Chronicle*'s text as very full, and certainly the fullest of the daily papers' accounts. If Wellesley was difficult to cover, Hazlitt and his colleagues seemed to find it more straightforward than did their peers. Moreover, it was not necessarily the worst speeches that were hardest to report; Hazlitt recalled that his favourite speech, Plunket's address on February 25, 1813, caused great problems for the journalists in the gallery.[109] Wellesley, as Hazlitt later mentioned, was a very loud speaker "who never lowers his voice for four hours from the time he begins": not perhaps a virtue in itself, but certainly useful for the reporters compared with the "low voice" of someone like Smith.[110]

Rather than manifesting some of Hazlitt's unique strengths, this report tends to reinforce the impression that he met the standards required by Perry and delivered by the *Morning Chronicle*'s team. At least two hands are involved in the production of the Wellesley report, yet there seems little difference between their styles. The sections excerpted by the editors of the *Parliamentary Debates*, for example, fall throughout the speech, and thus must have come from the pens of different reporters; so too do the sections that the *Debates* omitted. The style is also apparently consistent enough for Wu to attribute the whole piece to Hazlitt. Since sole

---

107 Wu, ed., *New Writings*, I: 31.
108 *Parliamentary Debates*, 1st ser., vol. xxv (1813): 675–99.
109 Hazlitt, "On the Present State of Parliamentary Eloquence," 14.
110 Hazlitt, "On the Present State of Parliamentary Eloquence," 21.

authorship is not a possibility, this stylistic consistency must arise from Hazlitt's thorough integration into the parliamentary corps.

Wu's analysis of the report of Macintosh's maiden speech manifests similar problems. Hazlitt's later recollections strongly suggest that he was in the gallery when Macintosh spoke in favor of a shortened adjournment period, as Wu outlines.[111] But reporting a speech is not the same as reporting a whole speech. As with the Wellesley example, the text of this report in the *Morning Chronicle* is almost certainly too long to be the work of a single hand. At more than four columns, around half of which is in a small, closely spaced type to squeeze in more content, this report would have encompassed more than one journalist's turn.

The evidence that places Hazlitt at the House on this occasion provides some insights into which part of the speech he might have covered. As Wu rightly points out, Hazlitt later recalled that Lord Castlereagh did not respond to Macintosh, and noted that the next speaker, Colonel St. Paul, characterized Macintosh's speech as "finical."[112] Such evidence does provide grounds for assuming that Hazlitt heard Macintosh speak, but it also provides compelling reasons for believing that he covered the latter part of the speech, and at least one of those which followed. It is possible that Hazlitt's turn begins at the point at which the *Morning Chronicle* shifted to a smaller type to print the speech, as this change might indicate that the previous journalist's report had already been set in type before it became clear that the speech (and indeed the debate) were going to last some time.

Again, this is an important point in terms of attribution, but it is also important in terms of the inferences that are then drawn from the journalistic style. Wu suggests that "[c]omparison of this report with those in other newspapers shows that great care was taken with it: it is comprehensive, detailed, and the style highly polished. This points to Hazlitt's involvement; it was typical of him to have rendered Mackintosh's speech with his utmost skill."[113] But the style of reporting this speech was probably established by another journalist, before Hazlitt took his seat. The decisions to report Macintosh in full, in the first person, and with due attention to the value of the speech, were not ones that Hazlitt took but rather ones with which he conformed. If great care was taken with this report, then that care belonged to others as well as Hazlitt. If it was

[111] Wu, ed., *New Writings*, 1: 94–95.   [112] Wu, ed., *New Writings*, 1: 94.
[113] Wu, ed., *New Writings*, 1: 95.

typical of Hazlitt to report with his utmost skill, then that was also typical of other *Morning Chronicle* reporters.

It is also somewhat doubtful that Hazlitt allowed his personal views of the speeches, as opposed to the views of his newspaper, to influence his decisions about how to report. Observers of the reports in the 1810s and 1820s suggested that the political views of both editors and individual reporters were a significant factor in the coverage; one source described the journalists as "living indexes of the sentiments of their respective papers."[114] Yet Hazlitt's practices as a reporter do not support this reading of his work. He was not a fan of Ponsonby, for example, whom he called "a bad orator."[115] Yet on both the occasions on which we know that Hazlitt reported Ponsonby, he produced quite full coverage, despite not having useful notes on one of these occasions. The *Morning Chronicle* had already come out in favor of a shorter adjournment than the government was proposing, urging members to consider a motion on the matter; Mackintosh's speech proposing a truncated adjournment was thus of interest to the paper and its readers.[116]

Wu does not specify which other newspaper accounts he used as the basis of his assessment that great care was taken with this report, but such a comparison is instructive. If we assume that Hazlitt reported the latter part of Macintosh's address, then its conclusion is the safest foundation from which to make a comparison. The *Morning Chronicle* reports Macintosh's final remarks as follows:

Thus, Sir, have I imperfectly submitted to the House, under the pressure of severe indisposition, such items as I have been enabled hastily to collect on this important subject. I sensibly feel the disadvantages under which I have laboured in the course of my address to you – disadvantages which I might perhaps have avoided, if I had listened to prejudice. I hope, however, that the House will do me the justice to believe, that in feeling what appears to me to be due to the civil liberty of Holland, I entertain no lukewarmness towards its national independence – that in wishing the Confederated Powers to exhibit strict justice to a neutral nation, I am nevertheless most anxious for their success on those honourable principles contained in their admirable Manifesto. Sir, I move as an amendment to the Noble Lord's motion, to substitute for the words, "Tuesday, 1st of March," the words "Monday, 24th January."[117]

[114] *The Periodical Press*, 139.
[115] Hazlitt, "On the Present State of Parliamentary Eloquence," 11. Barnes was similarly scathing; see "Criticus," "Parliamentary Criticism: Mr. Ponsonby," 572–74.
[116] *Morning Chronicle* (December 9, 1813): 3.
[117] *Morning Chronicle* (December 21, 1813): 3.

The *Morning Post*'s account is much less detailed, although Macintosh's sentiments are clear and some of the language he apparently used on the night is preserved.

He had but imperfectly expressed his ideas; but he hoped the House would do him the justice to believe, that his anxiety for the welfare of Holland made it impossible for him to contemplate with lukewarmness the subversion of the Constitution of the last republic in Europe. On this subject he had felt it his duty to express his apprehensions. He wished they might prove vain, and, at all events, hoped the conduct of this country would appear vindicated from any charge that might be preferred on this account. He had now only to move as an amendment to the motion of the Noble Lord, that the 24th of January should be substituted for the 1st of March.[118]

This section is heavily abbreviated in *The Times*, which only noted that "[a]fter some apologies for trespassing so long on the attention of the house, he concluded by moving, as an amendment, 'that the house, at its rising, do adjourn to the 24th of January'."[119] These comparisons do suggest that Hazlitt's contribution to the Mackintosh report was excellent, but this excellence was not unique to him; the *Parliamentary Debates* selected the *Morning Chronicle*'s entire text of the speech for its coverage of this debate in the Commons, making this the third instance in which Hazlitt's words became the official record, but also testifying to the overall quality of the report.[120]

Both of these reports deserve to be in a collection of Hazlitt's writing such as *New Writings*, but a better understanding of gallery practices and of Hazlitt's usual modes of reporting can help us refine the way we attribute and analyze such pieces. If we replace the image of the critical Hazlitt, making judgments about the relative worth of speeches and using these criteria to decide how to generate coverage, with the image of a successful member of the *Morning Chronicle*'s gallery corps, his achievement becomes more significant in journalistic terms.

CONCLUSION

The critical literature on Hazlitt's reporting is conspicuous in the way it overlooks both an analysis of his reports and a comparison with the work of other contemporary reporters, yet still offers a summary of his talents.

[118] *Morning Post* (December 21, 1813): 3.   [119] *The Times* (December 21, 1813): 3.
[120] *Parliamentary Debates*, 1st ser., vol. XXVII (1813): 301–23.

Birrell, in a biography that set the tone for much of the criticism that followed, proposed that Hazlitt "was no slavish stenographer – no *verbatim* man ... He listened to the speeches with the ear of a connoisseur in rhetoric, and he fixed upon the orator the eye of a portrait painter, and afterwards at his leisure reproduced such portions of their speeches as remained in his memory."[121] This comment, and the critical tradition that flows from it, hints at a comparison with contemporary norms and a working knowledge of Hazlitt's reportorial technique, which is inevitably praised. But no evidence is offered to support these claims, and the implications are actually erroneous. There were no verbatim reporters in the press gallery at this time; everyone produced reports that were versions of what they had heard. Hazlitt did not rely solely on his memory; he worked with a notebook and many of his reports reveal a strong reliance on the text of his notes. He did not approach the task as one of capturing striking rhetoric or compelling oratory, unlike Coleridge, Hazlitt was a regular member of the gallery with a very straightforward job to perform: take down the speeches and reproduce them as best you can. Connoisseurs and portrait painters need not apply.

[121] Birrell, *William Hazlitt*, 96, his italics.

CHAPTER 5

Charles Dickens and the ghost of speeches past

In an 1856 letter to Wilkie Collins, Charles Dickens looked back on his time as a parliamentary reporter in the early 1830s and noted his talent for working in the press gallery, writing that "I left the reputation behind me of being the best and most rapid Reporter ever known ... I could do anything in that way under any sort of circumstances and often did. (I dare say I am at this present writing, the best Short Hand Writer in the World)."[1] This view is backed up by the comments of his contemporaries in the gallery, such as Thomas Beard and James Grant, both of whom are cited in John Forster's *Life of Charles Dickens*, and by Charles Mackay, the subeditor of the *Morning Chronicle* from 1836, who remarked that Dickens "had the reputation of being the most rapid, the most accurate, and the most trustworthy reporter then engaged on the London press."[2]

By the 1830s, the role of the parliamentary reporter had become systematized and professionalized. Dedicated press galleries had been established for the first time in both Houses of Parliament in the early 1830s. In the twenty years since Hazlitt worked for the *Morning Chronicle*, the major London papers had, by some accounts, doubled or even trebled the size of their parliamentary corps, which now included between eight and fifteen reporters.[3] The one-hour turn that Hazlitt worked had shortened to forty-five minutes. It was possible by the 1830s to make between £300 and £400 a year working in the gallery, and the increased remuneration contributed to the growing appeal of parliamentary journalism as a career.[4]

---

[1] Dickens, *Letters*, VIII: 131.
[2] Forster, *Life of Charles Dickens*, 37, 41; and Kitton, *Charles Dickens by Pen and Pencil*, 133.
[3] For more information about the growth of the corps, see the *Morning Chronicle* (July 25, 1833): 3. Dickens depicted David Copperfield as part of a corps of twelve, which probably reflects the size of the *Morning Chronicle*'s team. See Dickens, *David Copperfield*, 535.
[4] A general account of the newspapers' normal practices can be found in Robson, *What Did He Say?*

An editorial in *The Times* pointed out that the previously disreputable press corps, made up largely of Irish immigrants who "came to England to be porters or *re*-porters, as luck might have it," had been replaced with teams of young lawyers, who used their time in the gallery to gain money and experience before pursuing their careers. The public could now have faith in "the high character, the unsullied integrity, and the talent, and extensive information of the great body of the existing reporters."[5] The press gallery was now attracting the right sort of young man – clever, ambitious and observant.

Charles Dickens was one of the new breed of parliamentary reporter. As well as possessing the requisite attributes, he had the right contacts to join the gallery journalists. His father had worked in this capacity for the *British Press* and the *Morning Herald* and his uncle, John Henry Barrow, had established the highly respected *Mirror of Parliament*, a weekly publication devoted solely to parliamentary news which ran from 1828 until 1841.[6] As part of his training for the press gallery, Dickens taught himself a popular system of shorthand from Thomas Gurney's *Brachygraphy*. As a teenager he began working in the courts of Doctors Commons before using his newfound ability as a shorthand writer to claim a place as a parliamentary reporter on his uncle's *Mirror of Parliament*, perhaps as early as 1831. He was certainly working for the *Mirror of Parliament* by 1832 while simultaneously doing some reporting for the *True Sun*, a radical London daily, between March and August.[7] The *Mirror*'s reporters were solely occupied as parliamentary journalists; when the House was not in session, the journalists did not get paid. During the session, the paper paid well; each reporter received a guinea per turn in the gallery, and was thus paid extra during the longest debates.[8] But Dickens's letters make it clear that he needed a more regular income.[9] In August 1834 he was offered a position at the *Morning Chronicle*, which had recently been

---

[5] *The Times* (July 29, 1833): 4. For an overview of impressions of journalists generally at this time, see Aspinall, "Social Status of Journalists," 216–32.

[6] More details about the *Mirror of Parliament* can be found in McBath, "Parliamentary Reporting in the Nineteenth Century," 29–30.

[7] Some of Dickens's letters suggest that he might have begun this work for the *Mirror* in early 1831. A letter to Mary Anne Leigh in March 1831 refers to "my week's exertions," which the editors of the *Letters* tentatively offer as evidence that he was working in the press gallery at this time (*Letters*, I: 2). Further evidence comes in a much later letter to Angela Burdett Coutts, in which Dickens remarks that he had told his son that "when I was a year older than he, I was in the gallery of the House of Commons" (*Letters*, VII: 245). If Dickens's maths and memory are correct here, it would mean that he had begun his parliamentary reporting career in early 1831.

[8] Grant, *The Great Metropolis*, II: 218.   [9] See for example *Letters*, I: 30.

purchased by a Whig consortium, and he served that paper as a parliamentary journalist and political correspondent until the end of the session in 1836.[10] By this time he was achieving success with his "Sketches by Boz" and had begun publishing *The Pickwick Papers*, making journalism a less necessary line of work.[11]

Dickens left behind several important testimonies that are frequently cited in accounts of his time in the gallery. His description in a speech to the Newspaper Press Fund in 1865 vividly conjures up the circumstances in which parliamentary reporters worked:

I have worn my knees by writing on them on the old back row of the old gallery of the old House of Commons; and I have worn my feet by standing to write in a preposterous pen in the old House of Lords, where we used to be huddled together like so many sheep ... kept in waiting, say, until the woolsack might want re-stuffing.[12]

Similarly, his fictionalized account of his efforts to become a parliamentary reporter in *David Copperfield* provides useful insights into the difficulty of mastering shorthand in preparation to enter the press gallery:

I bought an approved scheme of the noble art and mystery of stenography (which cost me ten and sixpence); and plunged into a sea of perplexity that brought me, in a few weeks, to the confines of distraction. The changes that were rung upon dots, which in such a position meant such a thing, and in such another position something else, entirely different; the wonderful vagaries that were played by circles; the unaccountable consequences that resulted from marks like flies' legs; the tremendous effects of a curve in the wrong place; not only troubled my waking hours, but reappeared before me in my sleep. When I had groped my way, blindly, through these difficulties, and had mastered the alphabet, which was an Egyptian Temple in itself, there then appeared a procession of new horrors, called arbitrary characters; the most despotic characters I have ever known; who insisted, for instance, that a thing like the beginning of a cobweb, meant expectation, and that a pen and ink sky-rocket stood for disadvantageous. When I had fixed these wretches in my mind, I found that they had driven everything else out of it; then, beginning again, I forgot them; while I was picking them up, I dropped the other fragments of the system; in short, it was almost heartbreaking.[13]

---

[10] Dickens had attempted unsuccessfully to secure a position with the *Chronicle* in 1833. For an excellent overview of the relationship between the *Morning Chronicle* and the Whigs, see Wasson, "The Whigs and the Press," 76–77.

[11] There had also been some conflict with the *Morning Chronicle*'s editors; see Denton, "Dickens the Beginner," 64.

[12] K. J. Fielding, ed., *The Speeches of Charles Dickens*, 347.

[13] Dickens, *David Copperfield*, 465.

Colourful sources such as these provide useful insights into Dickens's attitude to reporting and its challenges but they do not provide much guidance to scholars wishing to get to grips with the mechanics of his reportorial style and technique. On these points, accounts of Dickens's life often mention how little we know about his work as a parliamentary reporter.[14] Only one report has ever been conclusively attributed to him, and it has been assumed that his further contributions cannot be identified. This assumption perhaps arises from the anonymity of the reports, which make it impossible to establish a definite corpus for an individual journalist, and the notion that it was essential to learn and employ shorthand in order to work in the gallery, a necessity which in turn makes it all but impossible to isolate Dickens's contributions to the coverage among that of all the other parliamentary reporters who are also presumed to possess shorthand. In particular, little consideration has been given to the different expectations of Dickens's two primary employers, the *Mirror of Parliament* and the *Morning Chronicle*, and the ways in which these expectations might have influenced Dickens's accuracy.

The 1830s saw an increasing interest in the way that speeches of all sorts were reported. As Ivan Kreilkamp has perceptively noted, the Victorian era was characterized by concerns about the hegemony of print and the decline of authentic voices. In this context, Kreilkamp suggests that the invention of the phonographic method of shorthand by Isaac Pitman in 1837 revolutionized the way the early Victorians thought about the relationship between speech and the written text. From 1837 onwards, "the phonographic goal of transcribing voice and sound became seen as one of the most natural tasks of shorthand more generally, even its fundamental task ... Shorthand offered the promise of a reformed writing that would bear the trace of the living voice of speech."[15] Parliamentary reporting was naturally a central part of this highly scrutinized matrix of the oral and the written. The new potential for texts that captured the authentic spoken word led to an emerging disdain of the eighteenth-century notions of authenticity that guided Johnson, and, to a lesser extent, Coleridge and Hazlitt. Johnson's endeavours came in for specific criticism; Kreilkamp points to "the Victorian presumption that Johnson *should* have been attempting an *exact* transcription of speech."[16] The new

---

[14] See for example House, *The Dickens World*, 37.
[15] Kreilkamp, *Voice and the Victorian Storyteller*, 70.
[16] Kreilkamp, *Voice and the Victorian Storyteller*, 71–72.

Victorian standards were thus seen as a vast improvement in the field of parliamentary journalism, "as the representation of politics attains a new standard of mimetic accuracy, permitting the free workings of an unbiased fourth estate."[17]

Kreilkamp's compelling analysis raises an interesting question about Dickens's parliamentary reporting: if 1837 is the year in which this change in attitude became entrenched, how should we read the reports of someone whose career in the gallery ended in 1836? Was Dickens's experience of the gallery part of the new Victorian consciousness about orality, a remnant of the eighteenth century's ideas about accurate reporting, or somewhere in between? This chapter proposes not only that there is more evidence available about Dickens's reports than has been previously acknowledged, but that it is important to have a historically contextualized understanding of the value of accuracy in the gallery in this period, before Pitman's ideas had influenced the tenor of cultural expectations about accuracy. To gain that understanding, it is necessary to consider the reportorial styles of different periodicals.

THE *MIRROR OF PARLIAMENT* AND THE MORNING PAPERS

While many aspects of a reporter's job were the same regardless of his employer, there were significant differences between the *Mirror of Parliament* and the daily papers in terms of the potential audience courted and thus the reportorial techniques adopted. In the 1828 prospectus to the first volume of the *Mirror*, Dickens's uncle John Henry Barrow outlined the aims of his new weekly periodical:

EVERY MEMBER'S SPEECH upon *every question* shall be fully given, from short hand notes, in the *same* proportion of extent; without regard to the PUBLIC *or* PRIVATE *nature of the business discussed*; or to the party, the principles, or the greater or less reputation of the speaker.[18]

The *Mirror* thus aimed to fill a gap in the market by providing regular, comprehensive and corrected coverage from Parliament. It differentiated itself from *Hansard* by employing its own corps of reporters rather than attempting to compile coverage from the newspapers. Shorthand was clearly a necessity for anyone wishing to work for the *Mirror*, and Dickens would have been one of the journalists Barrow had in mind in 1832 when

[17] Kreilkamp, *Voice and the Victorian Storyteller*, 72.
[18] *Mirror of Parliament*, vol. 1 (1828): 2. Italics and capitals are in the original.

he referred to "the talents and perseverance of the several Reporters whose valuable services were retained" on the paper.[19]

The *Mirror* maintained an excellent reputation for its accounts among parliamentarians, and many of its subscribers were members of the legislature. Gladstone later commented that for the period that it covered, the *Mirror* was "the primary record, and not *Hansard's Debates.*"[20] Some MPs reprinted the *Mirror's* accounts in pamphlet form as the best versions of their speeches.[21] Although the *Mirror* struggled to attract general readers as regular subscribers, many people outside Parliament also respected the paper's accounts. The editor of *The Companion to the Newspaper* informed his readers that, on a particular debate, "[w]e quote from the *Mirror of Parliament*, and shall do so whenever we have occasion … to give the exact words employed by any member of either House."[22]

But the *Mirror* was far from flawless. As the comments above suggest, it was usually regarded simply as the best of the available accounts, not as an entirely reliable record. After reading the *Mirror's* version of one of his speeches, Thomas Macaulay wrote, "[i]t is middling – the report I mean: for the speech was capital. It is however the best report that there is of what I said."[23] The *Mirror* also courted controversy about the accuracy of its coverage through its policy of allowing MPs to correct their speeches. Barrow had highlighted this practice as one of the great virtues of his endeavour, noting that "[t]his mode of proceeding will be calculated to guarantee the authenticity of [the] reports beyond the possibility of impeachment."[24] However, as *The Times* pointed out, if the *Mirror's* version of a speech contained

passages which the noble lord or honourable member repents him of, or which may be disagreeable to his constituents, he strikes them out, of course; and if (which, after having heard the speeches of others, is not improbable) any good things occur to him, as things which he might have said with advantage, it is not to be expected that he will resist this temptation of inserting them, though he never thought of uttering them at the time.[25]

[19] *Mirror of Parliament*, vol. v (1832): iii.
[20] *Parliamentary Debates*, 3rd ser., vol. ccxxxiii (1877): 1576–77. Other comments that suggest that MPs valued the *Mirror's* coverage can be found in Aspinall, ed., *Three Early Nineteenth Century Diaries*, 150.
[21] See for example Buckingham, *Evidence on Drunkenness*, iv.
[22] "Political Retrospect of the Year 1833: Britain," 195.
[23] Macaulay, *Letters*, ii: 244.   [24] *Mirror of Parliament*, vol. i (1828): 2.
[25] *The Times* (July 6, 1832): 3. The *Morning Chronicle* expressed the same view on the same day (July 6, 1832): 3.

Attentive members of the public also queried the effects of correction; a correspondent in the *Quarterly Review* referred readers to one of Lord Brougham's speeches as reported in the *Standard*, "for in the report *corrected* for the *Mirror of Parliament* the point is lost."[26]

The potential weaknesses in the *Mirror*'s accounts were brought to readers' attention during the controversy that ensued when the Bishop of Exeter complained about the newspapers' coverage in 1832. The Bishop's assertion that the *Mirror of Parliament* was an authentic record of Parliament prompted an angry reaction in the morning papers. The *Chronicle* maintained that "[t]he Morning Papers are by much the most accurate record of the actual speeches on important questions," and published "The Bishop and the Reporter," a satirical poem about the events.[27] In the poem, Exeter plans to deny saying some of the words attributed to him in the newspaper reports.

> But when the newspapers the Bishop did see,
> "This is worse and worse," he mutter'd –
> "For *Chronicle*, *Times*, and *Herald* agree
> With *Ledger* and *Post*, in ascribing to me,
> – Yes every word that I utter'd.

> "Never mind. I've a chance, their Reporters, I'll swear,
> Are Mistaken in what I meant,
> And to prove the correctness of what I declare,
> I'll quote, and I warrant 'twill make the Whigs stare –
> *The Mirror of Parliament*."
> (lines 51–60)

As the Bishop goes on to point out in the poem, the *Mirror*'s clearly doctored account contained "[b]ut a very few sentences, there is my speech, / Whilst *The Times* makes it nearly a column to reach" (lines 68–69).

The *Mirror*'s approach was controversial, but the daily papers, like the *Morning Chronicle*, also faced considerable challenges when it came to accuracy. The system of turns, the inaudibility of certain speakers and the parliamentary prerogative of clearing the gallery all contributed to these problems. So too did the political biases of the papers. Thomas Barnes, the editor of *The Times*, was in constant contact with the Whigs about the paper's coverage before breaking with them in 1834, at which point

---

[26] "Article ix: Progress of Misgovernment," 576n, italics in the original.
[27] *Morning Chronicle* (July 6, 1832): 3 and (July 9, 1832): 3, respectively.

the Whigs took control of the *Morning Chronicle*. It was alleged that reporters demonstrated bias through the insertion of descriptions of the House's reactions; the *True Sun* denied "putting in unauthorized 'Hear, hears!' / And filling lines with 'Opposition cheers'," but such distortions were all too easy to achieve.[28] The working conditions of reporters also took their toll. They recorded their notes in a cramped, hot, noisy environment, and the difficulty of hearing the speeches was a constant limitation. In his sketch "The House," Dickens described the noise in the House as comprising

a hum of voices and confusion which would rival Babel but for the circumstance of its being all in one language ... [T]he body of the House and the side galleries are full of Members ... some going out, others coming in; all of them talking, laughing, lounging, coughing, o-ing, questioning, or groaning; presenting a conglomeration of noise and confusion to be met with in no other place in existence.[29]

But the most significant challenge to accurate reporting actually originated within the newspaper business itself. The daily papers did not have the space, nor the inclination, to cover the debates in full. This approach led to two significant controversies about the possibility of deliberately distorted reports in the 1830s. The first occurred when the MP George Dawson attacked *The Times*'s reports in the House and then in a letter to the paper in 1831.[30] *The Times*, in response, defended the notion of accuracy:

Let us be convinced that any reporter has wilfully misrepresented, or in any way unfairly dealt with, the speech of any member of any party, and that reporter from that moment shall cease to belong to our establishment. We fully admit that a baser fraud cannot be committed than deliberately giving a false account of any proceeding, public or private.[31]

But other letters on the Dawson controversy made it clear that, by accuracy, the newspapers only meant fair treatment, not full coverage. *The Times*'s reporter "J. T.," who had covered one of the speeches that Dawson felt had been mutilated, pointed out in a letter to the paper that "after 12 o'clock at night speeches, unless they are distinguished, either by their own extraordinary merit or by the paramount importance of the subject on which they are made, must of necessity be very considerably

---

[28] [A Rhyming Reporter], "Remonstrance to the Lower House," lines 18–19.
[29] "Boz," "The House," 3.   [30] *The Times* (March 28, 1831): 3.
[31] *The Times* (March 28, 1831): 3.

abridged."[32] The newspapers clearly did not aim for anything approaching verbatim coverage.

A second and more prominent controversy around the same issue occurred in 1833, when Daniel O'Connell attacked the papers for printing reports that were "designedly false." The papers' responses made it clear that they reserved to themselves the discretionary power of editing speeches and presenting debates as they saw fit. One of *The Times*'s reporters insisted that neither the House as a whole nor individual members had the right "to dictate to the press what speech it shall give, or what it shall omit, or to what length any speech shall be given."[33] The *Morning Chronicle* was equally strident, asserting that although

newspapers are not responsible, and cannot be responsible to Parliament for the mode in which they report the debates, the fact is, that a regard to their own interest forms a sufficient inducement to them to give day after day to the public a very ample account of what passes. If Members wish a more ample account, they are not precluded by the newspapers from supplying it themselves in a vehicle of their own; but the newspapers must themselves be the exclusive judges of what they shall and shall not publish.[34]

The Dawson and O'Connell controversies highlighted not only the ways in which accuracy was compromised in the parliamentary reporting of the day, but also the extent to which such compromise was considered both necessary and legitimate.

Various factors determined the extent to which speeches were abbreviated or otherwise modified in the newspapers. One of the most significant was the amount of space available. As a journalist in *Fraser's Magazine* had pointed out in 1830,

every gentleman that speaks wishes to be reported at length; and, if he be not so reported, he considers himself an injured man; he never considers that all which is spoken by that assembly in one night, (sitting, as it often did, from four in the evening to four in the morning,) could not be committed to writing, by twelve men, in a month, or printed in a week – or inserted in a paper ten times the ordinary size – or read within any period of time which a person of sound mind could, by the remotest possibility, be induced to devote to such a purpose.[35]

But there were also significant concerns about the public's interest in such full coverage. Grant, whose account always needs to be read with caution

---

[32] *The Times* (March 30, 1831): 5. "J. T." is almost certainly John Tyas, a well-known reporter.
[33] *The Times* (July 29, 1833): 4.   [34] *Morning Chronicle* (July 25, 1833): 3.
[35] "Ned Culpepper," "Place-men, Parliament-men, Penny-a-Liners, and Parliamentary Reporters," 290.

in light of some disagreement about the accuracy of his observations, argued that it was not simply space that needed to be considered but also the quality of the speechmaking:

Were the reporters not to exercise a sound discretion as to what speeches they ought to report and what not, and as to the relative length at which the speeches they do report ought to be given, – the mass of verbiage and nonsense which would daily appear in the morning papers, would, in the first place, make their readers turn away with disgust from the parliamentary reports.[36]

Some MPs appreciated the effects of the abridgements; during the debate on O'Connell's request that the newspapers produce verbatim reports, Robert Peel suggested that "in his opinion a verbal report of their speeches would not tend to raise the character of any Member of the House."[37] The *Morning Chronicle* was blunter, reacting to the suggestion of verbatim reporting by asking, "who will wade through fifty or sixty columns of heavy rubbish every day?"[38]

    Journalists argued that their editorial processes preserved the most noteworthy addresses and topics. Grant believed that reporters "know well who are the most influential speakers, and what is the measure of importance which the public attach to the question discussed."[39] Looking back on his work in the gallery during his 1865 speech to the Newspaper Press Fund, Dickens acknowledged that debates were shaped by reporters but stated that an MP was "reported according to the position he can gain in the public eye, and according to the force and weight of what he has to say."[40] In 1833 *The Times* was similarly insistent that "[t]he less important debate must give way to the more important, – the less able speakers to the more distinguished, so that something like an intelligible view of the whole may be presented to the public."[41] It was on precisely these grounds that Barrow justified the importance of the *Mirror of Parliament* as an improvement on the other papers' coverage:

In the daily Newspapers of London, a system of parliamentary reporting has been organized, – wonderful, indeed, considered in relation to their *plan*, to the means employed, and the disadvantages contended with; but decidedly ineffective as to the MAIN OBJECTS of COMPLETENESS AND CORRECTNESS. The same astonishing rapidity of publication which makes

---

[36] Grant, *The Great Metropolis*, II: 216. Kathryn Chittick points out that contemporary reviewers criticized the accuracy of Grant's accounts; see *Dickens and the 1930s*, 44.
[37] *Parliamentary Debates*, 3rd ser., vol. XIX (1833): 1250.
[38] *Morning Chronicle* (July 30, 1833): 3.   [39] Grant, *The Great Metropolis*, II: 215.
[40] Fielding, ed., *Speeches*, 346.   [41] *The Times* (July 26, 1833): 5.

them so invaluable to society, as perpetual channels of general intelligence, – is one cause of their obvious imperfection in this class of reports; and their limited space or capacity, to say nothing of the operation of party views, – another … the "want of room" inevitably compels the omission of numerous passages in an evening's debates, – the *full* report of which would more than occupy the *whole* of any newspaper's columns; whereas, on the most interesting occasions, it can appropriate not more than a *portion* of them (more or less considerable) to such a purpose.[42]

While the papers denied that their reporters were "giving speeches, that had much amused, / A serious tone; and rendering others martial, / That were intended to be very tame," other observers believed that the process of parliamentary coverage, with its emphasis on selectivity, space and timing, distorted the debates and the effect of individual speeches.[43] Charles Cavendish Fulke Greville complained that he had heard about a debate in the Lords that was "a magnificent display, and incomparably superior to that in the House of Commons, but the reports convey no idea of it."[44] On the other hand, Denis Le Marchant noted that one of William Cobbett's February 1833 speeches "was better in print than in delivery. For the reporters abridged it and thus cured its proxility."[45] Sometimes the newspapers even acknowledged that they had missed an opportunity to present an effective speech owing to their editorial processes, but such acknowledgments were usually unrepentant and explicit about the details of those processes; the *Morning Chronicle*, for example, remarked on one occasion that "[t]he lateness of the hour at which Lord JOHN RUSSELL spoke on Monday night" had prevented coverage of a speech that "produced, by all accounts, a strong impression on the House."[46]

Some creativity on the part of journalists was thus not just tolerated but encouraged. Grant noted, a little idealistically, that the parliamentary corps received

no instructions from the proprietors or editors of the different journals with which they are connected, as to what is to be reported, and what not; and when their reports are completed they are handed to the compositors, without the alteration of a single word, or anything in the shape of enlargement or abridgement being suggested by the editors.[47]

---

[42] *Mirror of Parliament*, vol. 1 (1828): 1, Barrow's italics and capitalization.
[43] [A Rhyming Reporter], "Remonstrance to the Lower House," lines 15–17.
[44] Greville, *The Greville Memoirs*, ii: 207.
[45] Aspinall, ed., *Three Early Nineteenth Century Diaries*, 299. For remarks in a similar vein, see Kriegel, ed., *The Holland House Diaries 1831–1840*, 63.
[46] *Morning Chronicle* (June 25, 1834): 3.
[47] Grant, *The Great Metropolis*, ii: 214–15.

This freedom was also acknowledged by those who criticized the news-papers' reports. Part of Barrow's justification for starting the *Mirror of Parliament* was that

the surprising *rapidity* with which all the operations of a daily newspaper are conducted, – from the moment of the reporters' beginning to transcribe their notes, until the publication at the earliest possible hour of the ensuing morn-ing, – precludes the exercise of any sound discretion in the selection to be made, out of the night's debates, of that *part* which it may be proposed to give.[48]

References to parliamentary oratory and reporting from the periodicals of the time suggest that readers were expected to be familiar with these con-ventions of speechmaking both in the House and on the page. In 1832, for example, the *Monthly Magazine* published a series of "Parliamentary Pastorals" that poked fun at particular MPs. One poem written in John Wilson Croker's voice had him lament:

> 'Tis in vain I am witty and wise,
> In my best and most eloquent mood;
> The reporters compress my replies,
> And omit all I thought was so good.
> (33–36)[49]

The *True Sun*, meanwhile, contributed to these satires on particular politicians in 1832 by putting the reporters' point of view. In the poem "Remonstrance to the Lower House," "A Rhyming Reporter" defended "his innocent and injured craft" (line 10):

> Imagine what we suffer. Goulburn speaks.
> How can we note down what he storms or stutters?
> Who could report what Sibthorpe thinks he utters?
> One Member whispers and another squeaks;
> Can any pen take notes of their abortions?
> Could Wetherell's self report his own contortions?
> Or Croker, who, when droll, is droll by dint
> Of dullness, put his restive jokes in print?
> (lines 44–51)[50]

These comments suggest the level of control newspaper reporters had within the confines of what actually occurred in the debate as a whole,

---

[48] *Mirror of Parliament*, vol. I (1828): I, Barrow's italics.
[49] "Parliamentary Pastorals," *Monthly Magazine*, vol. XIII (February 1832): 208. Another of the "Parliamentary Pastorals" made similar jokes at Sibthorp's expense; see the *Monthly Magazine*, vol. XIII (March 1832): 310.
[50] [A Rhyming Reporter], "Remonstrance to the Lower House," *True Sun* (June 22, 1832): 3.

but other observers noted that the reports included some fictionalized material, and regarded the ability to generate these creative passages as a key attribute in a reporter. Speaking specifically of the ideal *Morning Chronicle* or *Times* reporter, one correspondent remarked that, beyond note-taking skills and knowledge of both oratory and politics, "[h]e must besides possess a sound judgment and extreme facility of composition, to enable him on the moment to fill up the *lacunæ* which must necessarily exist in the most perfect note-book."[51] To some extent, it was understood by editors, journalists and readers alike that reporters were engaging in a mixture of factual transcription and fictional interpretation.

In light of the different editorial expectations imposed by his two employers, and the complicated attitude towards accuracy that each publication had adopted, Dickens's skill as a shorthand writer is perhaps more complex in its significance than has been noted. Although he would have needed shorthand to work for the *Mirror*, it was not the normal notation method for the newspapers' parliamentary reporters in the 1830s. It is not clear exactly when newspaper journalists began using shorthand in the gallery and it is a puzzling fact of the gallery's history that, despite the long history of printed shorthand manuals and systems, gallery journalists in the first half of the nineteenth century largely eschewed this approach to reporting; Hazlitt, for example, knew shorthand but did not use it, though it seems to have become more common by the early 1820s, perhaps because Parliament had appointed its own shorthand reporter in 1813.[52] Progress in this regard remained slow; writing at the end of Dickens's tenure at the *Chronicle*, Grant noted that only around a third of contemporary reporters were using shorthand and that among those who did not were some of the most highly regarded members of the gallery.[53]

Moreover, while the ability to write shorthand might have given Dickens an advantage in terms of accuracy, it was not the sole measure of a talented reporter. It was also important to be able to shape, select and interpret in order to produce effective copy. Contemporary accounts make it clear that

[51] "Culpepper," "Place-men, Parliament-men, Penny-a-Liners, and Parliamentary Reporters," 293.
[52] See Hazlitt, *Letters*, 70. For information about the 1820s, see [Coulson], "Review of *The Periodical Press of Great Britain*, 204.
[53] Grant, *The Great Metropolis*, ii: 229. As late as 1878, when a parliamentary select committee met to consider the future of parliamentary reporting, shorthand was still not universal in the gallery, and its use in other formal settings, such as inquests, was still being debated into the 1880s.

mechanical transcription of the speaker's words was not necessarily what newspaper editors valued. As one writer pointed out in 1833:

No reporter now thinks of depending merely upon his memory; all take notes, more or less extended. Few of them, however, write short-hand; the use of which is by many considered rather disadvantageous than otherwise, the object, in general, being to give, not so much the very words of the speaker, as the substance and spirit of his address.[54]

While the term "verbatim" was occasionally used in reference to the *Mirror of Parliament*, it was clear that this was not the standard expected from the newspapers; as Charles Ross of *The Times* later commented, "Verbatim reporting has never been known in the newspapers." It would be fairer, he claimed, to call the papers' style full and accurate.[55]

These ideas have important implications for our understanding of Dickens's career as a parliamentary reporter. His reputation needs to be seen within the context of contemporary expectations and debates about accuracy, but also within the context of the two publications that he served, one of which purported to be accurate but was the product of many outside influences, and one of which valued the ability to use discretion around presenting accurate material. Working for the *Mirror of Parliament* would have provided him with excellent training in shorthand reporting as well as an exposure to some of the complexities of producing accurate parliamentary journalism. These experiences in turn translated into a new opportunity in 1834, when the ability as a shorthand writer that he honed while working for the *Mirror* made him valuable not because it was an essential qualification but because it was something of a rarity. While he no doubt possessed the skill to be extremely accurate, at the *Chronicle* he would need to temper accuracy with selectivity.

The image of Dickens as a supremely accurate reporter has persevered, in part, because it is so difficult to attribute specific reports or speeches to him, and it has thus proved virtually impossible to do a stylistic analysis of them. Unlike the cases of Johnson, Coleridge and Hazlitt, where the attribution of at least some reports is relatively straightforward, the Dickens example poses considerable obstacles for researchers. No separate collection of his reports, in the manner of the *Debates in the Senate of Lilliput*, was ever made; no notebooks, along the lines of Coleridge's or Hazlitt's, have survived. Parliamentary reports were still unsigned and

---

[54] "Parliamentary Reporting," 20.
[55] *Report from the Select Committee on Parliamentary Reporting*, 44.

were in any case produced by a corps; as John M. L. Drew notes, this means that Dickens's parliamentary reporting seems to blend into the general coverage published by his employers, apparently leaving no trace of an individual hand, Dickensian or otherwise.[56] However, contemporary observers noticed that there were sometimes stylistic differences in the way reporters worked. One such observer believed that the impossibility of securing a corps of a dozen equally talented reporters meant

that the debates are necessarily reported unequally, and that such variations in style and spirit are observable in a single speech. Take up the *Chronicle*, and for a column of a speech of Brougham's, you are intuitively convinced that the very words he used have been set down with scrupulous fidelity; read the next – you find it might have been spoken by anybody. The dry branches of the tree are there; but the foliage which gave it grace and beauty, has disappeared.[57]

This variation is particularly important in the context of Dickens's shorthand abilities. Since it is clear that shorthand was not the norm, instances of something approaching verbatim reportage might help to point to Dickens's involvement in the relevant coverage; it was, we might say, his stylistic signature to have no idiosyncratic style, but instead to represent the words of the individual speakers with unusual fidelity. While his contributions remain very difficult to ascertain, it is in fact possible to speculate about some possible attributions by combining the information documented in hints from his letters, the recollections of peers and his own memories as told to friends with a more complete knowledge of the workings of the press gallery. With these details in mind, we can begin to trace Dickens's otherwise invisible reports.

DICKENS'S CORPUS AND THE CORPS

The *Mirror of Parliament* is both the most difficult and the easiest of the three publications in which to make an attribution to Dickens. The use of shorthand by all of its reporters produced the kind of full reports that cannot be broken down into the work of separate hands. Fortunately, the only report which Dickens claimed as his own dates from his time with the *Mirror*: Edward Stanley's February 27, 1833 address on Ireland, which famously attacked Daniel O'Connell. The anecdote about how Dickens came to report this speech for the *Mirror of Parliament* is often included

---

[56] Drew, *Dickens the Journalist*, 23.
[57] "Culpepper," "Place-men, Parliament-men, Penny-a-Liners, and Parliamentary Reporters," 293.

in biographies and studies of his journalism. The most reliable version of the story is probably that which Dickens himself related in a letter to Stanley in 1836:

> When I was connected with "The Mirror of Parliament" in the capacity of a Reporter, I had the honor to wait on Your Lordship, for the purpose of taking a faithful Report of a portion of Your Lordship's Speech, on moving the Second Reading of the Irish Disturbances Bill, from your own mouth: Your Lordship having been pleased to express so high an opinion of the Report of that part of your Speech which had originally fallen into my hands, as to select me for the task.[58]

Dickens's time at the *True Sun* is unfortunately even more mysterious. The best account of this period in his writing life can be found in Drew's excellent *Dickens the Journalist*, which provides compelling evidence of his verse contributions to the paper.[59] While there is little information to assist with attribution of parliamentary reports, Dickens's time at the *True Sun* did produce one important recollection about his approach to reporting; he apparently impressed the paper's owners with

> the succinctness of his reports, and the judicious, though somewhat ruthless, style with which he cut down unnecessary verbiage, displaying the substance to the best advantage, and exemplifying the well-known maxim of Perry, the famous chief of the *Morning Chronicle*, that "Speeches cannot be made long enough for the speakers, *nor short enough for the readers*."[60]

Dickens's accuracy apparently did not impede his ability to shape his coverage for the *True Sun*.

In the case of the *Morning Chronicle*, there is evidence about the dates on which Dickens worked which can be combined with the knowledge about the rarity of shorthand reporting in the daily papers to assist with attribution. There is also crucial information about the time at which he took his turn. Romance is the key to establishing a rough sense of some of his parliamentary reports for the *Chronicle*. In early 1836, in the lead-up to his marriage to Catherine Hogarth, Dickens wrote frequently to his

---

[58] Dickens, *Letters*, 1: 126–27. It was in fact on the occasion of the first reading of the bill that Stanley gave this speech, but there is no reason to dispute the other details Dickens mentions here. Forster questions whether Stanley actually requested Dickens's help or whether this was the normal procedure for taking speeches for the *Mirror of Parliament* (*Life of Charles Dickens*, 43). However, it is clear from the correspondence that Dickens certainly received a request based on the merits of his section of the original proof.

[59] Drew, *Dickens the Journalist*, 17–20.

[60] Hotten, *Charles Dickens*, 25–26, Hotten's italics.

fiancée to let her know whether he would be able to see her in the evening. A typical letter informs her that "as I have to be back at the house by half past eleven, it is impossible to escape between whiles."[61] We have the impending wedding to thank for these precious clues to an otherwise indefinable body of work; after the nuptials in April 1836 Dickens did not draft such useful love letters. From the information in his letters to Catherine, we can place Dickens at Parliament on five exact dates.[62] In the case of two of these five examples there is also crucial information about the time at which Dickens took his turn.[63]

This chapter will focus in particular on three pieces of coverage that can, in some cases only tentatively, be attributed to Dickens: the Stanley speech from the *Mirror of Parliament*, which he claimed as his own, and sections from the *Morning Chronicle*'s report for February 23 and March 11, 1836, in which the timing of Dickens's involvement is reasonably clear. The examples will be used as the basis for developing an understanding of his practices as a reporter, particularly the ways in which he adapted his highly accurate shorthand style to the editorial demands of a particular publication.

THE STANLEY SPEECH

While some version of the anecdote about Dickens's involvement with Stanley's speech on Ireland is routinely quoted by scholars to demonstrate his ability as a reporter, the full significance of the story has been somewhat underestimated.[64] The original *Mirror of Parliament* transcript of this speech, taken down in the House by the periodical's reportorial team, had included work by various hands taking their turns. But the speech ultimately published in the *Mirror*, which had gone through the normal process of correction by the speaker (a process modified to some degree by Stanley's request to restage the oration), was entirely Dickens's work. It is thus potentially a rare and invaluable insight into his reportorial practices because of the certainty of the attribution; the whole text can

---

[61] Dickens, *Letters*, 1: 142.
[62] Those dates are February 9, 10 and 21 and March 10 and 21, 1836. See Dickens, *Letters*, 1: 128–41. There are other speculative dates in this sequence of letters too.
[63] Other letters contain similar information about timing on the day but are too vague in terms of the date; see for example the letter that is tentatively dated March 8, 1836 in *Letters*, 1: 138.
[64] See for example Drew, *Dickens the Journalist*, 13–14.

be treated as Dickens's and compared with competing accounts. Despite this fact, the report has not been the subject of any sustained analysis.

Though the report deserves more attention as an authentic work from Dickens's pen, it does pose problems for scholars wishing to understand how he operated in the gallery. It was not taken down in normal parliamentary conditions and thus does not reflect the selective processes that parliamentary journalists were typically employing. Stanley had time, away from the bustle of the House, to present the speech as he wished, and presumably checked the whole to ensure that it read exactly as he wanted, meaning that it is nothing more than a mechanical transcription of his words and is also not an exact record of what he had originally said in Parliament. The real insights to be gained from this speech require us to step back to the draft that was submitted to Stanley for correction. While Dickens's letter to Stanley does not clarify which section of the report he originally produced, other sources point to either the opening and closing sections (as the product of two different turns), or just the final third of the speech, as Julian Charles Young proposes in his account, which was based on a conversation with Dickens:

> When Stanley fulminated his Philippic against O'Connell, it fell to young Dickens's turn to report the last third of it. The proof of the whole speech was forwarded to Mr. Stanley. He returned it to Barrow, with the remark, that the first two-thirds were so badly reported as to be unintelligible; but that, if the gentleman who had so admirably reported the last third of his speech could be sent to him, he would speak the rest of it to him alone.[65]

Since the final section of the speech is the one consistently mentioned in these stories, it seems that it is the most likely place to find Dickens's contribution. This final section concluded with Stanley's famous attack on O'Connell, which led to extraordinary scenes of animation in the debating chamber.[66] Presumably, as Young intimates in his account, Dickens did not take down this section a second time when he met with Stanley, but rather "the parts of the speech which had been bungled," which were then appended to "the rest of it."[67] In the published report, then, the

---

[65] Edgar Johnson, *Charles Dickens*, I: 65–66; Young, *A Memoir of Charles Mayne Young*, II: 112.

[66] For accounts of the effect of this speech see Broughton, *Recollections of a Long Life*, IV: 292; Russell, *Recollections and Suggestions*, 137–38; and Aspinall, ed., *Three Early Nineteenth Century Diaries*, 309 and 313.

[67] Young, *A Memoir of Charles Mayne Young*, II: 112–13.

final section probably preserves Dickens's initial efforts in the House. Of course, it is impossible to be sure at exactly which point in the speech Dickens began his turn in the gallery, but we can be sure that the closer we get to the end of the report, the more certain it is that we are dealing with his work, since both Young and Edgar Johnson identify this section as his. Stanley's concluding remarks are therefore the safest place to look for traces of Dickens's technique.

An examination of these remarks, as reported by different sources, shows the elements of the speech that Dickens apparently captured more effectively than his comrades. Quoting an inflammatory letter written by O'Connell, Stanley is made to say:

Does the Honourable Gentleman mean to say that he alone is Ireland – that two opinions may not exist – that a man may not excuse his judgment by voting on one side of an Irish question as on another? Or does he think that he is already installed as dictator of Ireland? (*Mirror of Parliament*)[68]

What, did the Honourable and Learned Gentleman mean to say that he and he alone is for Ireland? Did the Honourable and Learned Member mean to say that two opinions did not exist there, or that a man might not honestly and conscientiously exercise his judgment in supporting one side or the other – or did he mean to say that he had already arrived at that eminence at which he appeared to aim, and that he was already Dictator of Ireland? (*Morning Chronicle*)[69]

Did the hon. and learned gentleman mean to say that he and his adherents alone fought for Ireland? Why, he (Mr. Stanley) fought for Ireland. Did he mean to assert that one side of the house alone had the welfare of Ireland at heart; or did he mean to go further, and say that he (Mr. O'Connell) was already installed supreme dictator of Ireland? (*The Times*)[70]

An important difference stands out in these otherwise similar accounts. Only Dickens in the *Mirror* conveys the possibility that O'Connell thinks he is *synonymous* with Ireland, an idea that is translated into being "for Ireland" in the *Morning Chronicle* and having "fought for Ireland" in *The Times*. Dickens's interpretation was shared by the *Hansard* compilers, who recorded the comment as suggesting that O'Connell believed "that he, and he only, was to be considered as Ireland."[71]

---

[68] *Mirror of Parliament*, vol. VI (1833): 452. All of the subsequent references to the *Mirror*'s text of Stanley's speech can be found on this page.

[69] *Morning Chronicle* (February 28, 1833): 4. All of the subsequent references to the *Chronicle*'s text of Stanley's speech can be found on this page.

[70] *The Times* (February 28, 1833): 4. All of the subsequent references to *The Times*'s text of Stanley's speech can be found on this page.

[71] *Parliamentary Debates*, 3rd ser., vol. XV (1833): 1289.

There are similar subtle but crucial differences elsewhere in the versions of Stanley's summation. Only in Dickens's text does Stanley suggest that the Volunteer Society would bring everything under its "uncontrolled and uncontrollable dominion." The second adjective, which ought to have been easy to pick up, was omitted in both *The Times* and the *Morning Chronicle*. Only in Dickens's account is O'Connell accused of defending "a most unconstitutional and tyrannical interference" with the House's privileges; *The Times* picked up just the first adjective, the *Morning Chronicle* just the second one. These additional words might not have been heard by the other reporters; more likely they were treated as unnecessary flourishes that could be omitted without affecting the meaning and would only slow down a notetaker using longhand. Dickens's shorthand prowess might have allowed him to catch such small but significant details.

While these examples indicate differences between the versions, other phrases included in Dickens's *Mirror* report can be independently verified by using the two major dailies' accounts, particularly the *Morning Chronicle*'s, which is fuller and clearly more accurate than that of *The Times*. Stanley certainly referred to individuals who wore a "mask of liberty" and denounced O'Connell as a "frothy declaimer" who was the first person to "put forward so flimsy a veil" over corrupt practices, remarks which appear in both the *Mirror* and the *Chronicle*. He also definitely alluded to a "system of violence and prædial outrage" in Ireland, a phrase which was captured exactly by Dickens and his colleague at the *Chronicle*, although slightly mangled by the reporter from *The Times*.

But how do we account for the phrases that Dickens apparently misses? Why did he not record Stanley calling O'Connell a "noisy spouter about popular rights," as the *Chronicle*'s correspondent did? Why does his Stanley claim to have separated "the outrages against life and property from those against constitutional liberty" when the *Chronicle*'s Stanley claims to have separated "the outrages upon life and property, from those upon civil and constitutional liberty"? Why does his account truncate the *Chronicle*'s phrase "every germ of an unbiassed and independent public opinion" to "every germ of public opinion"? Why did he render what the *Chronicle* heard as the need "to protect honest and peaceable subjects" as the need to see "life itself protected"?

Two possible interpretations present themselves. If we regard the *Mirror of Parliament*'s text as the most accurate, taken down by a very proficient notetaker and corrected by the speaker himself, then the other papers' decisions can be regarded as journalistic interpolations, perhaps designed to inflate the drama of Stanley's rhetoric or to shape the speech to serve political ends. But the *Mirror*'s editorial practices complicate this picture, since they clearly involved producing an ideal text rather than a verbatim one. The second interpretation, then, is to accept the newspapers' accounts, particularly the *Morning Chronicle*'s, as the more accurate, since they were taken on the night and not interfered with by Stanley. The omissions in Dickens's reports can then be read as the products of Stanley's hindsight, the MP perhaps finding himself a little unsure about the wisdom of phrases such as "noisy spouter" once the excitement of the debate was over. Dickens's account certainly omitted some of the features that conjured up the experience of give and take in the House; in accordance with the *Mirror*'s policy he did not include the "Cheers" that peppered *The Times*'s report nor the references to "immense cheering" or "[l]oud and long-continued rounds of cheering" that concluded the accounts in the *Chronicle* and *The Times* respectively. Some minor rhetorical flourishes that worked better in debate than on the page were also modified; the "nay" in Stanley's reminder to MPs that "they wished to see property, nay, life itself secure" did not make it into Dickens's rendition.[72] The answer is probably a mixture of these two interpretations, with the editorial policies of the different periodicals converging and clashing at various points, rendering each of them factual in their own way.

The relationship between the *Mirror*'s text and those of the other publications demonstrates the complicated mixture of accuracy and abbreviation that was prevalent in 1830s reporting and that influenced Dickens's style. The different editorial strategies of the periodicals result in texts that are each imperfect but nevertheless have certain merits. Credibility in one area is sacrificed in order to maintain credibility in another, so that no report has all the virtues of exactness *and* immediacy. In this environment, Dickens's technique can be praised for some clear strengths. In particular, he seems to catch both subtleties of meaning and more of the specific content of a speech than his newspaper colleagues. While these strengths owe a great deal to his natural gifts for language and his proficiency in shorthand, the *Mirror*'s attempt to provide full and complete coverage of the speeches partly accounts for these virtues, especially the

[72] *Morning Chronicle* (February 28, 1833): 4. *The Times* has Stanley remind the MPs of the need for the "protection of constitutional right, of legal privilege, of property, – nay, of life itself" (February 28, 1833): 4.

level of detail that he included. But his accuracy was simultaneously compromised by the *Mirror*'s policies, which led to reports that had inevitably drifted further away from events on the night than those that were published by the daily papers and that were potentially further adulterated by political considerations. Dickens's accuracy thus adapts to commercial realities, becoming less absolute but, in some senses, more professional.

TITHING AND TRANSCRIBING

The Stanley speech is a relatively easy one to analyze, given that we know about Dickens's involvement. But what can we glean about his work for the *Morning Chronicle*? The sections that follow present the evidence that might lead to some attributions to Dickens. None of the evidence is conclusive, and these sections are not intended to constitute irrefutable arguments for his authorship of certain sections of the *Morning Chronicle*'s report. What I do attempt in the examples that follow, however, is to demonstrate that there is a substantial amount of circumstantial evidence about the way the gallery operated and Dickens's place within it that is rarely considered in the existing research, which simply repeats the idea that we do not and cannot know what he contributed.

Dickens's letters provide crucial information. For example, on February 21, 1836 he wrote to Catherine that "I hope and believe I shall be able to get out between my turns, tomorrow night – about half past 9."[73] In order to take such a break on February 22, he would had to have completed his turn and transcribed his work before leaving to meet Catherine. Grant described him as "one of the most rapid reporters of his day" but scoffed at the notion that Dickens could transcribe his turn in an hour.[74] Since Grant noted that it took the average reporter somewhere between three and four hours to write up a heavy forty-five-minute turn, Dickens probably would have taken somewhat more than one and less than three hours to complete his usual transcription.[75]

---

[73] Dickens, *Letters*, I: 133–34.
[74] Grant, *The Newspaper Press*, I: 301–2. Grant is probably referring to Charles Gratton, who claimed that Dickens was able to complete the copy for his turn in an hour, a task that was known to take as long as four or five hours. See Gratton, *The Gallery*, 100.
[75] Grant tells a story of writing up a heavy turn in three hours; see Grant, *The Newspaper Press*, II: 182–83. He elsewhere suggests that it took five minutes to write up every one minute of a turn, which would mean that a heavy forty-five-minute turn, from which the speeches needed to be transcribed in full, could be written up, by an average reporter, in a little over three and a half hours; see Grant, *The Great Metropolis*, II: 223.

To clarify further which part of the *Chronicle*'s reports on this date might belong to Dickens, it is necessary to understand his place within the system of turns. Reporters for the major morning papers worked in forty-five-minute shifts, taking down notes before leaving the House to transcribe them; on rare occasions, they took a second turn to complete coverage of the debate. The House of Commons usually began sitting at 5 p.m., and generally adjourned in the early hours of the morning, which suggests that the roster of turns for a newspaper such as the *Morning Chronicle* would have required one reporter to begin work at each of the following times: 5 p.m., 5.45 p.m., 6.30 p.m., 7.15 p.m., 8 p.m., and so on. It seems reasonable to assume that on February 22, 1836 Dickens knew he would be taking one of the early turns of the night, which would allow him time to complete his transcription before meeting Catherine; certainly he did not expect to be taking his first turn any later than around 8 p.m., putting him among the first four or five journalists on the *Chronicle*'s roster. Establishing the exact time at which he began work is neither possible nor necessary; it is sufficient to keep in mind that he was going to be producing some of the early coverage of the debate. In any case, two events at the House of Commons on February 22, 1836 would have affected the precise timing of the turns. First, the Commons began sitting early, commencing their debate at 3.45 p.m. instead of the scheduled 5 p.m., which Dickens could not have known when he wrote to Catherine the previous day. Second, the gallery was cleared for fifty minutes while taking a vote on the Brighton Railway. Although the sequence of turns would presumably have remained the same, with Dickens still in an early slot, these decisions would have altered the precise times at which turns occurred.

These details about timing are important because they can be compared with information about the publication schedule for one of the other dailies. The *True Sun* produced a second evening edition, which, as well as including coverage of the debates from the previous evening, printed a heavily abbreviated account of the first section of that day's deliberations in both Houses up until 6.30 p.m.[76] On February 22, the *True Sun* managed to cover all of the Commons' speeches before the division break. At the end of his report, the paper's journalist noted that "[t]he gallery was closed for the division for fifty minutes," establishing that he stayed long

[76] An announcement of these arrangements can be found in the *True Sun*, March 8, 1836, 2nd edn., p. 4. In the following day's paper, in keeping with the other papers, the *True Sun* would report the debate in full. The second edition coverage was always simply an outline of what was said that evening before the reporter left.

enough to ascertain the duration of the division, which must therefore have concluded by 6.30 p.m.[77]

The sequence of turns for a paper like the *Morning Chronicle* would have progressed in the following fashion. The early start would have meant that the first two reporters would have taken their turns at 3.45 p.m. and 4.30 p.m. respectively. At some stage during the third reporter's shift, which began at 5.15 p.m., the gallery must have been cleared, as we know that the fifty-minute division concluded not long before the *True Sun*'s reporter left at around 6.30 p.m. Later sources suggest that the reporter would not have counted the division break as part of his turn and would have resumed note-taking when the House returned.[78] The fourth and fifth reporters would then have taken their turns at some stage after the division break. While this information is imprecise, it does suggest that Dickens's turn would have taken place somewhere around the break, since it serves as a rough indicator of the time of night. The major debate that intervened between the end of the division and the much later Municipal Corporations Act Amendment Bill was a long discussion of the Tithes Commutation Bill. It is in this piece of the reportage that Dickens's contribution to the *Morning Chronicle*'s coverage probably resides.

The *Morning Chronicle* reproduced twenty-eight speeches from the debate on the Tithes Commutation Bill, to varying degrees of fullness. A comparison with the more detailed coverage in the *Mirror of Parliament* illustrates that the *Chronicle*'s journalists adopted one of four different approaches when deciding how to report an individual speech in this debate. These approaches produced accounts that were either almost verbatim; approximately the right length but with the language paraphrased; paraphrased and heavily abbreviated, with sections omitted or glossed over; or omitted entirely with just a reference to the fact that a particular MP spoke. Only five speeches fall into the first of these categories and were reproduced in near-verbatim versions in the *Chronicle*: Lord John Russell's opening address; a short speech by William Henry Fremantle; and then a sequence of three speeches in which Russell spoke, was answered by Robert Inglis, and then spoke again in response.

It is highly likely that these speeches are all the work of a single reporter. In 1833, *The Companion to the Newspaper* suggested that "[i]n the

---

[77] He did not get a chance, however, to cover any more of the debate, signing off instead with the note "Left sitting" to indicate that the House had resumed debating and had not yet adjourned (*True Sun*, 2nd edn. [February 22, 1836]: 4).

[78] *Report from the Select Committee on Parliamentary Reporting*, 40.

daily papers, the report of an hour's speaking, in a debate of interest, usually fills from one to two columns."[79] Grant's estimate, which *The Times* supported, was similar; he proposed that a typical forty-five-minute turn would be represented as around two columns of type, perhaps extending to two and a half columns if the parliamentarian being reported was a rapid speaker.[80] In a debate that was not too brutally abbreviated, then, an individual reporter probably generated up to two columns worth of type. The five detailed speeches in the *Chronicle's* report appear within the space of approximately two-thirds of a column. The remainder of the coverage on the bill occupies around two and a half columns but does not contain a single near-verbatim speech. The five near verbatim examples thus seem to constitute evidence of a particular reportorial style.

Reading these five addresses alongside the *Mirror of Parliament's* accounts illustrates their completeness. This is the full text of Inglis's speech, for example, from the verbatim *Mirror* and then from the *Chronicle*:

I wish to know whether, if the Bill be now read a second time, the Noble Lord will regard that second reading as merely *pro forma*; or is he disposed to think that, in permitting it to advance this stage, the House is pledging itself to the principle of the measure? Before resuming my seat, I beg to disclaim being bound by the opinion expressed by the Honourable and Learned Member for Ripon; and I wish it may be understood that, in addressing the House on the subject, that Honourable Member was expressing merely his own opinion, to which those who sit upon the same side with him are in nowise bound. The Honourable and Learned Member must not calculate upon having the unanimous support of Gentlemen upon this side to his proposition. (*Mirror of Parliament*)[81]

Sir R. INGLIS wished to know whether, if the Bill were now read a second time, the Noble Lord should regard that second reading as merely *pro forma*; or was he disposed to think that in permitting it to advance this stage the House was pledging itself to the principle of the measure! Before resuming his seat, he begged to disclaim being bound by the opinion expressed by the Honourable Member near him (Mr. Pemberton); and he wished it might be understood that in addressing that House, that Honourable Member was expressing merely his own opinion, to which those who sat upon the same side with him were in nowise bound [a laugh, and hear, hear!]. (*Morning Chronicle*)[82]

---

[79] The writer also pointed out that this would still only represent a portion of what was really said, since "the words actually contained in the most liberal of these allotments could certainly be uttered by a speaker of ordinary fluency in little more than the half of that time" ("Parliamentary Reporting," 20).

[80] Grant, *The Great Metropolis*, ii: 223; *The Times* (March 30, 1831): 5.

[81] *Mirror of Parliament*, vol. ix (1836): 259.

[82] *Morning Chronicle* (February 23, 1836): 2.

The tenses and pronouns reflect the different reporting styles of the two periodicals, and the *Morning Chronicle* account seems to lose the final sentence among the laughter and noise on the night, but the two accounts are strikingly similar. The *Chronicle*'s accuracy in reporting this speech is even more noticeable when one reads the account from *The Times*, which is largely paraphrased:

Sir R. INGLIS begged to deny the existence of that unanimity in favour of commutation in one form or another, on which his hon. and learned friend, the member for Ripon, insisted. The hon. baronet again urged the necessity of postponement, or at least that they might take the second reading *pro forma*.[83]

As already noted, the level of accuracy and fullness displayed by the *Chronicle*'s coverage of Inglis is not the norm in its report of the debate as a whole; Inglis's next speech, for example, which runs to slightly over 300 words in the *Mirror of Parliament*, is recounted in just 76 words in the *Chronicle*. While it is important not to overstate its accuracy and use it as the only benchmark for the daily papers, the *Mirror* did attempt to produce full accounts. If the *Chronicle* and the *Mirror* arrived at such similar versions independently on the night, it seems very likely that this is the speech that Inglis delivered. Alternatively, if the *Mirror* used the *Chronicle*'s text to improve and correct its own, or indeed if Dickens was actually moonlighting for the *Mirror* on this occasion, it demonstrates some certainty on the part of the *Mirror*'s reporters or editors, or of Inglis himself, that the *Chronicle* had produced the closest possible version.[84] In any of these cases, the *Chronicle*'s reporter had done an extremely good job and was obviously a shorthand writer. The rarity of this skill, combined with the proximity of these five near-verbatim speeches in the *Chronicle*'s account, the fact that near-verbatim reporting was not adopted anywhere else in the coverage, nor in the *Chronicle*'s coverage of the Lords that night, Dickens's acknowledged talent as a shorthand reporter and the likelihood that his turn on the night fell early within this debate, make it possible to propose that Dickens is the reporter of the sequence of speeches that begins with Sir John Russell's opening address

---

[83] *The Times* (February 23, 1836): 2.
[84] There is some evidence that the *Mirror* did make use of the daily papers' coverage. During the controversy around the Bishop of Exeter's remarks, *The Times* noted that there were instances in which "the reports in the *Mirror of Parliament* are the same as those in the morning papers, because they were executed by the same hands, or copied from the morning papers" (July 6, 1832): 3. In a speech in 1846, Robert Peel also suggested that there had been some collusion in the production of the *Mirror*'s reports; see *The Speeches of the Late Right Honourable Sir Robert Peel*, 706.

and ends with his reply to Inglis, although naturally this attribution cannot be proven conclusively.

Even such a tentative attribution is valuable, however, as it has been extremely difficult to so much as speculate about Dickens's contributions to the *Chronicle*. Moreover, it seems to confirm the impressive reputation for accuracy that he enjoyed during his time in the gallery and that has become the critical and biographical legacy of this period of his life. But, if this is Dickens's work, then it tells a more interesting story about his role within the parliamentary press corps. The sequence from Russell to Inglis contains not only the five near-verbatim speeches just discussed, but also a further six addresses that are paraphrased and another six that are omitted altogether.[85] It is possible that the accuracy of his reporting is thus intermittent; like all newspaper journalists in the gallery he made choices about whether and how fully to report a speech. It is likely that his normal practice in his original shorthand notes was to record the speeches in full, with the more subtle editorial decisions being made at the transcription stage. A certain amount of summarizing was required of even the most efficient newspaper reporter, both in terms of the inclusion or exclusion of speakers, and in terms of the content of their speeches.

The coverage of the February 22, 1836 debate contributes to our very scarce knowledge of Dickens as a reporter because it perhaps allows us to isolate him, albeit very tentatively, from the rest of the *Chronicle*'s gallery corps. It shows the way in which the skills he developed at the *Mirror of Parliament* might have helped to shape his later contributions to parliamentary journalism and make him a useful reporter, since his ability as a shorthand writer allows him to generate far more accurate accounts than might be expected. But it also demonstrates the ways in which he would have been shaped by and adapted to both the norms of the gallery and the expectations of a daily paper like the *Chronicle*. The reporter who produced these speeches cut and cropped his coverage where he saw fit. His report is not wholly accurate nor entirely paraphrased, but a compelling integration of the two tendencies that inevitably governed newspaper coverage in his time.

---

[85] The sequence of speakers according to the *Mirror of Parliament* was Russell (first speech), Knatchbull, Russell (second speech), Plumptre, Ayshford Sanford, Benett, Colonel Thompson, Brocklehurst, Granville Vernon, Pemberton, Althorp, Fremantle, Sir Matthew Ridley, Goulburn, Russell (third speech), Inglis, Russell (fourth speech). The *Morning Chronicle* makes reference to comments by an additional two MPs, Estcourt and Poulett Scrope, who may have simply made short asides that were not reproduced in the *Mirror*.

THE LORDS TEMPORAL AND SPIRITUAL

On March 10, 1836, a few weeks after the debate on tithes, Dickens wrote to Catherine that he had to be "in the House at a quarter to six … From what I see of the business of the Evening, I fear I shall have a heavy turn."[86] This information about timing squares with what we know about the system of forty-five-minute turns beginning from 5 p.m. It seems likely that on this occasion Dickens was required to work his first turn that evening in the House of Lords. The Lords' debate was reported at unusual length in the major dailies, which perhaps accounts for his weary suspicion that his turn would be a heavy one requiring lengthy transcription. The corresponding section of the Commons' debates, in contrast, renders a very brief transcription in the *Chronicle*; using the *True Sun*'s second edition, which cuts off at around 6.30 p.m., we can establish that approximately two-thirds of a column in the *Morning Chronicle* covers events at the Commons from the opening of the debate at the earlier time of 4 p.m. until 6.30 p.m., while the Lords' discussions from 5 p.m. to 6.30 p.m. account for around two and a half columns. It is also noticeable that there is no near-verbatim reporting in the early sections of the *Chronicle*'s coverage of the Commons, where Dickens's contribution would have to be located if he was in the Lower House that night, whereas there is a considerable amount of near-verbatim reporting in the coverage of the Lords.

The exact system of turns used by the newspapers at this time to ensure coverage of both Houses is not entirely clear. The best evidence can be found in the 1839 notebook of Thomas Campbell Foster, a reporter for *The Times*.[87] Foster's notebook shows that for two weeks in early February 1839 he reported from both Houses, before undertaking a second two-week stint of reporting only from the Commons.[88] Dickens's letters make it clear that he was expecting to be working in the Lords during the

---

[86] Dickens, *Letters*, 1: 138.

[87] News International Archive, Accn No. 95/6. For a discussion of the general procedures in the Lords that also makes reference to the way business was conducted in the Commons, see E. A. Smith, *The House of Lords*, 35–44.

[88] This practice differs from what we know of both earlier and later gallery systems. The newspapers' original plan involved using all of its journalists in both Houses where necessary. Charles Ross, for example, recalled that when he joined the gallery in 1820, "if the Lords were sitting, we took an hour's turn in each House … If the House of Lords was not sitting, we took three-quarters of an hour's turn" (*Report from the Select Committee on Parliamentary Reporting*, 39). An 1858 source, meanwhile, outlines *The Times*'s practice of dividing its corps in two and running two separate systems of turns, with reporters swapping Houses each week ("A Parliamentary

week in question; in a note that was probably composed on March 8, he wrote to Catherine: "My time is 8 o'Clock, supposing only one house sits."[89] If he did work in the Lords on March 10, the section of the report that would have fallen to him should also be included in the *True Sun*'s coverage, enabling us to focus on a narrowly defined group of addresses. Dickens's turn, from 5.45 p.m. to 6.30 p.m., would have ended at around the moment the *True Sun*'s coverage concludes (towards the end of the Archbishop of Canterbury's speech on the Ecclesiastical Commissioners' Report), given that the *True Sun* purported to cover the debates up to 6.30 p.m. in its second edition.[90] Since he was not the first reporter on duty, we can also discount the first part of the debate, which was taken up with numerous short items of business such as petitions and the tabling of reports, and instead focus on the first speech, which was Viscount Melbourne's address tabling the Ecclesiastical Commissioners' Report.

The *Morning Chronicle*'s version of Melbourne's speech is very similar to that produced by the *Mirror of Parliament*, allowing for the usual differences in pronouns and tenses that characterized the styles of the two publications. It would be incorrect to say that the *Chronicle*'s account was executed in a wholly near-verbatim fashion, since there are small but numerous differences in language and phrasing scattered throughout the report, but there are many sections that are reproduced word for word or with only minor alterations. It is also likely, of course, that the *Mirror*'s text is corrected, which would help explain some of the discrepancies in

Veteran," *Aids to Reporting*, 19–20). The 1830s system seems to mark a midway point between these two examples.

[89] Dickens, *Letters*, I: 138.

[90] There is some contradictory evidence about the timing of the debate that night that complicates attempts to fix Dickens's contribution. The *Times*'s report records that the House of Lords *adjourned* at 6.30 p.m., after the peers had finished discussing the Ecclesiastical Commissioners' Report and dealt with a small matter of business regarding affairs in Spain. Both papers cannot be right; either the *True Sun* reporter left much earlier than scheduled and the Lords then adjourned at 6.30 p.m., as *The Times* notes, or the *True Sun*'s reporter left at 6.30 p.m. and the adjournment happened later than *The Times* indicated. My interpretation of the reports assumes that the *True Sun* is more likely to be correct about this point, based on the evidence of the coverage. As my subsequent discussion will outline, there is a clear transition in reporting styles in both *The Times* and the *Morning Chronicle* only a few minutes before the *True Sun*'s coverage breaks off. This transition occurs far too late in the proceedings to be the start of the second reporter's shift at 5.45 p.m.; it is much more likely to mark the handover from the second reporter to the third at 6.30 p.m.. There was not much more business conducted after this transition point, however; the debate concluded perhaps fifteen or twenty minutes later. The reporter beginning his turn at 6.30 p.m. thus did not complete a full forty-five-minute shift and, by noting the adjournment time as "half-past 6" may simply have been indicating that the debate was over before 7 p.m.

the language, as Melbourne might have delivered his speech somewhat differently on the night.

A sample comparison between the texts of the *Mirror*, the *Chronicle* and *The Times* illustrates how closely the *Chronicle* text came to reproducing Melbourne's speech.

With respect to the minor canons, vicars' [*sic*] choral, and other officers of chapters, it is proposed that only so many shall be retained as shall be sufficient for the service of the cathedrals, and that they shall have such stipends as may preclude the necessity of their being paid by ecclesiastical patronage, – many of them, at present, holding benefices together with their offices in the cathedral. (*Mirror of Parliament*)[91]

With respect to the minor canons, vicars choral, and other officers of chapters, it was proposed that only so many should be retained as were sufficient for the service of the cathedrals, and they should have such salaries as might preclude the necessity of their being paid by patronage, many often holding benefices, together with their offices in the cathedral. (*Morning Chronicle*)[92]

As to minor canonships, it was proposed that no more should be retained than was absolutely necessary, and that those holding them should, in future, be paid by a regular stipend. (*The Times*)[93]

Small discrepancies like "salaries" in the place of "stipends" and the omission of phrases like "at present" might demonstrate that the *Chronicle* did not quite achieve a verbatim account, or perhaps that it is in fact the more correct rendition of what occurred on the night. In either case its report is an impressive attempt when compared not only with the apparently full text in the *Mirror* but also with the work of the other dailies. This level of accuracy persists throughout Melbourne's address and into the next speech by the Archbishop of Canterbury.[94]

The *True Sun*'s report helps to establish the end of Dickens's turn – if he is indeed the reporter in question – by providing a rough guide to the

---

[91] *Mirror of Parliament*, vol. IX (1836): 555.   [92] *Morning Chronicle* (March 11, 1836): 1.

[93] *The Times* (March 11, 1836): 3. All of the subsequent references to *The Times*'s coverage of this debate can be found on this page.

[94] The opening few sentences of the archbishop's address in the *Chronicle* do not correspond closely with the *Mirror*'s text, and were perhaps difficult to hear in the noise and movement that often characterized the transition between one speaker and the next; *The Times* records the shouts of "hear, hear" that greeted both the end of Melbourne's speech and the opening comments by the archbishop. After those cheers, however, the *Chronicle* resumes its impressively accurate coverage, closely following the *Mirror*'s apparently full transcription. The resumption of very accurate coverage occurs at the point at which the archbishop, in both the *Mirror* and the *Chronicle*, notes that he had "long been aware of the necessity of taking strong and vigorous measures"; see the *Mirror of Parliament*, vol. IX (1836): 556 and the *Morning Chronicle* (March 11, 1836): 1.

point at which the reporter who began his shift at 5.45 p.m. might have handed over to his incoming colleague.[95] Traces of this transition can be detected in the *Morning Chronicle*'s coverage. Slightly earlier than the moment at which the *True Sun*'s reporter signs off, a noticeable change of style appears in the *Chronicle*'s account. It is no longer in such close accord with the fullest available version in the *Mirror*.

The understanding, on which I consented to remain a member, was, that the integrity of the Episcopal Establishment of the Church should in every respect be preserved. To any reduction in the number of bishops I could never have given my consent. But concurring in the objections which have been frequently urged against the holding of benefices *in commendam* with bishoprics, and seeing, at the same time, the necessity of improving the incomes of the poorer bishops, I could find no other means of effecting the purpose than by adopting the plan of taking from the larger Sees some portion of those revenues, which in latter times have greatly increased, and transferring it to the smaller. (*Mirror of Parliament*)[96]

The condition on which he consented to remain a member was, that it should preserve the episcopal establishment of the Church in its integrity. Had it been proposed to have a smaller number of bishops than were necessary for the efficient discharge of the episcopal function, he should never have given his consent to the report. But having heard of the great objections that were made by many persons who were the real friends of the Church against bishops holding livings *in commendam* he agreed to put an end to that system, and it appeared to him that the least objectionable mode of making up the revenues of the smaller bishoprics, was by a taxation on, or rather a deduction from the revenues of the more opulent sees. (*Morning Chronicle*)[97]

These later sections from the Archbishop's speech represent a significant divergence from the close resemblance of the coverage of Melbourne's address, or the early part of the Archbishop's remarks. The *Chronicle*'s account is still very good, as one would expect from the best newspaper reporting team in London. But a change of journalistic approach is clearly evident.

This change of approach almost certainly indicates a change of reporter. It seems that this is the moment at which one turn ended and

---

[95] According to its heavily paraphrased account of this speech, the *True Sun*'s reporter left after the archbishop had said that "[i]f the suggestions in the report be acted upon, the Church would be placed in a position upon which it could easily be defended, and the country would be relieved from that excitement which consequent [*sic*] upon expected changes, and which excitement was prejudicial to religion" (*True Sun*, 2nd edn. [March 10, 1836]: 1).

[96] *Mirror of Parliament*, vol. IX (1836): 556.

[97] *Morning Chronicle* (March 11, 1836): 1–2.

another began. The alteration in reportorial style that can be detected in the *Chronicle*'s account is reinforced by the introduction, within a few sentences of the passage quoted above, of a scattering of "hear, hears." The early part of the Archbishop's speech in the *Chronicle* contains only one "hear, hear," and the account of Melbourne's address includes none, apart from the cheers at the end. *The Times*'s account of both speeches, by contrast, is liberally strewn with these atmospheric details, suggesting that cheering and barracking were indeed features of the debate that night that a reporter could choose to include. The reporter who covered Melbourne and the opening of the Archbishop's speech seems to omit almost all such references on principle, and their later inclusion strongly hints at a new pen.

The Times's account also suggests that a new reporter began his turn for that paper at around this point. The report in *The Times* is a fairly reliable paraphrase of the version in the *Mirror*, until the Archbishop begins to speak about sinecures. Suddenly *The Times*'s version becomes a much closer transcription, reproducing many exact phrases and sentences, although omitting occasional chunks of the speech. It is now *The Times* that is producing the most apparently accurate text among the newspaper reports.

I now wish to say a few words upon the objects which the Commissioners had in view in all their proceedings. Their great desire was to encourage and facilitate the diffusion and maintenance of pure religion throughout the country. For myself, I entirely disclaim any other motive than a sincere anxiety for the good of the Church. Neither I nor my fellow-Commissioners were actuated by any desire of popularity. (*Mirror of Parliament*)[98]

He now wished to say a few words upon the objects which the commissioners had in view when they made their report. He believed their great desire to be to encourage and facilitate the growth and increase of pure religion throughout the country. For himself, he entirely disclaimed any other motive than a sincere anxiety for the good of the church (Hear, hear.) Neither he nor his fellow-commissioners were actuated by any desire for popularity. (*The Times*)

The clear and sudden changes that occur in both *The Times* and the *Morning Chronicle* suggest that new reporters began their turn in the gallery at around the same point in the Archbishop's speech. The transition happens not long before the *True Sun*'s reporter finishes his coverage at approximately 6.30 p.m., a time which corresponds with the pattern of

---

[98] *Mirror of Parliament*, vol. IX (1836): 556.

forty-five-minute shifts beginning at 5 p.m. We know that Dickens was scheduled to work the turn that concluded at 6.30 p.m. We know that the *Chronicle*'s coverage moved away from being near-verbatim at around this point and that Dickens was one of the small number of reporters able to produce near-verbatim accounts. Once more, we might perhaps be able to trace his hand in the otherwise inscrutable newspaper columns.

While the coverage of the tithes debate in the Commons on February 22, 1836 showed a reporter who mixed accurate transcription with paraphrasing and omission of speeches, this example from the Lords demonstrates a different approach to reporting. The two speakers who appear in his coverage are accorded accounts that are at the very least near-verbatim, and might in fact have been closer to the delivered speeches than the *Mirror*'s corrected copy. However, the underlying motivations for covering Melbourne and the Archbishop in this way derive from the same mixture of journalistic discretion and newspaper imperatives that guided the journalist's choices in the earlier debate. The *Chronicle*'s reporter was not alone in regarding the discussion of the Ecclesiastical Commissioners' Report as a newsworthy moment in the Lords' proceedings that night. The *True Sun* produced a report of these two speeches that was paraphrased but, in terms of its usual standards of reporting in its second edition, relatively full. *The Times*'s reporters interpreted the significance of the debate in exactly the same manner as the *Chronicle*'s reporters, abbreviating the opening pieces of business before Melbourne rose to speak, and the concluding debate on Spain, and thus focusing their energies on the two key speeches of the night. Consulting the order of business, the gallery corps no doubt singled out this debate for special attention, requiring exactly the sort of "heavy turn" that Dickens so reluctantly anticipated that night. Covering these two speeches as fully as possible was less a question of reportorial independence and more a product of the quest for newsworthy material that influenced all of the gallery scribes.

CONCLUSION

Dickens was by reputation an extremely accurate reporter, but was he an extremely good one? Before 1837 and the growing focus on a truly verbatim record, some commentators, as was noted earlier in this chapter, believed that the best reporters were those who did not aim for an accurate account of the exact words of a speech, but rather used their discretion. As Charles Ross later told the Select Committee on Parliamentary

Reporting, "reporting and verbatim reporting are very different things."[99] Ross strongly agreed with the suggestion from the Committee that true verbatim reporting, which the newspapers had always eschewed, was simply "a mechanical art," whereas the full and accurate reporting for which good journalists strived was "an intellectual exercise."[100] Although he was himself a shorthand writer, Ross actually bemoaned the ubiquity of shorthand, which was universally used in the gallery by the time he gave his evidence to the Select Committee in 1878. He believed that contemporary reporting was not as elegant or polished as it had been in the early years of his career, when more creative license was allowed, and repeatedly told the Committee that full reporting was not desirable.[101]

Dickens's shorthand talents need to be seen in the context of the move away from such creative reporting and towards shorthand transcription in the lead-up to Pitman's invention of phonographic shorthand in 1837. Dickens offered the *Morning Chronicle* a relatively rare skill, but its value was in part determined by the fact that other members of the paper's gallery corps were offering something different: an artfully arranged précis of what had been said. The debates of February 22, 1836 and March 10, 1836 contain useful examples of this contrast. The highly accurate reports of Russell, Inglis and Fremantle on February 22 stand alongside the very full but largely creative interpretation of Peel's speech given by a different reporter later in the debate; the highly accurate reporting of the opening of the Archbishop of Canterbury's speech on March 10 gives way to what is apparently a loose version of his words as a new reporter takes over. But Dickens was probably able to engage in this kind of summarizing too; the sequence of speeches on February 22, 1836 also shows the blend of accurate transcription and paraphrase that he might have employed.

Newspapers in the 1830s were caught between an older generation of reporter, still working in longhand, and the new breed of shorthand writers who could take down every word. The standard that emerged in the ensuing decades of the nineteenth century was indeed a mixture of these approaches. While the public came to expect the more accurate reporting of speeches that shorthand delivered, they wanted less of it; short sections of accurate coverage came to be combined with sketches, summaries and light-hearted commentaries. The 1830s papers accommodated both

---

[99] *Report from the Select Committee on Parliamentary Reporting*, 46.
[100] *Report from the Select Committee on Parliamentary Reporting*, 46.
[101] See for example the *Report from the Select Committee on Parliamentary Reporting*, 41.

approaches, allowing their reporters some discretion to produce the kind of copy they thought was best and thus ensuring that each paper had a distinct version of the debate in question.

The nature of parliamentary reporting in the 1830s can be gauged in Dickens's remark to his colleague Thomas Beard that he intended to "exhibit in the Gallery next session."[102] There was an art to producing a report, as his pun on "Gallery" suggests, but that art, like a form of portraiture, was a blend of accurate recreation and imaginative reinterpretation. Longhand reporters had much more cause to master this art, but shorthand writers too had to manifest a certain artistry. A reporter who could take shorthand did not have to follow his longhand colleagues and invent material, but he still did have to decide which speeches, or even which sections of speeches, deserved full treatment, even if such decisions were overturned by an editor later on. These decisions were influenced by the nature and significance of the debate, the identity of the speakers, and the luck of the draw; a reporter could only report what he heard, and what he heard was not necessarily the high point of the debate.

In his novels, Dickens made comic mileage out of the problematic question of accuracy in the standard parliamentary report. Having tried unsuccessfully to take down a speech by "one of our crack speakers in the Commons," David Copperfield ends up setting up a mock Parliament on which to practice:

I should like to see such a Parliament anywhere else! My aunt and Mr. Dick represented the Government or the Opposition (as the case might be), and Traddles, with the assistance of Enfield's Speaker or a volume of parliamentary orations, thundered astonishing invectives against them. Standing by the table, with his left forefinger on the page to keep the place, and his right arm flourishing above his head, Traddles, as Mr. Pitt, Mr. Fox, Mr. Sheridan, Mr. Burke, Lord Castlereagh, Viscount Sidmouth, or Mr. Canning, would work himself into the most violent heats, and deliver the most withering denunciations of the profligacy and corruption of my aunt and Mr. Dick; while I used to sit, at a little distance, with my note-book on my knee, fagging after him with all my might and main ... My aunt, looking very like an immovable Chancellor of the Exchequer, would occasionally throw in an interruption or two, as "Hear!" or "No!" or "Oh!" when the text seemed to require it: which was always a signal to Mr. Dick (a perfect country gentleman) to follow lustily with the same cry. But Mr. Dick got taxed with such things in the course of his Parliamentary career, and was made responsible for such awful consequences, that he became

---

[102] Dickens, *Letters*, 1: 185.

uncomfortable in his mind sometimes. I believe he actually began to be afraid he really had been doing something, tending to the annihilation of the British constitution, and the ruin of the country.[103]

Dickens's portrayal of this scene conveys some important truths about the status of the speeches as fact. The addresses that Traddles reads are themselves the unofficial versions compiled, in the previous generation, from newspaper reports and corrected copies. They were not performed in any Parliament until this moment, when they become part of the record of Copperfield's eccentric family legislature. By taking the speeches down in shorthand as a reporter of this comic Parliament, Copperfield is investing them with a new factual status; paradoxically, they are authentic accounts of an inauthentic Parliament, whereas the original text from which Traddles reads is precisely the reverse. A similar point is made about the performance of a parliamentary debater as Copperfield's aunt employs the standard interjections that a reader would expect to encounter in coverage of a real debate and Mr. Dick, the other faux-MP, becomes convinced that he is actually affecting the course of history through his pretence. The subtlety of this scene suggests that Dickens was keenly aware of the struggle between accuracy and interpretation that characterized parliamentary reporting in his era. His reputation as an extremely accurate reporter deserves re-examination in light of this struggle. The Dickens that emerges from such a re-examination is more Copperfield than copyist; he is a journalist whose ability to work within expectations about accuracy made him an extremely useful member of a contemporary gallery team.

Modern critics have been largely dismissive of Dickens's reporting precisely because most take it that he cannot be considered to be both accurate and creative. Since his accuracy is not in question, his reports cannot be treated as creative works and therefore cannot be valued in the way a literary work might be. Fred Kaplan, for example, argues that "[t]he reporting genre demanded transcription rather than narration or interpretation, objective dryness rather than local color."[104] The creative part of Dickens's journalism is assigned, in these readings, to his simultaneous work as "Boz," to create the impression that, in Kathryn Chittick's words, "[t]he sketch-writer's fancy was kept separate from the reporter's reputation for accuracy."[105] Yet as Matthew Bevis has persuasively argued,

---

[103] Dickens, *David Copperfield*, 466.   [104] Kaplan, *Dickens*, 61.
[105] Chittick, "Dickens and Parliamentary Reporting," 156.

Dickens was working in a period of widespread debate about the distortions that characterized parliamentary reporting and the important political consequences that could arise from reportorial decisions.[106] Bevis shows how deeply Dickens engaged with both Parliament itself and with the vogue for representations of Parliament in the press, including the significance of the "imaginative recreation of speech."[107] As this chapter has demonstrated, Dickens probably participated in the often creative interpretation that was part of the process of reporting Parliament, which in turn would have influenced his mature style.

Dickens's achievement in the gallery should be somewhat reconsidered, not in terms of its impact but rather its component parts. There is no doubt that he was considered to be an excellent reporter. His sense that he would "exhibit" his talents implies that his type of artistry was identifiable and worth observing. This implication of success and perhaps even contemporaneous renown fits with his memory of making "a great splash" in the gallery.[108] But his accuracy, often held up by modern scholars as the sole wellspring of his achievement, was tempered by a host of professional, marketplace and logistical forces. The splash that he made, in a profession that valued judicious reportage, would have involved both an unusually high level of accuracy and an ability to pick and choose when to deploy it. It was never enough to be simply "the best Short Hand Writer in the World."[109]

In his detailed and compelling study of Dickens's journalism, John M. L. Drew has noted that "[a]s a reporter of speeches made within Parliament, Dickens remains more or less invisible."[110] This chapter has attempted to make him less invisible. Rather like a minor figure in one of his novels, Dickens the reporter is actually a recognizable character, apparently blending into but in fact distinguishable from a uniform and impenetrable cast of bit-players. The mass production of newspapers every day and the anonymity of the reporters who worked in the gallery give the impression of an undifferentiated textual landscape, a blur of print that cannot be broken down into smaller, more easily quantified parts. The notion of accuracy likewise suggests an objective, impersonal standard which is either reached or not reached by a gallery corps made up of drones.

---

[106] Bevis, "Temporizing Dickens," 171–91, and *Art of Eloquence*, 86–144.
[107] Bevis, "Temporizing Dickens," 172.   [108] Forster, *Life of Charles Dickens*, 39.
[109] Dickens, *Letters*, VIII: 131.   [110] Drew, *Dickens the Journalist*, 23.

The reality is entirely different. Dickens worked in a very specific moment in the history of parliamentary journalism, a moment whose characteristics are well-documented. There is, in fact, a wealth of evidence available to help us, from the debates about fair reporting and the competition between the different publications that covered Parliament, to the details about turns, second editions, and shorthand practices. Onto this detail we can then project the minutiae of Dickens's life: the dates and times at which he attended the gallery, and his sense of heavy and light turns. In the absence of manuscript evidence we cannot be sure which reports belong to Dickens, although sensible deductions are possible. At best, the two examples from the *Morning Chronicle* could be considered what Harold Love calls "tentative attributions," although perhaps it is fairer to place them in his category of "plausible speculation."[111] While there is the internal evidence of the remarkable likeness to the reports in the *Mirror of Parliament*, which suggests a highly skilled shorthand writer, and the external evidence about matters such as the dates and times of Dickens's turns, I am also mindful of Love's warnings about bias when one goes looking for items that might be the work of a particular writer.[112] Yet there is still much to suggest that Dickens is not only a less invisible figure than has been previously claimed but also a much more complicated figure, an accurate reporter who would not have always produced accurate reports.

---

[111] Love, *Attributing Authorship*, 216.   [112] Love, *Attributing Authorship*, 217.

CHAPTER 6

Conclusion: taking parliamentary reporting seriously

The creative Johnson, the poetic Coleridge, the critical Hazlitt and the accurate Dickens: this study has not aimed to overthrow such characterizations but to situate them within the business of journalism. Understanding these writers' careers as parliamentary reporters in the context of gallery journalism does not diminish their achievements, but rather reimagines them as journalistic, rather than pseudo-literary, successes. Moreover, it demonstrates that these authors drew strength from the standards of the gallery, whether such standards were conscientiously followed in the interests of pleasing existing readers or cleverly improvised upon in the interests of cultivating new ones. Johnson's creative interpretation of the debates drew directly on the house style of the *Gentleman's Magazine*, which was forged in the competition with the rival *London Magazine*. Although factual material was hard to come by, a premium was placed on any accurate information, and Johnson's creative contributions were either built around or displaced by such information. Coleridge occupied an unusual, though not entirely unique, place in the gallery, with the freedom to report creatively and to shape the *Morning Post*'s coverage, but this freedom, like Johnson's, derived from his editor's desire to promote the paper in the competitive world of parliamentary coverage. Hazlitt adapted to the gallery with ease, utilizing the mixture of full reportage, summary, omission, and reconstruction from memory that other reporters were also employing. Dickens had the ability to produce verbatim reports but probably tempered this approach with the abbreviations and selectivity that was characteristic of journalists at the time.

Scholars have been right, therefore, to suggest that the reports of each of these authors manifested one or both of the virtues of creativity or accuracy, but have not adequately explained the historical context for these values, nor shown how common they were in the normal gallery practices of each author's era, albeit shaped and modified by new developments in the gallery's operations and the market for parliamentary journalism. Too little of the extant scholarship has been informed by recent developments in periodical studies, developments which have led to a much more sophisticated and thorough consideration of the way journalism operates in the literary marketplace. The existing accounts instead promote the rather old-fashioned idea that literary talent allows these reporters to see beyond the norms of their time and create something superlative out of the unpromising material of a parliamentary address. The experience of working in the gallery can thus be easily accommodated into established narratives about the authors' lives and works by tracing their individual literary styles back to their reports.

I would like to suggest, however, that these four authors should be viewed primarily as journalists, not necessarily in terms of the relative amounts of journalism they composed in their lifetimes, nor in terms of the relative influence of their journalistic works compared with their literary works, but in terms of their writing habits and their attitude to the world of print. The formative experience of being fully integrated into a team that produced a form of writing which had to meet very specific standards imposed by readers must have influenced their thinking about the literary marketplace. All four authors were concerned throughout their careers with considering new ways to appeal to readers and live up to their expectations. Dickens is not only the most successful of the four in this regard, but is perhaps the most successful major writer ever. Johnson's achievement was perhaps less comprehensive, but he retained a lifelong sense of the importance of meeting the market. Hazlitt's innovations in criticism on art, drama and sport are still influential today, and while Coleridge might be regarded as a spectacular failure in this regard – witness *The Friend*, which was hardly designed to achieve mass readership – his continual experiments with projects aimed at attracting readers to his work suggest an awareness of the need to find new ways of engaging readers. Moreover, all four men remained wedded to journalism as a genre, according it a significant amount of their time and energy, and weaving their careers out of a mixture of literary and journalistic forms.

Parliamentary reporting also poses some fascinating questions about individual style. The collaborative nature of this sort of writing means that most reports actually manifest a composite style, generated by the combination of the parliamentarians' original words, different journalists working their turn, editorial demands and readers' desires. These are not simply the sort of generic influences which all readers are now encouraged

to see in the works of major writers, but rather the partial or total neg-
ation of one's own style in favor of a collaborative voice, with moments of
personal idiosyncrasy usually included in situations where creativity was
likely to enhance the collaborative product. While this study is not specifically concerned with rewriting the later literary careers of its subjects,
I would like to suggest that each of the authors examined in this book
was, throughout his career, a natural collaborator, always adjusting to
the rhythms and routines of different forms of writing and relationships
with other people in the literary marketplace as he had done in the gallery. In fact, it might be possible to view them *primarily* as collaborators,
whose individual style was always a composite of his own creativity and
the voices of others. Such an approach to style might change the way we
read Coleridge, for example, who so often imagined himself in conversation with his readers or fellow writers, and who struggled with the notion
of plagiarism, another form of collaboration. It might change the way we
read a piece of writing like Hazlitt's "The Fight," which is steeped in the
conventions of nineteenth-century boxing journalism despite being held
up as an exemplar of his unique journalistic style. It might even change
the way we think about what is "Dickensian" in Dickens, if we imagine
him as someone whose own voice is actually submerged in the collaborative voice of nineteenth-century London print culture.

But while scholars – and indeed most readers – are principally interested in these authors' reports only to the extent that they influenced their
literary careers, that is certainly not the only way in which one could
approach them. I have tried to argue in this book that the formal characteristics of parliamentary reports and the context in which they were
produced need to be thoroughly understood. It is surprising that among
a group of readers as acutely attuned to form as literary scholars, many of
whom are also literary biographers, the actual structures and techniques
of producing a parliamentary report receive so little attention when the
reporting careers of these writers are considered. If journalism is a genre
of its own, the parliamentary report is a recognizable sub-genre, a form
governed by rules of access, style, production, contemporary fashions
and readers' expectations. It makes no more sense to set aside these rules
than it would to ignore the characteristics of a sonnet when considering
Shakespeare's "Shall I Compare Thee to a Summer's Day?"

Yet it is the rules themselves that seem to cause disquiet. Duncan Wu's
image of "the straitjacket of parliamentary reporting" operates on two
figurative levels, each of which is emblematic of the way literary critics

and biographers tend to think about gallery journalism. The metaphor suggests not only the restrictions of the form, which are seen as inhibiting the creative talents of the author, but also a typically Romantic image of the writer as alienated, unappreciated, perhaps even a pariah, the genius-lunatic confined to a straitjacket. The parliamentary report is an altogether different garment, however. While it is certainly neatly tailored, and designed according to the dictates of contemporary fashion, it allows a freedom of movement that might not be obvious to anyone but the wearer. Moreover, while it potentially sets the wearer apart from the guild of literary authors, it does not therefore suggest utter isolation, but instead betokens membership of a different class of writers, one which perhaps does not deserve the stigma that the straitjacket suggests. In fact, it is difficult to see how a livery worn by four such accomplished journalists could be regarded as demeaning in the eyes of literary historians.

Recent scholarship on the relationship between literature and journalism has done an admirable job of making the case for the relevance of journalism in literary history. Perhaps the most successful example of this undertaking is Doug Underwood's 2008 work *Journalism and the Novel: Truth and Fiction, 1700–2000*. In this extremely wide-ranging and compelling book, Underwood makes the case for integrating journalism more thoroughly into our understanding of the lives and works of what he calls "journalist-literary figures."

That journalism sometimes turned out to be a place where ambition was frustrated and where the journalist-literary figures were kept from fulfilling their writing potential does not mean that the values and ideals of journalism did not impress themselves deeply upon them. As a foil for their satire, as a place to test their idealism about life and literature, as an introduction to the realities of the world, as a field where they were encouraged to indulge their intellectual curiosity and explore the possibilities of self-expression, as a place to learn the discipline of clear and appealing writing – in all these ways and more, journalism served the best known of the journalist-literary figures quite well, even if they often had to move beyond the journalistic workplace in order to write in ways that they felt were fully authentic.[1]

Yet while Underwood is no doubt right to suggest that journalist-literary figures had to leave journalism to fulfil their literary potential, that does not tell us much about how well they fulfilled their *journalistic* potential. The scope of his research and the thoroughness of his analysis make his

---

[1] Underwood, *Journalism and the Novel*, 6.

study an invaluable contribution to the field of literature and journalism, but it is a study that still assumes that the most important aspect of the reporting he considers is the part it played in the shaping of later literary careers.

What, then, is the proper way to situate work like parliamentary reporting within the oeuvre of a literary author? I have largely avoided engaging with this question in the body of this book in order that the substantial and focused analysis of each author's time in the gallery – which I consider to be overdue – does not become sidelined by conventional literary or biographical paradigms. But it is nevertheless an important question, one with a couple of possible answers. The first is that we need to accept the very real appeal of being a paid writer, working on one of the most prominent sections of an influential publication. There is a frisson to that experience that Coleridge, for example, knew all too well; as he wrote to a friend while working for the *Morning Post*, though "[w]e Newspaper scribes are true Galley-Slaves ... Yet it is not unflattering to a man's Vanity to reflect that what he writes at 12 at night will before 12 hours is over have perhaps 5 or 6000 Readers! To trace a happy phrase, good image, or new argument running thro' the Town, & sliding into all the papers! Few Wine merchants can boast of creating more sensation ..."[2] It is no coincidence that he wrote this letter the day after his first successful trip to the gallery to hear Pitt; the euphoria of influence, relevance, and professionalism is clear in every word. While an aspiring writer might prefer time to contemplate, and creative control, there is no reason to believe that he could not also take pride and pleasure in other kinds of writing, particularly writing that marked him out as a professional author.

Another answer to the question of how to place parliamentary reporting in an author's oeuvre is simply to query why we would accept lower standards of scholarship in some areas of literary and literary-biographical studies than we do in the purest forms of literary criticism. If the gallery careers of these authors are not relevant to a particular study, so be it. But when they are introduced, we ought to be able to expect a thorough consideration of the evidence, rather than assumptions about how such work *might* fit into a pre-ordained narrative. None of the evidence I have presented in this book is particularly obscure; the new materials, such as Lord Hardwicke's notes about the debates in the Lords in the eighteenth century, and Hazlitt's notebook, are held in some of the best-known

---

[2] Coleridge, *Letters*, 1: 569.

libraries and collections in the world, and the general information about
the system of parliamentary reporting in each era is widely available. The
neglect of Hazlitt's notebook strikes me as the most telling example of the
critical blind spot that this book has tried to highlight. The notebook has
been mentioned in recent scholarship and can be consulted by anyone
who wishes to see it in the Henry W. and Albert A. Berg Collection at
the New York Public Library. It is the most significant piece of evidence
available about Hazlitt's work as a reporter, and it is hiding in plain sight.

In the preface to this book, I asked why it was that evidence of this sort
had not been recovered or adequately assessed already, when the figures
it related to were so prominent and heavily researched. It seems that the
answer has to do with the way we make sense of literary lives, even in
light of influential theories that complicate the nature of authorship and
writing. Drudgery, hack work and neglected youthful genius are in many
ways essential ingredients in the portrait of the artist; they set the scene
nicely for the triumph which follows, even if that triumph is posthumous.
The ignorance and disrespect of the world – particularly the commercial or political world – become a kind of perverse confirmation of an
artist's true worth. This might seem like a very dated notion of the relationship between authors and society, but this study has demonstrated
how it continues to shape some of the darker recesses of literary and biographical scholarship, where little work has been done and little attention
is generally paid. Older notions of a divide between literature and journalism, which have largely been overturned in the wider realm of literary
criticism, continue to exercise a hold on scholars when confronted with
a challenging journalistic sub-genre like parliamentary reporting. While
the symbolism of working as a gallery journalist appeals to biographers,
critics and readers, the details do not; in fact, symbolism and an assumed
common perception that these apprentice tasks are not worth scrutiny,
or are worth scrutiny only if they shed light on later accomplishments,
actually substitutes for the kind of clear and thorough research we might
expect.

Journalism by literary figures is peculiarly prone to de- and re-con-
textualized interpretations. As her opening sentence in *Taking Journalism
Seriously: News and the Academy*, Barbie Zelizer writes: "Journalism is
most appreciated when it turns into a nonjournalistic phenomenon."[3]
Using Ernest Hemingway as an example, Zelizer shows how the early

---

[3] Zelizer, *Taking Journalism Seriously*, 1.

journalistic experiences of writers are presented as apprenticeships to the more important later literary work. She calls on scholars to rethink journalism, so that it can be "better appreciated for what it is, not for what it might be or what it turns into."[4] This book has attempted to meet that challenge in relation to parliamentary reporting. The motivation for the project was not a kind of cultural relativism, however – I too would rather have "The Rime of the Ancient Mariner" than Coleridge's report of Pitt – but rather a desire to consider these authors' reports alongside the real conditions and qualities of parliamentary reporting.

[4] Zelizer, *Taking Journalism Seriously*, 2.

Bibliography

(NB: This study involved consulting every issue of many newspapers and period-icals for the eras under discussion. The articles in these publications, which total in the thousands, are difficult to record in a bibliography in a way that would be meaningful to readers. They were often anonymous, untitled, or part of a series with a regular title in which an individual piece could be differentiated only by date. For these reasons, this bibliography does not contain every piece of jour-nalism or periodical verse consulted. Section C lists the principal newspapers and periodicals consulted and the relevant date ranges; readers should refer to the footnotes for further information about locating a specific article or item. The pieces of historical journalism listed in Section A are one-off articles, poems or series that were not part of the comprehensive comparative reading covered by Section C.)

SECTION A: BOOKS, ARTICLES, AND PAMPHLETS

Abbott, John Lawrence. *John Hawkesworth: Eighteenth-Century Man of Letters*. Madison, WI: University of Wisconsin Press, 1982.

Ackroyd, Peter. *Dickens*. London: Sinclair-Stevenson, 1990.

Anderson, Floyd Douglas, and Andrew A. King. "William Hazlitt as a Critic of Parliamentary Speaking." *Quarterly Journal of Speech* 67.1 (1981): 47–56.

Andrews, Alexander. *The History of British Journalism*. 2 vols. London: Richard Bentley, 1859.

"Article IX: Progress of Misgovernment." *Quarterly Review* 46 (92) (January 1832): 544–622.

Aspinall, A. *Politics and the Press c. 1780–1850*. London: Home and Van Thal, 1949.

   "The Reporting and Publishing of the House of Commons' Debates 1771–1834." In Richard Pares and A. J. P. Taylor, eds., *Essays Presented to Sir Lewis Namier*. London: Macmillan, 1956. 227–57.

   "The Social Status of Journalists at the Beginning of the Nineteenth Century." *Review of English Studies* 21.83 (1945): 216–32.

ed. *Three Early Nineteenth Century Diaries*. London: Williams and Norgate, 1952.

Asquith, Ivon. "The Structure, Ownership and Control of the Press, 1780–1855." In George Boyce, James Curran and Pauline Wingate, eds., *Newspaper History from the Seventeenth Century to the Present Day*. London: Constable, 1978. 98–116.

Axon, William E. A. *Charles Dickens and Shorthand*. Manchester: John Heywood, n.d.

Baker, Herschel. *William Hazlitt*. London: Oxford University Press, and Cambridge, MA: The Belknap Press, 1962.

Barker, Hannah. *Newspaper, Politics, and Public Opinion in Late Eighteenth Century England*. Oxford: Clarendon Press, 1998.

Barrell, Rex E. *The Correspondence of Abel Boyer, Huguenot Refugee, 1667–1729*. Lewiston, NY: The Edwin Mellen Press, 1992.

Bate, W. Jackson. *Samuel Johnson*. New York and London: Harcourt Brace Jovanovich, 1975.

"Bavius." *Memoirs of the Society of Grub Street*. London: J. Wilford, 1737.

Beetham, Margaret. "Open and Closed: The Periodical as a Publishing Genre." *Victorian Periodicals Review* 22.3 (1989): 96–100.

Bevis, Matthew. *The Art of Eloquence: Byron, Dickens, Tennyson, Joyce*. Oxford University Press, 2007.

"Temporizing Dickens." *Review of English Studies* 52.206 (2001): 171–91.

Birrell, Augustine. *William Hazlitt*. London: Macmillan, 1902.

Black, Jeremy. *The English Press 1621–1861*. Stroud: Sutton, 2001.

The English Press in the Eighteenth Century. London: Croom Helm, 1987.

Robert Walpole and the Nature of Politics in Early Eighteenth Century England. Basingstoke and London: Macmillan, 1990.

Bloom, Edward A. *Samuel Johnson in Grub Street*. Providence, RI: Brown University Press, 1957.

Boswell, James. *Boswell's Life of Johnson*. Eds. George Birkbeck Hill and L. F. Powell. 6 vols. Oxford: Clarendon Press, 1974.

Bourne, H. R. F. *English Newspapers: Chapters in the History of Journalism*. London: Chatto, 1887.

Bowen, John. *Other Dickens: Pickwick to Chuzzlewit*. Oxford University Press, 2000.

"Boz" [Charles Dickens]. "The House." *Evening Chronicle* (March 7, 1835): 3.

Bradbury, Nicola. "Dickens and the Form of the Novel." In John O. Jordan, ed., *The Cambridge Companion to Charles Dickens*. Cambridge University Press, 2001. 152–66.

Brake, Laurel, and Anne Humpherys. "Critical Theory and Periodical Research." *Victorian Periodical Review* 22.3 (1989): 94–95.

Brougham, Lord. *The Life and Times of Henry, Lord Brougham*. 3 vols. Edinburgh and London: William Blackwood, 1871.

Broughton, Lord [John Cam Hobhouse]. *Recollections of a Long Life.* 6 vols. New York: Scribner's, 1909–11. Repr. New York: AMS Press, 1968.

Buckingham, J. S. *Evidence on Drunkenness, Presented to the House of Commons, by the Select Committee Appointed by the House to Inquire into this Subject, and Report the Minutes of Evidence, with their Opinions Thereupon.* London: Benjamin Bagster, 1834.

Bulwer, E. L. and Sergeant Talfourd. *Literary Remains of the Late William Hazlitt.* 2 vols. London: Saunders and Otley, 1836.

Cannon, John. *Samuel Johnson and the Politics of Hanoverian England.* Oxford: Clarendon Press, 1994.

Carey, Brycchan. *British Abolitionism and the Rhetoric of Sensibility: Writing, Sentiment, and Slavery, 1760–1807.* Basingstoke and New York: Palgrave Macmillan, 2005.

Carlson, C. Lennart. *The First Magazine: A History of the "Gentleman's Magazine."* Providence, RI: Brown University Press, 1938.

Carlton, W. J. *Charles Dickens, Shorthand Writer: The 'Prentice Days of a Master Craftsman.* London: Cecil Palmer, 1926.

The Case of the Hanoverian Forces in the Pay of Great-Britain, Impartially and freely examined: With some Reflections on the Present Conjuncture of Affairs. London: T. Cooper, 1743.

Chittick, Kathryn. "Dickens and Parliamentary Reporting in the 1830s." *Victorian Periodical Review* 21.4 (1988): 151–60.

Dickens and the 1830s. Cambridge University Press, 1990.

Clifford, James. L. *Young Samuel Johnson,* London, Melbourne and Toronto: William Heinemann, 1955.

Cobbett, William. *The Political Proteus: A View of the Public Character and Conduct of R. B. Sheridan, Esq.* London: Cox, 1804.

Coleman, Deirdre. "The Journalist." In Lucy Newlyn, ed., *The Cambridge Companion to Coleridge.* Cambridge University Press, 2002. 126–41.

Coleridge, Samuel Taylor. *Collected Letters of Samuel Taylor Coleridge.* Ed. Earl Leslie Griggs. 6 vols. Oxford: Clarendon Press, 1956–71.

Essays on His Own Times, Forming a Second Series of The Friend. Ed. Sara Coleridge. 3 vols. London: William Pickering, 1850.

Essays on His Times. Ed. David V. Erdman. 3 vols. Princeton University Press, 1978.

The Friend. Ed. Barbara E. Rooke. 2 vols. Princeton University Press, 1969.

The Notebooks of Samuel Taylor Coleridge. Vol. 1. Ed. Kathleen Coburn. Princeton University Press, 1957.

The Watchman. Ed. Lewis Patton. Princeton University Press, 1970.

Colley, Linda. *In Defiance of Oligarchy: The Tory Party 1714–60.* Cambridge University Press, 1982.

Collier, John Payne. *An Old Man's Diary, Forty Years Ago.* 4 vols. London: Thomas Richards, 1871.

Colmer, John. *Coleridge: Critic of Society.* Oxford: Clarendon, 1959.

The Conduct of His Grace the D—ke of Ar—le for the Four Last Years Review'd. Together with His Grace's Speech April 15th, 1740. Upon the State of the Nation. London: Webb, 1740.

The Conduct of the Allies and the Management of the War. London: M. Cooper, 1744.

Coohill, Joseph. "Parliamentary Guides, Political Identity and the Presentation of Modern Politics, 1832–1846." *Parliamentary History* 22.3 (2003): 263–84.

[Coulson, Walter]. "Review of *The Periodical Press of Great Britain.*" *Westminster Review* 2 (July 1824): 194–212.

Coxe, William. *Memoirs of Horatio, Lord Walpole, Selected from his Correspondence and Papers, and Connected with The History of the Times, from 1678–1757.* 2nd edn. 2 vols. London: Longman, 1808.

    Memoirs of the Life and Administration of Sir Robert Walpole, Earl of Orford. 4 vols. London: Longman, Hurst, Rees, Orme and Brown, 1816.

A Critical History of the Last Important Sessions of Parliament, which Probably put a Period to B—sh Liberty. London: J. Huggonson, 1742.

"Criticus" [Thomas Barnes]. "Parliamentary Criticism." *The Examiner* (15 August 1813): 525–26.

    "Parliamentary Criticism: Mr. C. W. Wynne and Mr. Bankes." *The Examiner* (3 October 1813): 636–38.

    "Parliamentary Criticism: Mr. Ponsonby." *The Examiner* (5 September 1813): 572–74.

"Culpepper, Ned" [William Maginn]. "Place-men, Parliament-men, Penny-a-Liners, and Parliamentary Reporters." *Fraser's Magazine* (October 1830): 282–94.

Davis, Lennard J. *Factual Fictions: The Origins of the English Novel.* New York: Columbia University Press, 1983.

A Defence of the People: Or, Full Confutation of the Pretended Facts, Advanc'd in a Late Huge, Angry Pamphlet; call'd Faction Detected. 2nd edn. London: J. Robinson, 1744.

Denton, F. J. Harvey. "Dickens the Beginner." *Quarterly Review.* 262 (519) (January 1934): 52–69.

The Desertion Discussed; Or, the Last and Present Opposition Placed in their True Light. London: M. Cooper, 1743.

The Detector Detected; Or, The Danger to which our Constitution now lies Exposed, set in a True and Manifest Light. London: M. Cooper, 1743.

DeVries, Duane. *Dickens's Apprentice Years: The Making of a Novelist.* New York: The Harvester Press, 1976.

Dickens, Charles. *David Copperfield.* Ed. Nina Burgis. Oxford: Clarendon Press, 1981.

The Letters of Charles Dickens. Eds. Madeline House, Graham Storey, Kathleen Tillotson, K. J. Fielding, Nina Burgis and Angus Eason. 12 vols. Oxford: Clarendon Press, 1965–2002.

Dodsley, Robert. *The Correspondence of Robert Dodsley 1733–1764*. Ed. James E. Tierney. Cambridge University Press, 1988.

Drew, John. M. L. *Dickens the Journalist*. Basingstoke and New York: Palgrave Macmillan, 2003.

Erdman, David. V. "Coleridge in Lilliput: The Quality of Parliamentary Reporting in 1800." *Speech Monographs* 27 (1960): 33–62.

"Editor's Introduction." In Samuel Taylor Coleridge, *Essays on His Times*. Ed. David V. Erdman. 3 vols. Princeton University Press, 1978. lix–clxxix.

Escott, T. H. S. *Masters of English Journalism: A Study of Personal Forces*. London: T. Fisher Unwin, 1911.

A Farther Vindication of The Case of the Hanover Troops. London: M. Cooper, 1743.

Fielding, Henry. *Amelia*. The Works of Henry Fielding. Vol. VII. London: Frank Cass, 1967.

The History of the Life of the Late Mr. Jonathan Wild. The Works of Henry Fielding. Vol. II. London: Frank Cass, 1967.

Fielding, Henry and Sarah Fielding. *The Correspondence of Henry and Sarah Fielding*. Ed. Martin C. Battestin and Clive T. Probyn. Oxford: Clarendon Press, 1993.

Fielding, K. J., ed. *The Speeches of Charles Dickens*. Oxford: Clarendon Press, 1960.

Folkenflik, Robert. "Johnson's Politics." In Greg Clingham, ed., *The Cambridge Companion to Samuel Johnson*. Cambridge University Press, 1997. 102–13.

Ford, P. and G. Ford. *Luke Graves Hansard's Diary 1814–1841*. Oxford: Blackwell, 1962.

Forster, John. *The Life of Charles Dickens*. London: Chapman and Hall, 1892.

Gerrard, Christine. *The Patriot Opposition to Walpole: Politics, Poetry, and National Myth, 1725–1742*. Oxford: Clarendon Press, 1994.

Gillman, James. *The Life of Samuel Taylor Coleridge*. London: Pickering, 1838.

Goldgar, Bertrand A. *Walpole and the Wits: The Relation of Politics to Literature, 1722–1742*. Lincoln: University of Nebraska Press, 1976.

Grant, James. *The Great Metropolis*. 2nd edn. 2 vols. New York and London: Saunders and Otley, 1837.

The Newspaper Press. 2 vols. London: Tinsley Brothers, 1871.

Random Recollections of the House of Commons from the Year 1830 to the Close of 1835. London: Smith Elder, 1836.

Gratton, Charles J. *The Gallery: A Sketch of the History of Parliamentary Reporting and Reporters*. London: Pitman, 1860.

Grayling, A. C. *The Quarrel of the Age: The Life and Times of William Hazlitt*. London: Weidenfeld and Nicolson, 2000.

Greene, Donald J. *The Politics of Samuel Johnson.* New Haven, CT: Yale University Press, 1960.

"Samuel Johnson – Journalist." In Donovan H. Bond and W. Reynolds McLeod, eds. *Newsletters to Newspapers: Eighteenth-Century Journalism. Papers Presented to a Bicentennial Symposium at West Virginia University, Morgantown, West Virginia.* Morgantown, WV: The School of Journalism, West Virginia University, 1977. 87–101.

Greville, Charles Cavendish Fulke. *The Greville Memoirs: A Journal of the Reigns of King George IV, King William IV and Queen Victoria.* Ed. Henry Reeve. 8 vols. London, New York and Bombay: Longmans, Greene and Co., 1898–99.

Grubb, Gerald G. "Dickens's First Experience as a Parliamentary Reporter." *Dickensian* 36 (1939/40): 211–18.

Gunther, A. E. *An Introduction to the Life of the Rev. Thomas Birch D.D. F.R.S., 1705–1766.* Suffolk: The Halesworth Press, 1984.

Gurney, Thomas. *Brachygraphy.* 15th edn. London: W. B. Gurney, 1825.

Haig, Robert. L. *The Gazetteer 1735–1797: A Study in the Eighteenth-Century Newspaper.* Carbondale, IL: Southern Illinois University Press, 1960.

Hall, S. C. *A Book of Memories of Great Men and Women of the Age, from Personal Acquaintance.* London: Virtue, 1871.

Retrospect of a Long Life: From 1815 to 1883. 2 vols. London: Richard Bentley, 1883.

Hansard, Luke. *The Auto-Biography of Luke Hansard, written in 1817.* Ed. Robin Myers. Wakefield: The Fleece Press, 1991.

Hardcastle, Mrs, ed. *Life of John, Lord Campbell.* 2nd edn. 2 vols. London: John Murray, 1881.

Harris, Bob. *Politics and the Rise of the Press: Britain and France 1620–1800.* London: Routledge, 1996.

Harris, Michael. *London Newspapers and the Age of Walpole: A Study of the Origins of the Modern English Press.* London and Toronto: Associated University Presses, 1987.

"The Structure, Ownership and Control of the Press, 1620–1780." In George Boyce, James Curran and Pauline Wingate, eds., *Newspaper History from the Seventeenth Century to the Present Day.* London: Constable, 1978. 82–97.

Hawkins, Sir John. *The Life of Samuel Johnson, LL.D.* Ed. O. M. Brack, Jr. Athens, GA: University of Georgia Press, 2009.

Haydon, Benjamin. *The Autobiography and Journals of Benjamin Robert Haydon.* Ed. Malcolm Elwin. London: Macmillan, 1950.

Hazlitt, William. *The Eloquence of the British Senate: Being a Selection of the Best Speeches of the Most Distinguished Parliamentary Speakers, from the Beginning of the Reign of Charles I to the Present Time.* 2 vols. London: J. Murray, 1808.

The Letters of William Hazlitt. Ed. Herschel Moreland Sikes. London and Basingstoke: Macmillan, 1979.

"On the Difference Between Writing and Speaking." In P. P. Howe, ed., *The Complete Works of William Hazlitt*. 21 vols. London: J. M. Dent, 1930–34. Repr. New York: AMS Press, 1967. Vol. XII. 262–79.

"On the Present State of Parliamentary Eloquence." In P. P. Howe, ed., *The Complete Works of William Hazlitt*. 21 vols. London: J. M. Dent, 1930–34. Repr. New York: AMS Press, 1967. Vol. XVII. 5–21.

"The Periodical Press." In P. P. Howe, ed., *The Complete Works of William Hazlit*. 21 vols. London: J. M. Dent, 1930–34. Repr. New York: AMS Press, 1967. Vol. XVI. 211–39.

"The Spirit of the Age." In P. P. Howe, ed., *The Complete Works of William Hazlitt*. 21 vols. London: J. M. Dent, 1930–34, repr. New York: AMS Press, 1967. Vol. XI. 5–184.

Hazlitt, William Carew. *Memoirs of William Hazlitt*. 2 vols. London: Richard Bentley, 1867.

Herd, Harold. *The Making of Modern Journalism*. London: Allen, 1927.

The March of Journalism: The Story of the British Press from 1622 to the Present Day. London: George Allen and Unwin, 1952.

Press Days and Other Days: Recollections and Impressions. London: Fleet Publications, 1936.

A Press Gallery. London: Fleet Publications, 1958.

Hessell, Nikki. "Coleridge and Column Inches." *Romanticism on the Net* 40 (2005). www.erudit.org/revue/RON/2005/v/n40/012457ar.html.

Hill, Brian W. *Sir Robert Walpole: "Sole and Prime Minister."* London: Hamish Hamilton, 1989.

Hill, George Birkbeck, ed. *Johnsonian Miscellanies*. 2 vols. New York: Barnes and Noble, 1966.

Hindle, Wilfrid. *The Morning Post 1772–1937: Portrait of a Newspaper*. London: Routledge, 1937.

The History of The Times: *"The Thunderer" in the Making 1785–1841*. Vol. 1. London: The Times, 1935.

Holmes, Richard. *Coleridge: Early Visions*. London: Flamingo, 1999.

Hoover, Benjamin Beard. *Samuel Johnson's Parliamentary Reports: Debates in the Senate of Lilliput*. Berkeley and Los Angeles: University of California Press, 1953.

Hotten, John Camden. *Charles Dickens: The Story of His Life*. London: John Camden Hotten, [1870].

House, Humphry. *The Dickens World*. 2nd edn. London, Oxford and New York: Oxford University Press, 1942.

Howe, P. P. *The Life of William Hazlitt*. 2nd edn. London: Hamish Hamilton, 1947.

Hughes, Linda. "Turbulence in the 'Golden Stream': Chaos Theory and the Study of Periodicals." *Victorian Periodicals Review* 22.3 (1989): 117–25.

Hunt, F. Knight. *The Fourth Estate: Contributions Towards a History of Newspapers, and of the Liberty of the Press*. London: Bogue, 1850.

Hunt, William. *Then and Now; or, Fifty Years of Newspaper Work.* London: Hamilton, Adams, 1887.

The Interest of Great Britain Steadily Pursued. In Answer to a Pamphlet, entitl'd The Case of the Hanover Forces Impartially and Freely Examined. London: J. Roberts, 1743.

"Investigator." "Civic Consistency and Justice." *The Satirist* (March 1811): 234–36.

Jerdan, William. *The Autobiography of William Jerdan, With His Literary, Political, and Social Reminiscences and Correspondence During the Last Fifty Years.* 4 vols. London: Arthur Hall, Virtue and Co., 1852–53.

Johnson, Edgar. *Charles Dickens: His Tragedy and Triumph.* 2 vols. Boston and Toronto: Little, Brown & Co., 1952.

Johnson, Samuel. *Debates in Parliament.* Ed. John Stockdale. 2 vols. London: J. Stockdale, 1787.

The Letters of Samuel Johnson: With Mrs. Thrale's Genuine Letters to Him. Ed. R. W. Chapman. 3 vols. Oxford University Press, 1952.

Samuel Johnson's Prefaces and Dedications. Ed. Allen T. Hazen. New Haven, CT: Yale University Press, 1937.

Jones, Kennedy. *Fleet Street and Downing Street.* London: Hutchison, 1920.

Jones, Stanley. *Hazlitt: A Life. From Winterslow to Frith Street.* Oxford: Clarendon Press, 1989.

Kaminski, Thomas. *The Early Career of Samuel Johnson.* New York and Oxford: Oxford University Press, 1987.

Kaplan, Fred. *Dickens: A Biography.* New York: William, Morrow, 1988.

Kernan, Alvin. *Samuel Johnson and the Impact of Print.* Princeton University Press, 1989.

Keynes, Geoffrey. *Bibliography of William Hazlitt.* 2nd edn. Godalming, Surrey: St Paul's Bibliographies, 1981.

Kitton, Frederic G. *Charles Dickens By Pen and Pencil.* London: Frank T. Sabin, 1890.

The Minor Writings of Charles Dickens: A Bibliography and Sketch. London: Elliot Stock, 1900.

Kramnick, Isaac. *Bolingbroke and His Circle: The Politics of Nostalgia in the Age of Walpole.* Cambridge, MA: Harvard University Press, 1968.

Kreilkamp, Ivan. *Voice and the Victorian Storyteller.* Cambridge University Press, 2005.

Kriegel, Abraham D., ed. *The Holland House Diaries 1831–1840: The Diary of Henry Richard Vassall Fox, third Lord Holland, with Extracts from the Diary of Dr. John Allen.* London, Henley and Boston: Routledge and Kegan Paul, 1977.

Lamb, Charles and Mary Anne. *The Letters of Charles and Mary Anne Lamb.* Ed. Edwin W. Marrs. 3 vols. Ithaca and London: Cornell University Press, 1975–78.

Latané, David E. "The Birth of the Author in the Victorian Archive." *Victorian Periodicals Review* 22.3 (1989): 109–17.

Law, William. *Our Hansard; Or, The True Mirror of Parliament.* London: Pitman, 1950.

Leader, Zachary. "Coleridge and the Uses of Journalism." In Jeremy Treglown and Bridget Bennett, eds., *Grub Street and the Ivory Tower: Literary Journalism and Literary Scholarship from Fielding to the Internet.* Oxford University Press, 1998. 22–40.

Lipking, Lawrence. *Samuel Johnson: The Life of an Author.* London and Cambridge, MA: Harvard University Press, 1998.

Love, Harold. *Attributing Authorship: An Introduction.* New York: Cambridge University Press, 2002.

Loveman, Kate. *Reading Fictions, 1660–1740: Deception in English Literary and Political Culture.* Aldershot and Burlington, VT: Ashgate, 2008.

Lynch, Jack. *Deception and Detection in Eighteenth-Century Britain.* Aldershot: Ashgate, 2008.

Macaulay, Thomas Babington. *The Letters of Thomas Babington Macaulay.* Ed. Thomas Pinney. 6 vols. Cambridge University Press, 1974–81.

Macdonagh, Michael. *The Book of Parliament.* London: Ibister and Company, 1897.

  The Pageant of Parliament. 2 vols. London: T. Fisher Unwin, 1921.

  Parliament: Its Romance, Its Comedy, Its Pathos. London: P. S. King, 1902.

  The Reporters' Gallery. London, New York and Toronto: Hodder and Stoughton, [1913].

MacKenzie, R. Shelton. *Life of Charles Dickens.* Philadelphia: T. B. Peterson, 1870.

Maclean, Catherine Macdonald. *Born Under Saturn: A Biography of William Hazlitt.* London: Collins, 1943

Martin, Peter. *Samuel Johnson: A Biography.* London: Weidenfeld and Nicolson, 2008.

McBath, James H. "Parliamentary Reporting in the Nineteenth Century." *Speech Monographs* 37.1 (1970): 25–35.

Meyers, Jeffrey. *Samuel Johnson: The Struggle.* New York: Basic Books, 2008.

Mitchell, Sally. "Victorian Journalism in Plenty." *Victorian Literature and Culture* 37.1 (2009): 311–21.

Montagu, Lady Mary Wortley. *The Complete Letters of Lady Mary Wortley Montagu.* Vol. II. Ed. Robert Halsband. Oxford: Clarendon Press, 1966.

Morison, Stanley. *The English Newspaper: Some Account of the Physical Development of Journals Printed in London Between 1622 and the Present Day.* Cambridge University Press, 1932.

Mulvihill, James. "Hazlitt on Parliamentary Eloquence." *Prose Studies* 12.2 (1989): 132–46.

Murphy, Arthur. *An Essay on the Life and Genius of Samuel Johnson, LLD.* London: Longman, 1787.

The New Opposition Compared with the Old in Point of Principles and Practice. London: W. Bickerton, 1744.

Newbould, Ian. *Whiggery and Reform 1830–41: The Politics of Government.* London: Macmillan, 1990.

"A Newspaper Editor." *Journalism.* London: n.p., 1831.

Nichols, John. *Literary Anecdotes of the Eighteenth Century; Comprizing Biographical Memoirs of William Boyer.* 6 vols. London: Nichols, 1812.

Opposition Not Faction: Or, the Rectitude of the Present Parliamentary Opposition to the Present Measure, Justified by Reason and Facts. In Answer to a Late Book, Intitled, Faction Detected. London: M. Cooper, 1743.

"Parliamentary Pastorals." *Monthly Magazine* 13 (February 1832): 208.

"Parliamentary Pastorals." *Monthly Magazine* 13 (March 1832): 310.

"Parliamentary Reporting." *The Companion to the Newspaper* 2 (April 1833): 17–20.

"A Parliamentary Veteran." *Aids to Reporting; or, The Student's Guide to Press Occupation.* London: Groombridge, 1858.

Patmore, P. G. *My Friends and Acquaintance.* Vol. II. London: Saunders and Otley, 1854.

Rejected Articles. London: Henry Colburn, 1826.

Patten, Robert L. "From *Sketches* to *Nickleby*." In John O. Jordan, ed., *The Cambridge Companion to Charles Dickens.* Cambridge University Press, 2001. 16–33.

Peacey, Jason. "The Print Culture of Parliament, 1600–1800." *Parliamentary History* 26.1 (2007): 1–16.

Peel, Sir Robert. *The Speeches of the Late Right Honourable Sir Robert Peel, Bart., Delivered in the House of Commons.* Vol. IV. London: George Routledge and Co., 1853.

[Perceval, Lord]. *Faction Detected, by the Evidence of Facts.* London: J. Roberts, 1743.

The Periodical Press of Great Britain and Ireland: An Inquiry into the State of the Public Journals, Chiefly as Regards Their Moral and Political Influence. London: Hurst and Robinson, 1824.

Pettit, Alexander. *Illusory Consensus: Bolingbroke and the Polemical Response to Walpole, 1730–1737.* Newark, DE: University of Delaware Press, 1997.

"Political News and Notes." *Evening Post* (September 24, 1897): 6.

"Political Retrospect of the Year 1833: Britain." *The Companion to the Newspaper* 13 (January 1834): 193–214.

Public Discontent Accounted For, From the Conduct of Our Ministers in the Cabinet, and of our Generals in the Field: Wherein Proper Observations are Made on the late Ministerial Apology, intitled, Faction Detected. London: M. Cooper, 1743.

Pykett, Lyn. *Charles Dickens.* Basingstoke and New York: Palgrave, 2002.

"Reading the Periodical Press: Text and Context." *Victorian Periodicals Review* 22.3 (1989): 100–108.

The Question Stated with Regard to Our Army in Flanders: and the Arguments for and against this Measure compared. London: Roberts, 1743.

Reasons Founded on Facts for a Late Motion. In a Letter to a Member. London: T. Cooper, 1741.

Redding, Cyrus. *Fifty Years' Recollections, Literary and Personal, with Observations on Men and Things.* 3 vols. London: Skeet, 1858.

Past Celebrities Whom I Have Known. 2 vols. London: Charles J. Skeet, 1866.

Reid, Christopher. "'Community of Mind': Quotation and Persuasion in the Eighteenth-Century House of Commons." *The Age of Johnson* 17 (2006): 317–40.

"Whose Parliament? Political Oratory and Print Culture in the Later 18th Century." *Language and Literature* 9.2 (2000): 122–34.

Reitan, E. A., ed. *The Best of the "Gentleman's Magazine."* Studies in British History 4. Lewiston: The Edwin Mellen Press, 1987.

Report from the Select Committee on Parliamentary Reporting; Together with the Proceedings of the Committee, Minutes of Evidence, and Appendix. London: House of Commons, 1878.

A Review of the Late Motion for an Address to his Majesty Against a Certain Great Minister, and the Reasons for it; With Some Remarks upon the Minister's Speech, in Defence of Himself. London: W. Ward, 1741.

A Review of the Whole Political Conduct of a Late Eminent Patriot, and His Friends; for Twenty Years last past in which is contained A Complete History of the Late Opposition and a Full Answer to a Pamphlet, entitled, Faction detected by the Evidence of Facts. London: M. Cooper, 1743.

Robinson, Henry Crabb. *Diary, Reminiscences, and Correspondence of Henry Crabb Robinson.* Ed. Thomas Sadler. 3rd ed. 2 vols. New York: AMS Press, 1967.

Henry Crabb Robinson on Books and their Writers. Ed. Edith J. Morley. 3 vols. London: J. M. Dent, 1938.

Robson, John M. *What Did He Say? Editing Nineteenth-Century Speeches From Hansard and the Newspapers.* Lethbridge, AB: University of Lethbridge Press, 1988.

Russell, John, Earl. *Recollections and Suggestions 1813–1873.* London: Longmans, Greene and Co., 1875.

Sandford, Mrs. Henry [Margaret]. *Thomas Poole and His Friends.* 2 vols. London: Macmillan, 1888.

Sherbo, Arthur, ed. *Memoirs of the Life and Writings of the Late Dr. Samuel Johnson, by William Shaw, and Anecdotes of the Late Samuel Johnson, LL.D. during the Last Twenty Years of His Life.* London: Oxford University Press, 1974.

Sheridan, Richard Brinsley. *The Letters of Richard Brinsley Sheridan.* Ed. Cecil Price. 3 vols. Oxford: Clarendon Press, 1966.

Slater, Michael. *Charles Dickens.* New Haven and London: Yale University Press, 2009.

Smith, E. A. *The House of Lords in British Politics and Society, 1815–1911.* London and New York: Longman, 1992.

Smith, Grahame. *Charles Dickens: A Literary Life*. Basingstoke and London: Macmillan, 1996.

Sparrow, Andrew. *Obscure Scribblers: A History of Parliamentary Journalism*. London: Politico's, 2003.

Stanhope, Philip Henry. *Life of the Right Honourable William Pitt*. 3rd edn. 4 vols. London: John Murray, 1867.

Stanley, Edward. *Ireland. Speech of the Right Hon. E. G. Stanley, M. P., Chief Secretary for Ireland, in the Debate on the Disturbances (Ireland) Bill, in the House of Commons, on Wednesday, February 27th, 1833. Extracted from the Mirror of Parliament. – Part CLXXXIX*. London: Charles Knight, 1833.

Stephen, James. *The Memoirs of James Stephen, Written by Himself for the Use of His Children*. Ed. Merle M. Bevington. London: The Hogarth Press, 1954.

Straus, Ralph. *Dickens: The Man and the Book*. London: Thomas Nelson and Sons, 1936.

A Portrait of Dickens. London: J. M. Dent and Sons, 1928.

Stuart, Daniel. "Anecdotes of the Poet Coleridge." *Gentleman's Magazine* ns 9 (May 1838): 485–92.

Taylor, John. *Records of My Life*. 2 vols. London: Edward Bull, 1832.

Taylor, Stephen, and Clyve Jones, eds., *Tory and Whig: The Parliamentary Papers of Edward Harley, 3rd Earl of Oxford, and William Hay, M.P. for Seaford 1716–1753*. Woodbridge: The Boydell Press, 1998.

Thomas, Peter D. G. "The Beginning of Parliamentary Reporting in Newspapers, 1768–1774." *English Historical Review* 74.293 (1959): 623–36.

The House of Commons in the Eighteenth Century. Oxford: Clarendon Press, 1971.

Trewin, J. C. and E. M. King. *Printer to the House: The Story of "Hansard."* London: Methuen, 1952.

Two Speeches on the Late Famous Motion, by the Right Honourable the Lord L—k. London: J. Millan, 1743.

Underwood, Doug. *Journalism and the Novel: Truth and Fiction, 1700–2000*. Cambridge University Press, 2008.

Van Noorden, Charles. *Off the Tourist Track in London: A Morning's Stroll Among the Places of Literary and Historical Interest Round about the Strand, Fleet Street and Holborn*. London: H. A. Bowman, 1911.

A Vindication of a Late Pamphlet entitled, The Case of the Hanover Troops considered: with some Observations upon those Troops; being A Sequel to the said Pamphlet. London: T. Cooper, 1743.

Wahrman, Dror. "Virtual Representation: Parliamentary Reporting and Languages of Class in the 1790s." *Past and Present* 136 (1992): 83–113.

Walker, John. *The Academic Speaker; or, a Selection of Parliamentary Debates, Orations, Odes, Scenes and Speeches, from the Best Writers, Proper to be Read and Recited by Youth at School*. 3rd edn. London: J. Walker, 1797.

Walpole, Horace. *The Yale Edition of Horace Walpole's Correspondence.* Eds. W. S. Lewis, A. Dayle Wallace, Robert A. Smith, and Joseph Reed, Jr. 48 vols. New Haven, CT: Yale University Press, 1937–83.

Wasson, Ellis Archer. "The Whigs and the Press, 1800–1850." *Parliamentary History* 12 (2006): 68–87.

Werkmeister, Lucyle. *The London Daily Press 1772–1792.* Lincoln, NE: University of Nebraska Press, 1963.

A Newspaper History of England, 1792–1793. Lincoln, NE: University of Nebraska Press, 1967.

Windham, William. *The Windham Papers: The Life and Correspondence of the Rt. Hon. William Windham, 1750–1810.* 2 vols. London: Herbert Jenkins, 1913.

Wolff, Michael. "Charting the Golden Stream: Thoughts on a Directory of Victorian Periodicals." *Victorian Periodicals Newsletter* 4.3 (1971): 23–28.

"Damning the Golden Stream: Latest Thoughts on a Directory of Victorian Periodicals." *Victorian Periodicals Review* 22.3 (1989): 126–29.

Woodfall, William. *My Note-Book; or, Sketches from the Gallery of St. Stephen's. A Satirical Poem.* London: G. and W. B. Whittaker, 1821.

Wu, Duncan, ed. *New Writings of William Hazlitt.* 2 vols. Oxford University Press, 2007.

William Hazlitt: The First Modern Man. Oxford University Press, 2008.

Young, Julian Charles. *A Memoir of Charles Mayne Young, Tragedian.* 2 vols. London and New York: Macmillan, 1871.

Zellzer, Barbie. *Taking Journalism Seriously: News and the Academy.* Thousand Oaks, CA: Sage, 2004.

SECTION B: MANUSCRIPT COLLECTIONS

Auckland Papers, British Library

Thomas Barnes Papers, News International Archive

Thomas Birch Collection, British Library

Egmont Papers, British Library

Papers from the Consistory Court of London, 1830, Guildhall Library MS 20778

Thomas Campbell Foster's Parliamentary Shorthand Notebook, News International Archive

Gladstone Papers, British Library

W. B. Gurney and Sons Papers, Parliamentary Archives

Thomas Curson Hansard Papers, Parliamentary Archives

Hardwicke Papers, British Library

Hazlitt Family Memoir, British Library

Sarah Stoddart Hazlitt Poetry Commonplace Book, Henry W. and Albert A. Berg Collection, New York Public Library

Huskisson Papers, British Library
Liverpool Papers, British Library
Martin Papers, British Library
Spencer Perceval Papers, British Library
Press Gallery Papers, Parliamentary Archives
Thomas Secker's Notebook, British Library
Papers Chiefly Relating to Richard Brinsley Sheridan, British Library
Parliamentary Papers of Lord Strafford, British Library
James Tyas Papers, News International Archive
Walter Family Papers, News International Archive
Windham Papers, British Library
Philip Yorke's Parliamentary Journal, British Library

SECTION C: NEWSPAPERS AND MAGAZINES

Champion 1742
Common Sense 1741
The Craftsman 1739–1741
Daily Gazetteer 1738–1744
E. Johnson's London Gazette 1800
Gentleman's Magazine 1732–1744
London Daily Post 1741–1743
London Evening Post 1738–1741
London Magazine 1732–1744
Morning Chronicle 1800, 1812–1813, 1831–1836
Morning Herald May 1803
Morning Post 1800, May 1803, 1812–1813
Oracle 1800
Star 21 September 1796, 1800
The Times 1800, 1812–1813, 1831–1836
True Briton 1800
True Sun 1832–1836
Universal Spectator 1741–1742
Westminster Journal 1742–43
Whitehall Evening Post 1800

SECTION D: PARLIAMENTARY RECORDS

Cobbett's Parliamentary History of England
*A Collection of the Parliamentary Debates in England, from the Year 1668 to the
    Present Time*
*The History and Proceedings of the House of Commons from the Restoration to the
    Present Time*

The History and Proceedings of the House of Lords from the Restoration in 1660, to the Present Time

Mirror of Parliament

The Parliamentary Debates, from the Year 1803 to the Present Time Forming a Continuation of the Work Entitled "The Parliamentary History from the Earliest Period to the Year 1803"

The Parliamentary Register; or History of the Proceedings and Debates of the House of Lords and Commons

Index